WHEN CANADIAN LITERATURE MOVED TO NEW YORK

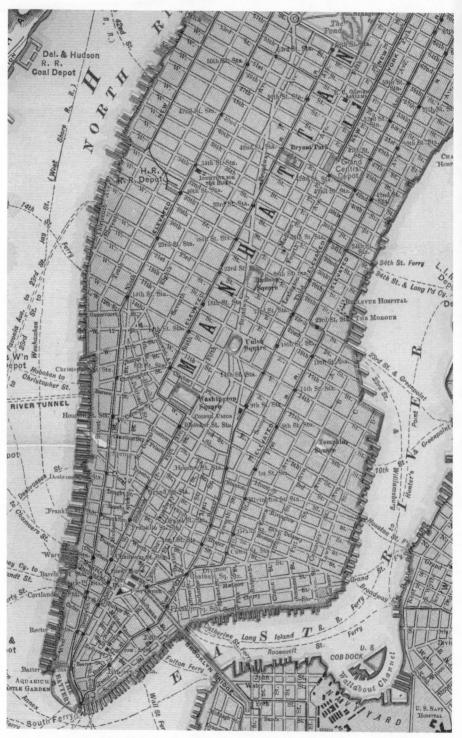

'The market for Canadian literary wares of all sorts.' Manhattan, 1902.

When Canadian Literature Moved to New York

Nick Mount

UNIVERSITY OF TORONTO PRESS
Toronto Buffalo London

PS 8071.2 .M68 2005

© University of Toronto Press Incorporated 2005
Toronto Buffalo London
Printed in Canada

ISBN 0-8020-3828-X

(Studies in Book and Print Culture)

Printed on acid-free paper

Library and Archives Canada Cataloguing in Publication

Mount, Nicholas J. (Nicholas James), 1963–
    When Canadian literature moved to New York / Nick Mount.

(Studies in book and print culture)
Includes bibliographical references and index.
ISBN 0-8020-3828-X

1. Canadian literature – Publishing – New York (State) – New
York – History – 19th century.   2. Authors, Canadian – United
States – History – 19th century.   3. Canadian literature – 19th
century – History and criticism.   I. Title.   II. Series.

PS8071.2.M68 2005   C810.9′004   C2005-900609-9

The introduction was previously published in different form as 'The Expatriate
Origins of Canadian Literature' in *Recalling Early Canada: Reading the Political
in Literary and Cultural Production*, ed. Jennifer Blair et al., © 2005 The University of Alberta Press.

University of Toronto Press acknowledges the financial assistance to its publishing
program of the Canada Council for the Arts and the Ontario Arts Council.

This book has been published with the help of a grant from the Canadian
Federation for the Humanities and Social Sciences, through the Acid to Scholarly
Publications Programme, using funds provided by the Social Sciences and
Humanities Research Council of Canada.

University of Toronto Press acknowledges the financial support for its publishing
activities of the Government of Canada through the Book Publishing Industry
Development Program (BPIDP).

For Bernadette

'What are the only two books in the Old Testament that describe Canada?'
Answer: 'Lamentations and Exodus.'

—Canadian joke, circa 1890s

Contents

x   Contents

Illustrations follow page 86

WHEN CANADIAN LITERATURE MOVED TO NEW YORK

Introduction

They laid Bliss Carman in his grave and Canadian literature began almost immediately.

It began, as these things do, with an argument over a body. Canada's first and until recently only poet laureate died in his sixty-eighth year on the morning of 8 June 1929 after stepping out of the shower in his rooming house in New Canaan, Connecticut. By the time of his death Carman had spent over forty years in the northeastern United States, studying at Harvard in the late 1880s, working in Boston and New York throughout the 1890s, and from 1908 on residing more or less permanently in New Canaan, then as now a New York commuter community. Almost all of his hundreds of poems and essays had first seen print in American periodicals and American books; his first Canadian book didn't appear until 1921, two dozen books and a quarter-century after his first. In his heyday in the mid-1890s the *New York World* had called him 'The American High Priest of Symbolism.' In rural Prince Edward Island on the eve of 1911 Lucy Maud Montgomery wrote in her journal that Carman was 'the foremost American poet' of a poetically unremarkable age; that same winter in midtown Manhattan a visiting Ezra Pound concluded that of the present crop of American poets, Bliss Carman was 'about the only one of the lot that wouldn't improve by drowning.'[1]

It is understandable, then, that when Carman died that morning in June his executor, neighbour, sometime lover, and closest companion for over thirty years, Mrs Mary Perry King, should have arranged for him to be buried in America, right there in New Canaan, in the King family plot. The next day, a Sunday, the *New York Times* reported that the poet's body would lie at the home of Dr and Mrs King until services on Tuesday, with burial to follow in New Canaan's Lake View Cemetery.[2]

A lecturer in physical education and the founder, with Carman's help, of the

Unitrinian School of Personal Harmonizing, Mary Perry King was Canadian poetry's Yoko Ono. When Carman met her in the late 1890s, his closest friends were his cousin Charles G.D. Roberts and their shared circle of writers and artists. But as Carman and King's relationship developed from a simple affair into a full-blown artistic and spiritual collaboration, his old friends drifted away, and he and Roberts grew apart, even quarrelled over her influence. For years after Carman's death Roberts continued to blame 'the shadow of Mrs King' for the decline of Carman's art into mystical mediocrity.[3]

But that weekend in June Roberts's immediate concern was with Mrs King's influence over his cousin's physical remains. Roberts learned of Carman's death through the Toronto Sunday papers, and in company with his publisher Lorne Pierce and Carman's Canadian editor Rufus Hathaway he left for New Canaan the following morning. Like others of Carman's Canadian family and friends, Roberts was outraged at Mrs King's failure to consult with relatives about Carman's last resting place. Carman had been born and raised in Canada – he had his own family plot waiting for him in Fredericton, New Brunswick. And there was more at stake than family tradition: through his popular Canadian reading tours of the early 1920s Carman had recently become a Canadian poet again, indeed the official Canadian poet, elected by the Canadian Authors' Association in 1921, and it would hardly do for Canada's version of Poets' Corner to be inaugurated in a Connecticut cemetery. Mindful of these embarrassments, the premier of New Brunswick and the mayor of Fredericton wired Mrs King asking her to return Carman's body to his birthplace, while the Associated Press reported that 'the city of Fredericton has made plans for bringing the body to his native city and the New Brunswick government will make arrangements for the funeral.'[4] The announcement was premature, the result of the wire service mistaking Canadian editorial desire or government press releases for consensus among the parties. Carman's funeral was held as originally planned at St Mark's Episcopal Church in New Canaan and his body sent to Brooklyn for cremation.

Upon returning to Canada, Roberts, Pierce, and others renewed the campaign to bring Carman's remains home. Three days after the funeral, the *Hamilton Herald* scolded Mrs King for refusing the New Brunswick government's offer of a state funeral. 'Naturally,' the editors wrote, 'she would as belonging to the United States, have little consideration for his native land or the feelings of his countrymen.' Far from enlisting her sympathy as the editors intended, the editorial infuriated King, who attributed it in a letter to Pierce to 'evil from the ignoble Roberts.'[5] In the end, it was Pierce, not Roberts, who persuaded King to give up Carman's ashes by writing her a series of consoling letters and by convincing both Premier Baxter and Prime

Minister Mackenzie King to wire another round of official requests for the ashes' return. By the end of July, Roberts could write to a friend, 'As you have doubtless seen by the papers, we of New Brunswick are likely, after all, to get B's ashes to Fredericton. Mrs. K. seems to be relenting.'[6]

It hurt her to do it – 'I am agonized tonight lest I should have kept the beloved ashes here,' she wrote Pierce before leaving – but on 20 August 1929, Mrs King arrived for Carman's second funeral at Fredericton's Christ Church Cathedral, carrying his ashes in an urn and weeping behind her veil. After the service the ashes were interred with state recognition in a concrete tomb in Forest Hill, a Loyalist cemetery that would also become Roberts's final home. A little over a year later, contributors to a memorial fund in Carman's name erected a granite shrine over his grave as 'a permanent token of the gratitude of our nation to one who enriched the traditions of our literature.'[7] The body of Bliss Carman had been repatriated. It would take somewhat longer to do the same for his literary corpus.

All literatures have three beginnings. A literature's first beginning is the moment of its emergence, often in quasi- or extra-literary forms: oral celebrations of gods and heroes, chronicles of distant legend or current crop conditions, narratives of exploration and travel (or captivity and slavery), and so on. Its second beginning is marked by its writers' self-conscious recognition of themselves as writers (rather than, say, explorers who write), and of their membership in or connection to a community of others who share that recognition. Much more so than the first, this second beginning depends upon the existence of those who will produce, distribute, and consume the literature – conventionally, the publisher, the bookseller, and the reader, though it hasn't always been so, and occasionally modern communities of writers have found substitutes for one or more of these functions. Because of its dependence upon a market, a literature's second beginning is most clearly announced by the professionalization of its writers, by the moment at which they begin to earn their living from, or mostly from, their writing. Finally, a literature undergoes its third beginning when it receives critical or institutional recognition as *a literature*, that is, as a discrete body of writing, with its own history and its own set of works and characteristics. In its actual life any literature is far too internally disparate and too interwoven with other literatures to admit such definition. When we say 'a literature,' what we really mean is an object that exists only in perception, an object whose birth was simultaneous with its recognition and that survives only in restatements of that recognition – Aristotle's *Poetics*, the year's Pulitzer prizes, a university course on Caribbean literature, or the claim to ownership of a poet's last remains.

This book is about the last two of these beginnings for Canadian literature. It is about the first communities of professional Canadian writers and their markets, and about the subsequent reclaiming of those writers as the beginning of a Canadian literature. One of these is a Canadian story; the other is mostly a story of elsewhere – a story, especially, of New York.

Bliss Carman wasn't the first Canadian writer to pursue a career in America. Canada's self-declared 'first and only' author, John Richardson, had loudly given up on Canadian readers forty years before and moved to New York, where he fared little better, dying of malnutrition two years later.[8] More successful if also fated for an early death, the country's first best-selling novelist, May Agnes Fleming, left Saint John for Brooklyn in 1875. Both before and after Confederation, many other Canadian writers sought and found positions with American magazines, newspapers, or publishing firms, while many more routinely published their work in Boston, New York, or Philadelphia.

But in Carman's generation, the 1880s and 1890s, something over a million Canadians left Canada for the United States, the greatest such emigration in Canadian history. With these emigrants went more Canadian writers, practising and hopeful, than ever before or since. Canadian census statistics give some idea of the size of the literary exodus in these years. In 1881, the Department of Agriculture (then responsible for the census) reported the existence in Canada of 601 'artists and litterateurs.' Ten years later, in the census of 1890–1, that number had slipped to 279. By the first year of the new century, just fifty-six Canadians – forty-one men and fifteen women – were identifying themselves as full-time authors. Of the hundreds of occupations abstracted from Canada's 1901 census for comparison in the following census, the only one to have attracted fewer adherents than literary work was the manufacturing of 'fancy goods and notions.'[9]

These numbers are probably less dramatic than they appear. For one thing, the 1881 figure likely includes some of the country's full-time journalists, who don't show up as a separate profession until the census of 1890–1. For another, both the 1881 and 1890–1 figures almost certainly include an unspecified number of librarians, who weren't reported separately until 1901. But even allowing for these and other differences between censuses, the figures still indicate a serious decline in the number of working Canadian authors in the last two decades of the nineteenth century. The rate of that decline can only be estimated, but the census figures together with the expatriation rate for better-known authors of the period suggest a rate of about 50 per cent. (Of the forty-five English Canadian writers born before 1880 profiled in W.H. New's *Canadian Writers, 1890–1920*, for instance, twenty-two left Canada permanently or for an extended period.) Numbering the decline is more difficult: after adding in natural additions to the profession by birth or immigration, I would hazard the conservative estimate that between 1880 and 1900 upwards of two hundred Canadian writers either quit their profession or quit their country.

Canadian censuses of this period don't record how many of these writers changed professions rather than left, or where those that left went. But American records provide some answers to these questions. In New York alone, eleven Canadian writers became prominent enough to merit entries in the first edition of *Who's Who in New York City and State*, published in 1904. Alongside the Astors and the Vanderbilts appear Canadians Palmer Cox, Sophie Almon Hensley, Charles Brodie Patterson, Charles G.D. Roberts, and Ernest Thompson Seton, among others (Seton's entry fills almost two full columns, the same space accorded native New Yorker and sitting president Theodore Roosevelt). That same year, Oscar Fay Adams's *Dictionary of American Authors* contained entries on over eighty Canadian-born authors then living in the United States.[10] And although too late to register the boom years of the Canadian literary emigration, the American census of 1910, the first to enumerate foreign-born workers by occupation, still recorded 93 Canadian-born authors and a further 570 editors and reporters.[11]

The disappearance of their writers did not pass unnoticed in Canada. In the spring of 1893, a contributor to the Toronto *Week* complained that 'More than one of our most prominent writers have left Canada permanently: in more fortunate climates they may find the soil and the atmosphere more congenial and more supporting ...' Ottawa poet Archibald Lampman made similar observations in his column in the next morning's *Globe*, noting the success of Grant Allen, Gilbert Parker, and Sara Jeannette Duncan in England, and of E.W. Thomson, Walter Blackburn Harte, and Bliss Carman in the United States. 'They probably bring more honour to their country in the fields which they have chosen,' wrote Lampman, 'than they would if they had remained at home. Here their energies might have withered away in petty and fruitless occupations, and their talent have evaporated in the thin sluggishness of a colonial atmosphere.' (Lampman's bitterness stemmed in part from his own failure to improve his situation, despite petitions by Toronto papers the year before for Ottawa to intervene after rumours that the post office employee had been offered a chair at an American university: 'Don't Let the Yankees Have Our Poet,' the *World* urged.[12])

More enthusiastic were several articles that appeared in the Canadian press by the expatriates themselves. In 1893, the *Dominion Illustrated Monthly* opened its May number with a contribution from Nova Scotia expatriate Sophie Almon Hensley on Canadian writers in New York. Canadians, wrote

Hensley, boast of the work of their writers, but 'we must not forget that there is a large number of writers, born Canadians, Canadians in heart, and hope, and ambition, who have been obliged to make their homes in other countries but who still assert their claim to be sons and daughters of Canada, and who should unquestionably come under the designation of Canadian writers.' Former University of Toronto student Frank L. Pollock contributed a detailed sketch to his alma mater's *Acta Victoriana* in April of 1899 on New York's 'flourishing Canadian artistic colony,' including portraits of its 'chief,' Charles G.D. Roberts, his brothers William and Theodore, and their cousin Bliss Carman. Arthur Stringer's 'Canadian Writers Who Are Winning Fame in New York,' printed in the *Montreal Herald* in March of 1901, provided a more gossipy account of Canadian writers in the city. By his time, Stringer joked, Canadian writers were so common in New York that 'New Yorkers have an idea that you can't throw a snowball in Canada without hitting a poet. When a New York editor has all the poetry he wants he hangs out a sign, "No Canadians Admitted." In the same way, when he runs short of verse, he swings out a placard with a red mitten on it.'[13]

Boston, literary America's elder statesman, attracted its own Canadian contingent. Toronto journalist E.W. Thomson accepted an editorial position with the long-running *Youth's Companion* in 1891, writing to his friend Archibald Lampman that he was 'nicely situated, with agreeable people, in an agreeable city,' and complaining only that Bostonians did not celebrate the Queen's birthday with enough zeal.[14] Walter Blackburn Harte, a London-born immigrant to Toronto, lasted just three years before declaring literary success in Canada an impossibility and decamping for the States, becoming assistant editor of Boston's *New England Magazine* after a year of reporting work in New York. Hersilia Keays of Woodstock, Ontario, moved to Cambridge around 1897 and turned to fiction for a living, producing at least eight novels before her death. The Reverend William Benjamin King of Charlottetown, Prince Edward Island, elected to remain in Boston after retiring from his Cambridge ministry in 1900 and became (as Basil King) a best-selling novelist. Novelist Marshall Saunders deplored the Maritime migration to Boston, calling it 'a huge pulp mill into which Nova Scotia throws many of her sons and daughters,' but herself spent several years in the city before leaving in 1898 on an extended trip across America to her sister's home in California.[15] Bliss Carman worked in Boston for most of 1894–6, editing a new little magazine, the *Chap-Book*, and writing a weekly literary column for the *Boston Evening Transcript*. Like many other Canadian writers, he and his cousin Charles visited the city regularly throughout the 1890s and the first decade of the new century, placing manuscripts, looking for work, and meeting with their publishers.

Busy Chicago, especially strong in the 1880s and '90s in the publishing and newspaper industries, drew more Canadian publishers and journalists than novelists and poets. After a lucrative career of pirating popular British and American authors (most famously, Mark Twain), Alexander and Robert Belford moved the headquarters of their Toronto publishing firm to Chicago around 1880 and became the largest publishers west of New York. George Doran quit his job with Toronto's Willard Tract Depository in 1892 for a position with Chicago's Fleming H. Revell and Company, rising to vice-president by age twenty-four. Fredericton native Slason Thompson arrived in Chicago via San Francisco and New York in 1880 as western agent for the Associated Press and thereafter occupied a dizzying number of editorial positions in the city, including co-founder and editor of the *Chicago Herald*, manager of the *Chicago Daily News*, founder and co-editor of the weekly *America*, and contributing editor for the *Journal* and the *Evening Post*. Ontario journalist Eve Brodlique quit her position on the *London Advertiser* (for which she was Canada's first female parliamentary correspondent) and moved to Chicago around 1890, becoming a staff writer for the *Chicago Times-Herald*, arts reviewer for the *Times* and *Evening Post*, and president of the Chicago Women's Press Club. Constance Lindsay Skinner, a British Columbia writer who later became a popular American historian, was the Chicago *Evening American*'s drama critic from 1908 to 1910. Poet and critic Thomas O'Hagan, another late arrival to the city, served as chief editor of the Catholic *New World* from 1910 to 1913 before returning to his native Toronto after more than twenty years of teaching and writing in the States.

In fewer numbers, Canadian writers also migrated to Baltimore, Detroit, Philadelphia, Cleveland, Seattle, San Francisco. History recapitulated geography: Maritime writers moved in greater numbers to Boston, central Canadians to Chicago and New York, and so on westward, in diminishing numbers as the population decreased. A handful left the continent altogether. Nova Scotia journalist Daniel Logan, breaking regional tradition, migrated not to Boston but to Montreal and from there to the editor's desk at the *Honolulu Daily Bulletin*. Humorist Robert Barr originally left Toronto in 1876 for a position on the *Detroit Free Press*, but five years later his employers sent him to London to launch an English edition of the paper, and when the relationship ended Barr stayed. Like Barr, Ontario novelist Sara Jeannette Duncan left Canada for an American position, on the *Washington Post* in 1885–6, but after a museum curator she met on her travels proposed to her (outside the Taj Mahal, by moonlight no less), she married and settled in Calcutta. A frequent visitor to both Great Britain and the northeastern United States, Montreal novelist Lily Dougall settled permanently in England in 1900. Ontario native Gilbert Parker, the most well known in his day of Canada's English expatriates, arrived in London via Australia as an unknown journalist in 1890; ten years later, the popularity of his novels and short stories helped elect him to a seat in the British Parliament.

Of all the literary centres of the English-speaking world in the last decades of the nineteenth century, New York City beckoned most brightly. By century's end New York was publisher to the nation, home to almost a thousand book publishing and printing firms. But in these years the primary medium for new writers and the mainstay for many established writers was not books but magazines, and here New York dominated the continent. Partly because of the size of its domestic market, and partly because the reputation and distribution of its major monthlies had by this time secured markets across the States and into Canada, New York was the undisputed leader of the magazine boom of the 1880s and 1890s. By 1900, the state was producing almost fifty million dollars annually in periodical sales, subscriptions, and advertising revenue – thirty million more than next-ranked Pennsylvania, and nearly twice that of its own book and job business.[16] Literary historians are fond of dating New York's replacement of Boston as the literary centre of America from William Dean Howells's move from Boston to New York in 1891 to assume the editorship of John Brisben Walker's *Cosmopolitan* magazine. Such things no doubt matter, but what mattered more, to Howells as much as anyone, was New York's dominance over the industry that brought him to the city in the first place.

Canadian writers were neither ignorant of nor immune to the forces that brought Howells to New York. They saw the same publishers' imprints on the same books he did, read the same magazines with the same addresses on their mastheads, and in both their own and American periodicals followed the same literary currents and gossip from the city that Stringer called 'the busiest literary market in the world.' By far the largest single group of Canada's literary expatriates of the 1880s and 1890s made the same choice Howells did, and this book is mostly their story – the story of why they left Canada, of what they did in New York, and of what happened to them afterward. Its main cast numbers about two dozen, with walk-on parts by another dozen or so. All were English Canadians from the Maritimes, Quebec, or Ontario. Most played multiple roles in this story: as members of the then relatively new profession of letters, they wrote in various genres for various audiences, and from one day to the next might also be editors, publishers, illustrators, lecturers, activists, and 'metaphysicians.'

Among the first of the Maritime arrivals in New York was Craven Langstroth Betts of Saint John, a poet, bookseller, and friend and patron of American poet Edwin Arlington Robinson. Charles Brodie Patterson of Pictou, Nova Scotia, became one of the American founders of the million-strong cult of the New Thought, and with two other Canadians in New York, metaphysician Ella Walton from Toronto and her third husband John Emery McLean from Orangeville, Ontario, ran a school, a publishing house, and two magazines devoted to the cult's teachings. Aspiring poet Sophie Almon Hensley of Windsor, Nova Scotia, arrived in New York in 1890 and there transformed herself into feminist activist Almon Hensley. That same year, Bliss Carman left Fredericton to take an editorial position on the New York *Independent*; seven years later, his cousin Charles joined him in the city as the assistant editor of the *Illustrated American*, bringing with him younger brothers William and Theodore and later his son Lloyd. Within a year of his arrival the eldest Roberts became a charter member of America's National Institute of Arts and Letters.

From Quebec came Mary Elizabeth McOuat of Brownsburg, a staff writer for the *New York Recorder* in the 1890s and for the *Tribune* the following decade, and Acton Davies of St Jean, who earned his reputation as drama critic for the *New York Evening Sun* for over twenty years, but his fifteen minutes of fame as the *Sun*'s unlikely correspondent in Cuba and Puerto Rico during the Spanish-American War of 1898. Easily the most famous Canadian writer in New York in the 1880s and '90s, and one of the least well known today, was Granby's Palmer Cox, a humorist and illustrator who came to New York via San Francisco in the mid-'70s and reinvented himself as 'the Brownie Man,' the creator of the fantasy world most popular with American children until L. Frank Baum sent Dorothy to Oz at the turn of the century. Arguably more infamous than famous, Montreal publisher John W. Lovell arrived in New York about the same time as Cox and by the early '90s had become known to the trade as 'Book-a-Day Lovell,' the largest, most aggressive publisher of cheap books in America.

Toronto, then as now the centre of publishing in Canada, was also the epicentre of the literary exodus. Especially hard hit was the city's fledgling *Saturday Night*, which could probably claim the title of the Canadian magazine most likely to be abandoned for an American paycheque. Two friends from the magazine's first years, humorist Peter McArthur and literary editor Duncan McKellar, left for New York in 1890 and 1891, respectively. The weekly's outdoors writer Edwyn Sandys left in 1891 to accept an editorial position on the New York sporting magazine *Outing*, and a year later its sometime society columnist Graeme Mercer Adam, the post-Confederation era's most tireless promoter of Canadian letters, left to work for his former partner John W. Lovell in New York.

Mary Bourchier Sanford, a humorist from Barrie, Ontario, arrived in New

York the same year as McArthur and published her sketches and jokes in many of the same periodicals. In 1891, the success of Toronto lawyer Stinson Jarvis's first novel precipitated a career change and a move to New York, where Jarvis's upper-class Toronto recreations sustained additional careers as a yachting reporter, a drama critic, and an authority on psychic phenomena. By 1896 New York was home to Toronto naturalist Ernest Thompson Seton, author and illustrator of the animal stories that paid for a midtown studio overlooking Bryant Park and a hundred-acre country estate near Greenwich, Connecticut. The following year saw the arrival of Norman Duncan of Brantford, a former University of Toronto student whose first taste of literary success came with a series of stories about lower Manhattan's Syrian colony. By century's end three more University of Toronto students – Arthur McFarlane, Harvey O'Higgins, and Arthur Stringer – shared an attic in an old Fifth Avenue brownstone that, like the Robertses' family addresses, became a centre for Canadians in the city. McFarlane became a well-paid investigative journalist, a so-called muckraker, while O'Higgins won the title 'prose laureate of the commonplace man' for his stories of New York's Irish community and Stringer broke the best-seller lists with fast-paced adventure novels about the city's criminal underworld.

There were, of course, other Canadians whose work has been lost in the unsigned columns of the city's dailies and weekend 'specials,' or whose literary ambitions became careers in advertising, banking, plumbing. The New York literary industry experienced an unprecedented boom in these years, the kind of prosperity that attracts many but rewards few and remembers even fewer. This book has some success stories to tell, but there are many failures in its silences.

History has left a better record of the failure that caused the exodus in the first place, the inability of post-Confederation Canada to sustain and thus retain its writers. The union of Britain's northern colonies in 1867 excited a burst of domestic literary energy, but as Graeme Mercer Adam later remarked, 'the flush on its face ere long passed off,' largely because the source of that energy was political need (for founding father Thomas D'Arcy McGee, a national literature was 'a state and social necessity'), not a critical mass of writers and readers. The generation of Canadians who came of age in the 1880s and 1890s inherited a literary culture with very few domestic models, and with substantial material impediments to domestic authorship, among them a publishing industry more intent on reprinting familiar English and American authors than encouraging new Canadian authors; inadequate copyright protection for books first published in Canada; higher postage rates for magazines shipped within Canada than imported into Canada; and, its writers claimed, a readership too preoccupied with economic progress to care about imaginative literature – about anything but 'wheat, railroads and politics,' as one fired back from exile.[17]

Post-Confederation Canadians with an interest in fostering a native literature were acutely aware of and repeatedly lamented the problems specific to Canadian literary culture. To focus too closely on their complaints, however, is to lose sight of the full dimensions of that culture and therefore to misunderstand the conditions of authorship in late-nineteenth-century Canada. Traffic in literary goods and influences moved more freely across Canada's borders in this period than in any other, and like other forms of economic and intellectual traffic was especially fluid across the country's only land border. The problems confronting domestic literary production were real, but the domestic market wasn't the only option for Canadian writers of this generation: they also had access by mail or in person to the much larger American market, a market that by this time *included* Canada. Canadians had few home-grown literary models, but the flood of American magazines and American books into Canada provided models for them, models that had become features of a North American literary landscape. At a professional level, the decision by so many Canadian writers of these years to move to American cities wasn't about giving up one national literary culture for another; it was about moving from the margins to the centres of a continental literary culture. She wasn't entirely happy about it, but for Sara Jeannette Duncan in the summer of 1887 the literary predicament of her generation was clear: 'The market for Canadian literary wares of all sorts is self-evidently New York, where the intellectual life of the continent is rapidly centralising.'[18]

The market Duncan described had consolidated its reach, not its products. Literature at the time of its production doesn't consist of anything like T.S. Eliot's 'ideal order' of classic monuments, but is instead the highly diverse product of a constantly changing set of different artistic communities.[19] These communities are rarely devoted to a single literary genre or confined to a single literary mode (fiction or non-fiction, realism or romance), or even to a single artistic medium. Their main organizing principles are content and sensibility: people who are interested in animal conservation write and read literature sympathetic to animals, but that interest ranges from factual studies of real animals to romantic stories of fictional animals, and is likely to include making, collecting, or simply enjoying animal-sympathetic art in a variety of media. Each of these communities develops recognizable characteristics that help to promote it (the artistic equivalent of branding) and that allow others to join by successfully reproducing those characteristics: if, in Eliot's day, you were interested in becoming a modern poet, you should have known better than to write poems about how happy daffodils made you feel. Eventually, those characteristics become entrenched and susceptible to challenge and revision, or to boredom, parody, and abandonment.

The American literary landscape of the 1880s and 1890s consisted of many such 'cultures of letters,' as their historian Richard H. Brodhead calls them. But what Brodhead calls American cultures of letters were actually North American cultures of letters, cultures based in the literary centres of the United States but with a transnational and in some cases transatlantic membership and audience. The dimensions of the American literary market ensured the visibility of these cultures in Canada, and therefore that Canadians could acquire, with the same facility as Americans, the familiarity required to reproduce their forms. Some Canadian writers participated from a distance, sending their work to American magazines and publishers hospitable to their interests, but many took the next logical step and moved to the American centres of these literary cultures.

The best way, I think, to make sense of the variety of American-based literary communities that Canadian writers joined in this period is through the cultural map provided by Jackson Lears in his *No Place of Grace: Antimodernism and the Transformation of American Culture, 1880–1920*. Lears argues that many turn-of-the-century Americans rebelled against what they saw as the morally, spiritually, and physically attenuating forces of modern culture. Concerned that modernization had created a life that was overcivilized and strangely unreal, antimodernists prescribed regenerative, more 'authentic' models of experience, models that included the preindustrial craftsman, the medieval warrior, the big-game hunter, the simple rustic, and the Eastern mystic. Both Lears's antimodern rebels and his modern guardians were mostly well-educated, middle-class whites from the North, and Canada's literary expatriates, mostly well-educated, middle-class whites from the other North, settled comfortably into the cultural contest he describes. Some found homes in literary communities supportive of the official culture, reporting its milestones in the daily press, feeding its citizens' insatiable desire for self-improvement with informative magazines and books, and using humour to celebrate its achievements and laugh off its failures. Perhaps because of their less modern origins, however, Canadian expatriates played especially prominent and in several cases leading roles in antimodern literary cultures, including that face of its therapeutic movement that came to be known as New Thought, its cult of the outdoors (whether as animal-worshipper or animal-hunter), and its postrealist versions of romantic adventure and local colour fiction. Like Lears's American antimodernists, Canadian contributors to the rebellion unintentionally helped their audiences not to remedy but to accept modernization: Carman's

Vagabond poems, McLean's and Patterson's program of psychic rejuvenation, Seton's and Sandys's outings with the animals, and Stringer's and Roberts's romantic adventure stories weren't cures but effective and popular tonics for a tired modern America.

Canadian writers who moved to New York in this period joined these and other literary cultures, but they also formed their own social and professional communities within and across these cultures. Older arrivals like Lovell, Betts, and Halifax theology student turned dime-novel publisher George Munro joined the Canadian Club of New York, by 1887 occupying an ornately equipped four-story clubhouse on East Twenty-ninth Street and listing over four hundred resident and non-resident members.[20] Younger, less solvent expatriates frequented cafés like Maria's spaghetti house on West Twelfth, the favourite of the city's Bohemian set, or Flouret's, a popular French restaurant at Eighteenth and Fifth where Carman first introduced 'Mary Perry' to his friend and publisher Mitchell Kennerley. In working hours they met at each other's professional addresses, at the lower Broadway offices of Peter McArthur's *Truth*, or at Carman's office at the *Independent* five blocks north, or at what Roberts called 'the down-town Canadian Club,' the offices at 140 Fifth Avenue where Kennerley managed the American interests of London publisher John Lane.[21] They gathered too at each other's homes, notably the East Fifty-eighth Street boarding house that was the Robertses' first address in the city (just a few blocks from where Howells had landed, on West Fifty-ninth overlooking the Park), their next home on East Seventeenth, and the attic flat above Kennerley's offices where Stringer, McFarlane, and O'Higgins covered the walls with rejection letters and mixed drinks on credit for Carman, Roberts, McArthur, and other visitors to their 'Chamber of a Thousand Sorrows.'

Here, in New York, Canadian writers formed their country's first professional literary communities. At these and other gathering places they shared setbacks and successes, read and discussed each other's work, exchanged literary gossip, and argued new literary trends. They helped each other into print, passing on tips about copy-hungry editors and warning about those slow with a paycheque. Most directly, they published each other's work in the magazines they edited, in McArthur's *Truth*, or in Carman's *Independent* and Sandys' *Outing*, or in Thomson's *Youth's Companion* and Harte's *New England Magazine* in Boston. And, crucially for some Canadian writers, they extended the reach of these communities beyond New York, using their positions and connections to promote and publish the work of friends still at home and in other literary centres.

These communities weren't exclusively Canadian: professionally and socially they included American and transplanted English members, editors like

Richard Watson Gilder of the *Century*, publishers like the English-born Kennerley, mentors like the New York critic Edmund Clarence Stedman, and co-writers like Carman's companion in Vagabondia, the American poet Richard Hovey, or Harvey O'Higgins's several American collaborators. But for the first time, Canadian writers found in New York professional literary-social communities composed primarily of other Canadians, at the centre of a large and receptive market for their products, and with members who were proving it possible for a Canadian writer to earn a living and even fame from writing alone. For twenty-two-year-old Toronto writer Frank Pollock, a visitor in the winter of 1898–9 to the Robertses' busy rooms at 105 East Seventeenth, the effect of this combination of circumstances upon the city's colony of Canadian writers was 'the most amazing *esprit de corps* imaginable.'[22]

Its effect upon Canadian literature was equally dramatic. From the late 1890s to the First World War Canadian literature experienced its own boom, a phenomenon that Ontario historian Lawrence Johnstone Burpee diagnosed in 1899 as 'what promises to be the genuine and thorough awakening of the long dormant spirit of Canadian fiction,' and that the Canadian Institute for Historical Microreproductions has since quantified, more generally, as an increase in language and literature titles from 9 per cent of its pre-1900 collection to 25 per cent of its collection from 1900 to 1920.[23] Canada's expatriate writers were directly responsible for much of this growth: they represented over half of the country's more prolific writers in these years, and all but a few of its best-sellers. All five of the well-known novelists that prompted Burpee's prediction, for instance, were expatriates. More important for Canadian literature, the commercial and critical recognition the expatriates received from non-Canadian publishers, reviewers, and readers helped to legitimize the writing, publishing, and reading of imaginative literature in Canada. By their own work and by the example of that work, the literary expatriates of the 1880s and 1890s did more than any other individual or group to lead Canada to a self-aware, self-sustaining, and eventually self-defining domestic literature.

At first, most Canadian references to the expatriates proudly claimed their work as Canadian, usually by proudly claiming their authors as Canadian. But the domestic literary boom rekindled nationalist imperatives to celebrate writers within Canada and to distinguish their work from other literatures, especially American. To meet these imperatives Canadian literary critics and historians used the same logic as their European and American predecessors. To be Canadian, they argued with increasing confidence, a work of literature must show the impact of the Canadian environment – the spirit of the soil, in one of their favourite figures. The consequence of this argument was the excision of many of the expatriates from the literature they had made possible.

In 1896, the New Brunswick-born historian Thomas Guthrie Marquis defended Carman against a critical review in the New York *Bookman* by arguing that its (American) reviewer needed experience of the (Canadian) land to appreciate the poem he'd found fault with. Seventeen years later, in 1913, Marquis argued in English Canada's first comprehensive literary history that Carman and the other expatriates of his generation had 'lost their Canadian colour and atmosphere and become a literary part of the country in which they have made their home.'[24] The land giveth, and the land taketh away.

The story doesn't end there, of course – if it did, Carman's ashes would still be lying in a Connecticut cemetery. As the domestic literary scene gained momentum, and especially during the war years, those expatriates still known in Canada went though a period of neglect from which most never recovered. When Carman and Roberts returned to Canada in the 1920s, however, they were neither ignored nor dismissed as American or English writers; they were welcomed popularly and officially as conquering Canadian heroes, one crowned poet laureate and the other knighted. Carman and Roberts were welcomed home because they had succeeded where it has always mattered most to most Canadians, in the literary centres of the United States and England. For Canadians to sacrifice home-grown celebrities to the nationalist demand for an indigenous literary tradition was too great a price to pay: Marquis may have thought the expatriates were no longer purely Canadian, but he included their books in his study all the same, because without them the short and humble story that he saw as Canada's literary history to date would have been shorter and humbler.

Over the long term, though, 'Canadian colour' proved more important than commercial or critical success in deciding which of the expatriates, and which of their works, would be repatriated. The principle that an authentic national literature reflects the special qualities of its homeland ensured, for instance, that Carman's nostalgic lyrics about his Maritime home, Seton's biographies of doomed animals, and Norman Duncan's stories about the hard life of a Newfoundland outport would become part of Canadian literature, and that Duncan's stories about the blending of cultures in Manhattan's Syrian quarter, Roberts's New York love poems, Stringer's racy urban crime novels, and any others that didn't fit the developing perception of that literature, would not. In the end, the expatriates gave Canada more than a literature: they gave it a past in which critics could find both the Canada they wanted and the Canada they didn't, a process of selection and definition that expressed itself in histories like Marquis's and in acts like the claiming of Carman's body, and that ultimately produced a recognized if perennially contested national literature. Very few of the expatriates were as enthusiastically reclaimed as Carman. And yet, in outline, his story is typical of their fate: celebrated at home when they were needed, dismissed as not sufficiently Canadian when they weren't, and selectively repatriated and reinvented after their deaths as contributors, whether as founders or footnotes, to a discretely Canadian literary tradition.

In the last decades of the nineteenth century, powerful obstacles to a domestic literature together with powerful attractions to other literary centres caused most Canadian writers who mattered, and many who didn't, to leave Canada, most for the United States, most of those for New York. As a profession, as the inspiration for a domestic literature, and as the groundwork of a national canon, Canadian literature began here: not in the backwoods of Ontario, not on the salt flats of New Brunswick, but in the cafés, publishing offices, and boarding houses of late-nineteenth-century New York.

But first, how it got there.

Chapter 1

Lamentations

In 1906, two articles appeared in the American press that belatedly confirmed the Canadian literary presence in the United States. In June, Columbia University's *Political Science Quarterly* published a study of Canadians in America by University of Toronto economist Samuel Morley Wickett. Mostly statistical, Wickett's study alludes to several well-known individual Canadians in the States, including New York businessman Erastus Wiman and Cornell University president Jacob Gould Schurman, and adds that a full list of distinguished Canadians living in that country would have to include 'littérateurs, clergymen, actors, members of Congress and even one diplomatic representative of the Republic' (probably Hamilton King, Newfoundland-born American consul general to Siam from 1898 to 1912). A month later, New York's *Munsey's Magazine* ran an illustrated article on Canadians in the States as part of a series on the immigrant races of America by staff writer Herbert N. Casson, an Ontario native who had recently come to *Munsey's* from the *New York World*. Casson lists the names and accomplishments of some two hundred Canadian-born educators, preachers, doctors, public officials, soldiers, lawyers, engineers, actors, authors, artists, and businessmen then living in the United States. Authors Bliss Carman, Norman Duncan, Palmer Cox, Charles G.D. Roberts, and Agnes C. Laut appear, as do journalists Slason Thompson, Herbert F. Gunnison, Acton Davies, James Creelman, and Hubert P. Whitmarsh. 'In proportion to her population,' notes Casson, 'Canada has perhaps been more generous to us than any other country, with the exception of Ireland. There are comparatively few families in Canada which have not given at least one citizen to the United States.'[1]

As Wickett's and Casson's articles suggest, Canada's literary expatriates were part of a massive wave of Canadian emigration to the United States in the final decades of the nineteenth century. Canada kept no serious record of its departing citizens, but the most cautious estimates, based on American census returns of the Canadian-born resident in the States, put the number who emigrated to the United States between 1880 and 1900 at over three-quarters of a million. Other sources, first among them the noted American immigration historian Marcus Lee Hansen in his *The Mingling of the Canadian and American Peoples*, claim that Canadian emigration to the States exceeded a million people in the 1880s alone.[2] (The natural increase in the Canadian population for both decades was just 1.46 million.) Whichever figure we now accept, to the Canadian of the day Goldwin Smith's remark in his controversial *Canada and the Canadian Question* of 1891 must have seemed to express a bitter reality: 'The Americans may say in truth,' wrote Smith, 'that if they do not annex Canada, they are annexing the Canadians.'[3]

Canadian historians have identified a number of reasons for this exodus. The economy of the period suffered a series of financial panics and outright depression. Droughts on the prairies forced farm foreclosures. High freight rates hurt existing businesses and discouraged new ones. Protective tariffs, ironically intended to foster the domestic economy and 'retain in Canada thousands of our fellow-countrymen, now obliged to expatriate themselves in search of the employment denied them at home,' ultimately forced Canadians to buy more expensive 'Made in Canada' manufactured goods.[4] Maritimers and Westerners, unhappy with the broken promises of Confederation, grumbled and talked of succession and annexation. Throughout all this, newspapers, friends, and relatives told of jobs just a border away with better pay, better conditions, and better prospects. In sum, says one observer, the period 'demanded a high price for being a Canadian and a great number chose not to pay.'[5]

Canadians of the day tended to offer simpler, if sometimes stranger, explanations for the southern drift. In May of 1884, one J.H.S. argued in Toronto's *Week* that the emigration of young Canadian men to the United States was due to certain key professions in Canada being overstocked (medicine and the law), underpaid (railway clerks and stenographers), or 'sneered at ... as one scarcely suitable to a *gentleman*' (journalism).[6] Five years later, a *Week* editorial attributed the 'much-talked-of "exodus"' of young Canadians to the States to the general urbanward movement of all populations, and to Canada's lack of enough large cities to satisfy the demand. For his part, K.L. Jones of Kingston, Ontario, credited the exodus to America's better climate – much of Canada, wrote Jones, is 'a fit home only for the Laplander and reindeer' – and to the inherent greed of the Scottish-Canadian, lured statesward by the rags-to-riches fairy tales of the Astors, the Vanderbilts, the Goulds. In response, 'Redfern' of Weston, Ontario, argued that Mr Jones would have come nearer the truth had he said that 'a young man is treated better, paid better, works better, in our neighbouring Republic.'[7]

Whether caused by a faltering economy, discontent with the political bargain, the lure of better prospects, or the Canadian winter, Canadian emigration to the United States between 1880 and 1900 exceeded any twenty-year period in Canadian history. By the turn of the century, the Canadian-born resident in America numbered about 1.2 million – almost a quarter of Canada's total population at the time. Boston, with over 84,000 citizens of Canadian birth or parentage, was Canada's third largest city, behind only Montreal and Toronto.[8] In his speech formally opening the Canadian Club of New York on 1 July 1885, founding president Erastus Wiman estimated the number of Canadians in the city to be about six thousand; by 1900, the Canadian-born population of New York City had almost quadrupled, to just under 22,000.[9] French Canadian immigrants, who amounted to some 400,000 of the Canadian-born in the United States, tended to settle in a concentrated area – the mill towns of Massachusetts, New Hampshire, and Rhode Island, with a smaller group in Michigan. English Canadians could be found in considerable numbers throughout the States, except in the South.[10] Massachusetts, Michigan, and New York had the highest number of first-generation English Canadian residents, but there were also large concentrations in Illinois and California and a more evenly spread group across the entire Midwest. After tallying the statistics for the Canadian exodus in his 1907 *The Americanization of Canada*, American historian Samuel E. Moffett was moved to facetiousness: 'Greater Canada – the home of the Canadian people – reaches down to Long Island Sound, westward south of the Great Lakes, and on to the Pacific Coast.'[11]

The same motives that compelled so many other Canadians to seek their fortune in America played upon the minds of Canadian writers. In time, too, the size of the migration became its own cause, as individual and collective success stories made their way back to Canada via letters, the press, and rumour. But for Canada's literary emigrants, there were additional incentives for the move. There must have been. Even accepting the highest estimates, the national emigration rate over the 1880s and 1890s was under 17 per cent, while the Canadian literary community was reduced over the same period by something approaching 50 per cent.

In the Camp of the Philistines

The first requirement for the survival of a professional writer is a publisher. While not quite in crisis – not consistently, anyway – the publishing industry in Canada of the 1880s and '90s suffered with other industries from the period's economic difficulties. The census of 1881 had recorded 395 printing and publishing establishments in the country (that is, printers and publishers not just of books and periodicals, but of stationary, sheet music, and so forth), employing 6,423 people and producing an aggregate value of products of 4.7 million. Although the ensuing decade did see growth in the trade, it was also marked by a series of prominent failures. Toronto's James Campbell and Son went bankrupt in October of 1884. The Dawson Brothers of Montreal dissolved their partnership in 1889. William Clark's Canada Publishing Company, a sometime employer of future expatriate Graeme Mercer Adam, had disappeared by 1890. As late as 1894, London's *Publishers' Circular* reported that bankruptcies in the Canadian printing and publishing industry were 40 per cent above all previous records.[12] Despite these failures, by the end of the 1880s the number of Canadian printers and publishers had climbed to 589, employing 8,614 people and producing 8.3 million dollars' worth of product annually. But by 1900 that number had decreased to 419, and both employment and production had increased much less than in the previous decade. The declining number of establishments in the 1890s is partly attributable to consolidation in the industry, something that was also occurring south of the border. But the relatively small gain in the value of products (24 per cent, compared to 75 per cent in the 1880s) suggests that the industry failures of the 1880s were followed in the 1890s by a period of regrouping, of scaled-back expectations and production.[13]

More important to Canadian writers, the domestic publishing industry was neither devoted to nor dependent upon the publication of original Canadian work. According to George L. Parker's *The Beginnings of the Book Trade in Canada*, Canadian publishers from the mid-1870s to the mid-'90s relied upon one of three methods for economic survival: 'by becoming fiction reprint houses, by innovative merchandising that consisted of distributing books by mail and by subscription, or by developing monopolies as textbook printers.'[14] None of these methods required original Canadian creative work to succeed. Some few Canadian publishers, such as Saint John's J. and A. McMillan, Montreal's Dawson Brothers, and Toronto's William Briggs, published a smattering of Canadian fiction and poetry in the eighties and early nineties. But most Canadian publishers of imaginative literature were content to keep to the lucrative field of reprinting well-known British and American authors. By 1889, for instance, John Ross Robertson of Toronto, publisher of Robertson's Cheap Series, claimed to have printed (others said pirated) over a million books.[15] Of the sixty-eight titles I've been able to locate in this series, most are reprints of popular American authors of the period, including E.P. Roe, E.D.E.N. Southworth, Mary J. Holmes, and Mark Twain. Only eight are of known

Canadian authorship, and all but one of those are reprints of novels by May Agnes Fleming, better known and much more widely published in America than in Canada, and by then dead and buried in Brooklyn.

With little publisher support or interest at home, the more successful Canadian writers of the period followed Fleming's example, sending their manuscripts to publishers outside the country. After privately printing his first book, Archibald Lampman finally placed his second and last with a Boston firm in 1896: 'We really have no publishers in the country except Briggs,' he wrote that year. A few years later, Sara Jeannette Duncan confessed that she had 'given up as hopeless any attempt to get my books on the market of my own country. They always seem to fall between the two stools of the London & New York publishers.'[16] Less-established Canadian writers could print their work themselves, or pay a publisher to bring it out for them, but none made a living from such arrangements. In early 1892, Walter Blackburn Harte, by then in Boston, argued in the London *Literary World* that young Canadian writers had no choice but to emigrate because 'in Canada it is impossible to find a publisher willing to assume the risk of publishing a book; and if the author defray the cost of production it is ridiculous to look for a public in Canada which will buy his book sufficiently to reimburse him.' Or as Harvey O'Higgins had one hopeful writer and soon-to-be expatriate say of Canadians in his autobiographical novel *Don-A-Dreams*, 'They don't charge you anything for printing your stuff – unless you want to bring out a book. You have to pay for a book. There's money in writing school readers, I understand – and City Directories. If they want anything to read after they leave school, they buy a set of Dickens or Thackeray, and enjoy the latest thing in literature. I'd sooner write ads for a New York department store on a salary of three thousand a year.'[17]

The market for magazine publication in late-nineteenth-century Canada wasn't much better than that for books. Religious periodicals went forth and multiplied, but there were few secular magazines, and even fewer that strayed from the tried-and-true practice of reprinting syndicated work by well-known British and American writers. In Montreal, the *Canadian Illustrated News* (1869–83) and its successor, the *Dominion Illustrated* (1888–93), regularly published Canadian artists and writers. In Toronto, Goldwin Smith's *Rose-Belford's Canadian Monthly* (1878–82) and the *Week* (1883–96) published original articles on Canadian culture and history, Canadian poetry, and the odd short fiction by a Canadian author. *Saturday Night*, founded in 1887, was a Canadian version of the by then numerous British and American mass-market fiction weeklies. T.H. Best's *Canadian Magazine* (1893–1939), a popular monthly devoted to current affairs, short fiction, and photographic essays, made it a special policy to publish Canadian writers. In Manitoba, the *Winnipeg Free Press* (1872–) published some original poetry, fiction, and essays. In part because its most energetic editor, George Stewart Jr, had moved to central Canada, the Maritimes in the 1880s and 1890s experienced an unusual gap in periodical publication. *Stewart's Literary Quarterly* and the *Maritime Monthly* of Saint John hadn't been published since the mid-1870s, and the first issue of the *New Brunswick Magazine* wouldn't appear until 1898.

If Canadian writers of the 1880s and 1890s had only a half-dozen or so mainstream, general interest magazines to choose from, it was harder still to find an outlet for writing aimed at three of the largest splinter markets of the magazine era: juvenile literature, avant-garde work in the manner of London's *Yellow Book*, and humour. The only Canadian competitors for giants of the children's magazine industry such as Boston's *Youth's Companion* and New York's *St. Nicholas* were Sunday school periodicals the likes of *Pleasant Hours* (Toronto, 1881–1929) and the odd short-lived secular paper. For Canadians who might want to publish more experimental writing than that favoured by the mainstream magazines, there were even fewer choices: Toronto's *Tarot*, an illustrated monthly that featured 'rather esoteric writing for Victorian Toronto,' appeared for just two issues in 1896, and Theodore Goodridge Roberts edited the equally short-lived *Kit-Bag* in Fredericton in 1902.[18] As for humour, in 1906 Herbert Casson asked readers of *Munsey's Magazine* to Imagine a land of nearly four million square miles, an not one comic paper! If a Canadian writer does pen a humorous article in a moment of weakness, he is obliged to send it out anonymously. If he confesses his guilt, the consequences are sometimes serious. Recently a professor in an Ontario college, so a Canadian editor tells me, wrote a witty story for a New York magazine. As soon as it appeared, he was solemnly requested to send in his resignation.'[19] Casson overlooked Toronto's *Grip* (1873–94), by that time defunct, but his point stands, and presumably wasn't lost on aspiring Canadian humorists like Robert Barr and Peter McArthur.

Also not lost on Canadian writers was the all too well-known fact that Canadian periodicals could not, or would not, pay competitive prices to their contributors. As George Stewart Jr wrote in a letter to the *Week* in 1894, 'until Canadian publishers make up their minds to pay their contributors a fair honorarium, they cannot expect to get the best productions of their pens.' Those contributions, Stewart warned, have been and will be published instead in British and American periodicals.[20] Some Canadian writers continued to offer some of their work to Canadian periodicals out of a sense of charity or duty, but as with their books, many – and most of those who lived by their writing – sent their work elsewhere. Between 1882 and 1902 Boston's *Youth's*

Companion alone published some three hundred articles, poems, and stories by known Canadian writers.[21] Ottawa poet Wilfred Campbell, a contributor to the *Companion* in the early nineties, had by the end of 1893 earned over $350 for his periodical verse – 'not a cent of it,' writes his biographer, 'appears to have been Canadian money.' Even those who continued to submit their work to Canadian periodicals occasionally bridled. As late as 1906, Halifax university professor Archibald MacMechan wrote the *Canadian Magazine* to describe the eight dollars he had received for his article on James De Mille as 'starvation wages,' and to warn that Canadian magazines 'will not be supported from motives of patriotism alone.' When the magazine offered the same amount to Toronto writer Marjorie Pickthall for a short story, Pickthall withdrew it, saying she expected at least fifteen dollars. The story appeared in Boston's *Atlantic Monthly.*[22]

Next to money, the most common complaint among Canadian authors of the 1880s and 1890s was the country's deficient readership. Duncan called her native Ontario 'one great camp of the Philistines.' Harte noted bitterly that Canadians 'only care for wheat, railroads and politics.' Barr nominated Canada 'the poorest book market in the world outside of Senegambia.'[23]

Duncan, Harte, and Barr were right in one respect: Canadians of their day were less literate than Americans. At the start of the 1890s the Canadian census reported a literacy rate of 80 per cent, while American returns showed an 87 per cent literacy rate. The actual difference is certainly greater, for although the American figure included non-whites – with, on average, a far lower literacy rate than the white population – the Canadian pointedly did not: 55,401 Natives were 'eliminated' from the reckoning.[24]

But contrary to the complaints of their departing writers, literate Canadians had access to and appear to have enthusiastically supported a growing number of bookstores, amateur educational associations, and literary societies. As early as the 1860s, says Parker, there were bookstores in 'every important town in the country.' In 1884, to give a local example, four bookstores served Victoria's population of ten thousand – a greater ratio than the city enjoys today. By 1880 the English-founded Mechanics' Institutes, mutual-instruction societies for working men, numbered about a hundred in Ontario alone. The institutes lent works in technical instruction, practical science, and so on, but also, by popular demand, fiction: in the Toronto Institute, almost 80 per cent of the books borrowed in the 1878–9 season were fiction.[25] As book historian Heather Murray has recently shown, late-nineteenth-century Ontario saw a boom in amateur educational societies with a literary focus, from single-author book clubs to eclectically interested literary societies and more structured mutual-improvement associations such as the Mechanics' Institutes and Canadian versions and chapters of the American-based Chautauqua Institution. Murray identifies over three hundred literary societies in nineteenth-century Ontario, and it's the size of that figure that confined her work to Ontario, not the absence of similar societies elsewhere in Canada.

In deference to Barr's complaint about the Canadian book market, it should be said that Canadian booksellers of this period faced real difficulties: competition with the low-overhead subscription houses and the Mechanics' Institutes, public libraries, and literary societies (all formed to avoid buying books by sharing their cost among subscribers); the new bookstalls on trains and in train stations; the entry of department stores into the loss-leader book business; and the ability to skip the Canadian middleman and import books directly from other countries. But none of these hurdles suggests that Canadians didn't read books: the very fact that Canadian booksellers repeatedly bemoaned their losses tells us there was a market to be lost. As Murray shows, Canadians of the period read a great deal: they just didn't read, in the eyes of Duncan, Harte, and Barr, the *right* books. By the late 1880s the market in Canada for imaginative literature was based on cheap, pirated reprints or 'colonial editions' of standard English and American authors. In this active but highly competitive arena there couldn't have been much room for original Canadian books, the one field in which publishers had to consider the author in determining their costs and therefore their prices. Fortunately for the reprint houses, the Canadian readership had tastes as conservative as its spending habits. There are no societies dedicated to Canadian writers among Murray's three hundred, and very few that read any Canadian writing at all. When an independent Chautauqua formed at Niagara-on-the-Lake in the summer of 1887, it named the streets of its grounds after the figures who, as Murray says, represented their 'intellectual, educational, political, and spiritual orientations': the surviving map shows streets named for Addison, Dickens, Longfellow, Homer, Milton, Shakespeare, and Tennyson, but none for Canadian poets or novelists, though Ontario educator Egerton Ryerson did get a park in a 'secluded corner.'[26]

Even if published, even if paid, even if read, Canadian writers still faced the problem of how to protect their work. The full story of the copyright problem in early Canada is too complex to relate here; it takes its best historian, George Parker, the better part of a book to relate. But to summarize, borrowing from Parker, nineteenth-century Canada was governed by two bodies of copyright law, the first imperial and the second local. From 1842 to 1911, copyright in the British empire was controlled by the Copyright Act of 1842. Intended like most early copyright acts to protect publishers more than the international rights of authors, the Copyright Act protected throughout the empire only those works that were first published in London or Edinburgh. It also prohibited pirated reprints of British copyright books from entering British territory. In 1847, under heavy pressure from the Canadian colonies, in particular, for 'cheap books,' this prohibition was lifted in the Foreign Reprints Act, which remained in effect until 1894. Under the terms of this act, each colony would pass its own act to govern the collection of a special duty placed on each pirated reprint, which would then be paid to the copyright owner (in practice this duty was rarely collected and even more rarely paid). In addition to this colonial version of imperial copyright law, local acts extended limited protection to locally produced and usually locally authored books. Such acts, which protected works only within their province or region, were passed in Quebec in 1832, Nova Scotia in 1838, the united Province of Canada in 1841, and the Dominion of Canada in 1868.

The upshot of all this for post-Confederation Canadian authors was that their work, if first published in Canada, was protected from piracy only within the relatively small market of Canada itself. For the vast majority of Canadian authors, the economic effect of this failure to protect Canadian works beyond the Canadian border was zero: although a phenomenon like Ralph Connor could, and did, lose thousands of royalty dollars to foreign reprints, London and New York publishers weren't waiting in line to pirate the latest literary sensation from Etobicoke. Besides, Canadian authors could circumvent the problem by publishing their work first in England or, after 1891, in the United States and then arranging for a Canadian edition to secure copyright in their own country. But along with Connor, some Canadian authors who published at home were undoubtedly hurt by the lack of international protection – exactly how many may never be known, given the ephemeral nature of the reprint establishments and their products. Just as important, with the 'Copyright Question' continually debated in Canadian newspapers and magazines, aspiring Canadian writers knew that success for a home-printed book included the possibility of being pirated abroad and sold at home with no remuneration to themselves. To a lesser extent, this was also true for books printed in the United States, which provided authors with full national but limited international protection because of its refusal to sign the Berne Convention. But given the size of the American market, the choice between losing copyright in, say, Holland, and losing it in the United States can't have been hard to make.[27]

In addition to the financial effects, the copyright problem had other, less tangible, effects on Canadian authors. In the long and labyrinthine quarrel that is the history of Canadian copyright in the nineteenth century, it was the author alone among the interested parties – the government, the reading public, the retailers, the wholesalers, the printers, and the publishers – whose interests were, as Parker puts it with characteristic understatement, 'pretty well ignored.'[28] The reprint publishers in particular, with their cries for the protection of Canadian industry, simply swung a much larger stick. Eventually, too, the effect became a cause: so many high-profile Canadian authors had left by the end of the century that few remained to speak on their behalf, though some, like Gilbert Parker in England, did so from exile. Finally, it is one of the unfortunate accidents of history that the principal debates on the 'Copyright Question' came at a time when Canadian politicians went to the international bargaining table more intent on demonstrating Canadian autonomy than on any other objective. If England wanted international protection for authors, then, perversely, Canada did not: 'We have the right,' proclaimed Minister of Justice Sir Charles Hibbert Tupper in September of 1895, 'to misgovern ourselves if we choose as to copyright, as we have in tariff and everything else.'[29] In such a climate the wonder is not that so many Canadian authors left, but that any stayed.

The Continental 'We'

Few Canadian writers of the post-Confederation era knew better the problems they faced than Toronto's Graeme Mercer Adam. Adam tried it all: bookseller, publisher, editor, writer. At nineteen, he managed a Toronto bookstore. In the early 1870s he almost single-handedly wrote and published the trade journal *Canada Bookseller*. He started his own publishing house, and lobbied extensively for improvements to Canadian copyright law. He founded, edited, and saw the demise of some of the most important Canadian magazines of his day, including the *British American Magazine*, the *Canadian Monthly*, and *Rose-Belford's Canadian Monthly*. He edited the Royal Canadian Readers series for Canadian schools, compiled bibliographies for Canadian libraries, and reviewed new books for Canadian newspapers and magazines. He wrote a popular history of the North-West, a school history of England and Canada, and a scholarly history of Canadian literature. In his spare time, he wrote travel books on Toronto, Quebec City, Halifax, and Ontario's Muskoka region, and co-authored a historical romance of Upper Canada. In short, Adam knew every aspect of the Canadian publishing scene, and everyone in it knew him. 'Not to have heard of Mr. Graeme Mercer Adam,' wrote Sophie Hensley in 1893, 'would be to prove oneself not a Canadian, so many years has he been identified with Canadian thought and literature.'[30]

By the summer of 1890, after three decades of literary labour in Canada, Adam was ready to pass judgment on the fruits of that labour. Speaking at a banquet of the Employing Printers' Association in Toronto, he remarked, 'It is not so long since one of the most gifted of Australian poets blew his brains out just after the publication of his "Bush Ballads" in Melbourne. Of the literary fraternity in the Colonies, the wonder is that he alone has sought to put a speedy and tragic close to the burden of life.'[31]

Adam may have been the most qualified to speak on Canada's literary problems, but he wasn't the only one to do so. Virtually all those who left, and many who stayed, voiced their complaints. Arthur Stringer told Montrealers that 'no man can live by praise alone. The young Canadian dreamer who grows up under the blue skies of his Dominion is going to have a hard road to travel if he thinks he can prance his Pegasus between Montreal and Toronto, and pay for oats and horse-shoes when the travelling is over.' Marshall Saunders, probably the first Canadian author to sell over a million copies of a single book (*Beautiful Joe*, 1894), recalled years later for a Toronto audience that 'when I started writing I met with so little encouragement in Canada that I went to American earth – but without,' she discreetly added, 'the slightest resentment.' Constance Lindsay Skinner justified her American residence to a friend by saying 'alas! Canada has, as yet, failed to provide a market for her writers; and writers must live – at least we *think* we must!' Thomas O'Hagan wrote home to charge Canadians with praising their poets but not providing any '*practical* appreciation of their worth' – money, or, as O'Hagan had found in Chicago, the security of a university chair. 'It is not voices to sing the praises of Canadian poets that are wanting,' said O'Hagan: 'it is the means to buy bread while the "fit is on them."'[32]

No support, no readers, no money – reasons enough to leave Canada, but there were others that Canadian writers were unable or unwilling to express. By 1880, the old guard, the first rank of Canadian writers, was past or passing. In Halifax, Howe had been dead for seven years, and De Mille would die in January. In Saint John, Fleming had left for New York five years before. In Montreal, McGee, Heavysege, and Leprohon were in their graves, the last dying just the year before. In Ottawa, Sangster hadn't published a book in twenty years and was eking out his remaining years in the post office. In rural Canada West, what was to be Moodie's last book was now five years old, McLachlan had published nothing for six years, and Kirby had just lost his royalties from *The Golden Dog* and with them any inclination for writing more Canadian fiction. Of the more visible English Canadian literary figures born between the century's beginning and 1840, only Goldwin Smith, Graeme Mercer Adam, Charles Mair, Agnes Machar, Catharine Parr Traill, and George Stewart Jr were still active. And of these, Mair was spending more time at a succession of failing businesses in the West than he was at poetry, Traill had written no fiction in almost thirty years, and the remainder were too few and too scattered to form any kind of community.

With some local exceptions, the generation of Canadian writers who came of age in the 1880s and early 1890s had few domestic literary models. They were not born into what Richard Brodhead calls 'cultures of letters,' literary-social communities that define their audience and project a profile of the kind of authors they invite. And yet, if Canadians lacked home-grown literary cultures, they had imported cultures, cultures that in a very real sense had become their own. The expatriates of the eighties and nineties grew up in a literary landscape occupied not only by reprints of standard British authors, not only by the Canadian writers so carefully documented in the *Literary History of Canada*, but also and especially by American books and magazines. As a youth in Toronto in the early 1870s, Ernest Thompson Seton swapped marbles for 'the little contraband books known as Beadle's Dime Novels, a large number of which were lurking in the dark places of the school.' A few years later and sixty miles west, a teenaged Sara Jeannette Duncan spent her ten-dollar composition prize from Brantford Ladies College on the same 'questionable fare of dime novels.' Much further west, a young Constance Lindsay Skinner scratched a peephole in the frosted window of her father's Cariboo trading post so she could watch for her copy of *St. Nicholas* to arrive by dog sled.[33] In 1867, Thomas D'Arcy McGee had complained that the minds of half of Canada's most intelligent citizens were swayed by 'Boston books and Boston utterances.' By 1887, the adult Duncan could report in the Toronto *Week* that 'any bookseller in the city will tell us that for one reader of Blackmore or Meredith he finds ten of Howells or James; any book reviewer will testify to the largely American sources from which the volumes of his praise or objurgation come; any newsdealer will give us startling facts as to the comparative circulation of the American and the English magazines ...'[34]

As the scarcity of legitimate publishers and the prevalence of bookstores suggest, post-Confederation Canada was a consumer culture, and America was what it mostly consumed. 'We have not been *producers*, to any extent,' conceded the everywhere evident Adam in the *Canada Bookseller*, 'but that as re-producers, in the publication of American reprints, &c., our book firms have been active to an unusual degree.'[35] The positive consequence of this literary trade deficit was that aspiring Canadian writers in the decades after Confederation had ready, cheap, and plentiful access to American-based literary cultures – to what those cultures asked of a writer, and to what they offered that writer. To many Canadians, of course, this benefit of access was and is a problem of influence: as the *Ottawa Free Press* put the Canadian complaint in 1905, American periodicals 'have already moulded our language, are shaping the character of the young, and giving us our national ideals.'[36] But however legitimate a concern for cultural nationalists, for the literary historian, national divisions hide more than they reveal. A national focus was essential for recognizing Canadian literature's arrival, and it remains essential for periodically reaffirming its health, but it cannot explain the actual circumstances of much of that literature's production. No national model can account for Carman writing the first of his Vagabondia poems after reading an English law book in a New York library, or for Palmer Cox creating his Brownies by combining the Scottish legends he heard as a child in Quebec with the skills he acquired as a cartoonist in California, or for Ernest Thompson Seton submitting his career-launching story about a New Mexico wolf to a New York magazine because he was urged to do so by a Toronto economist – or indeed for the circumstances that produced any literary work, in any literature.

From a national perspective, Canadian writers of this period lacked literary cultures; from a transnational perspective, they were surrounded by such cultures. Raised on imported books and magazines, as young adults they read in their own as well as English and American magazines about the new regionalist movement led by westerners and southerners (men and women, like them, from the continent's cultural margins), about young literary adventurers such as the English Rudyard Kipling and the American Richard Harding Davis, about the new journalism being created by Joseph Pulitzer and William Randolph Hearst. And they read of the attention these literary celebrities received, attention unheard of in Canada. Readers of the *Week*'s Literary Table, for instance, were greeted in each issue with summaries and comment, almost always favourable, on the lead articles in major monthlies, with special mention of any by Canadian authors. Many of the magazines so abstracted were British; a sporadic few were Canadian. But most were American, among them the *Atlantic Monthly, St. Nicholas, Forum, Outing, Harper's*, the *New England Magazine, Lippincott's*, and the *North American Review*. The attention given contributors to these American magazines couldn't have been lost on hopeful Canadian writers, any more than could the conspicuous absence of Canadian periodicals on the Literary Table. Canada's literary expatriates of the eighties and nineties may not have been especially outspoken about this particular motive, but surely most wished for more than just survival, more than just 'the means to buy bread.' Bread could be had in Canada; fame was the province of elsewhere. And Canadian writers chose elsewhere.

For most, elsewhere meant America, the literary metropolises of the United States rather than those of the United Kingdom or continental Europe. Travel to the States was cheaper and easier than travel overseas: in 1876, to give an early example, Ontario visitors to the Centennial Exhibition in Philadelphia could for a fare of between sixteen and twenty dollars choose from among thirty rail and steamer routes to the exhibition grounds.[37] But America was also closer to home in more fundamental ways. The author of an 1889 essay on Canada's political future spoke for a growing number of Canadians when he argued that if the young Canadian goes to England, 'though a British subject of perhaps wealth and education, he knows that he and his countrymen have no influence on her councils, are not really sharers in British trials and British glories, and he actually feels on the whole less at home than in Ohio or New York.'[38] For the young heroine of Sara Jeannette Duncan's *Cousin Cinderella*, a visit to England forces the recognition that 'we were strangers really, though we knew the flag so well, and had sung "Rule Britannia" since we could sing anything; such strangers that I felt sometimes as if we had rifled the flag out of Westminster Abbey, and found the song in a book of Runic rhymes.' Prototypically anti-American, Mary Trent and her brother nonetheless realize that as Canadians they have more in common with Americans than with the English. In one scene, Mary consoles another visitor, an American woman who, like Mary, has had her speech corrected by their English hosts. 'Let them laugh at us as much as they can. We can laugh at them a great deal more, because we're made that way, and they aren't, are they?' 'I used "we" continentally,' adds Mary in an aside to the reader.[39]

Like the defeated hero of Duncan's better-known novel *The Imperialist*, post-Confederation Canadians had to confront England's growing indifference to Canadian objectives, political or literary. In 1889, publisher John Lovell, reporting to Ottawa on his failure seventeen years ago to secure reprint rights for British works, told the Privy Council that 'the English publishers would not yield an inch ... Their ignorance of Canada was profound. They treated Canada as if it was part and parcel with the United States.'[40] In June of 1896, poet Duncan Campbell Scott protested in the New York *Bookman* that 'the indifference with which the colonies have been treated in the past by the English people and its government is almost inconceivable; and Canada has suffered peculiarly from the apathy and want of heart which seems to pervade all dealings with colonial dependencies.' A decade later, Scott warmed to the subject again in a letter to his friend, Pelham Edgar. 'Why think of sending [your article] to an English review?' wrote Scott. 'They are inhospitable to us and have no interest in anything we do.' Instead, Scott urged Edgar to send his work to the *Atlantic*, the *North American*, or *Harper's*.[41]

Lovell and Scott may have had personal reasons for their charges of English indifference – a failed business deal for the one, or a rejected manuscript for the other. But there is evidence to suggest they didn't exaggerate. According to Samuel Moffett, turn-of-the-century best-seller lists from the New York and London *Bookman* show that while Americans were reading Canadian books, the English were not. Comparing the top six best-sellers in each country from

September 1900 to December 1902, Moffett found that Canadian-authored books accounted for 10 per cent of the Toronto best-seller lists, just under 7 per cent of the New York lists, and not one title of the London lists.[42] Widening Moffett's dates doesn't significantly change the results: my own search of the London *Bookman* between January 1895 and December 1902 turned up just three Canadian-authored books in the top six, Grant Allen's *The Woman Who Did* in March and April of 1895 and Gilbert Parker's *The Seats of the Mighty* in September of 1896 and *The Right of Way*, which Moffett missed, in November of 1901 (both Allen and Parker were by this time living in England).

Like the million or so other Canadians who crossed the line between 1880 and 1900, Canadian writers who chose America over England – or for that matter, over Toronto – did so because it was the customary choice. Then as now the continent's cultural fault-lines ran from north to south, not from east to west. A line on a map could not undo the cumulative effects of a common climate, a common geography, a common language, and for many a common heritage. For Maritimers, especially, Boston and New York seemed closer, more familiar than the cities of central Canada: it's worth remembering that in the late 1880s, around the time Sophie Hensley, Bliss Carman, and other Maritime writers left for the States, the premier of Nova Scotia was openly advocating secession from the Dominion. For the head of Prince Edward Island's largest school at the time, 'easy communication by correspondence or travel tends to obliterate national boundaries, and rather to erect them against Central Canada, which is more and more considered the overbearing, self-seeking sister province.'[43] Even in central Canada, though Scott's *Bookman* essay argued strenuously that Canadians wouldn't support any form of union with the States, his own observations demonstrated the extent to which culture and commerce had already effected that union: 'Upon the frontiers of the countries there is hardly an atom of difference between them. The farmer of Stanstead and Mississquoi has the same characteristics as his neighbour of Vermont. He even speaks with a similar drawl. One passes the borders of Maine and does not discover that he is in the county of Charlotte or of York. The peninsula of Southern Ontario is swept by railway trains which shuttle across the border free as spiders upon the strands of their own webs; and the vernacular and the accent in which it is conveyed is hardly distinguishable on the northern and southern shores of Lake Erie.' As Moffett would later write, 'The English-speaking Canadians protest that they will never become Americans – they are already Americans without knowing it.'[44]

By the end of the nineteenth century multiple and well-established ties bound Canada to America – bound, more exactly, Halifax and Saint John to Boston, Toronto and Montreal to Chicago and New York, Victoria and Vancouver to Seattle and San Francisco. Rail connections between eastern Canada and the northeastern states had been in place since the 1850s, decades before the completion of the CPR, even before the first line between the Maritimes and Quebec. Ecclesiastical districts overlapped the political border; Canadian and American clergy transferred back and forth from the Maritimes and New England to the Canadian North-West and the American West. Because of the high incidence of writers among clergy of this period, this particular cross-border link was responsible for the American residence of several Canadian writers, including Basil King and Arthur Wentworth Eaton (Episcopalian), Charles Aubrey Eaton (Baptist), and Arthur John Lockhart (Methodist). Touring theatrical companies out of Boston and New York regularly visited the cities of eastern and central Canada, enticing many young Canadians to the American stage, such as singer-comedienne May Irwin of Whitby, Ontario, remembered in film lore for having shared the first on-screen kiss, or Ontario native James K. Hackett, by 1895 the leading man at the New York Lyceum and the youngest leading man in the city's theatrical history. Professional associations and labour unions recruited on both sides of the border: at its 1905 convention in Toronto the International Typographical Union declared that it 'knew no boundaries, and that so far as their aims and objects were concerned, no line existed between Canada and the United States.'[45] Canadian and American natural scientists published in each other's journals, joined each other's societies, conducted field work in each other's countries, and developed continental vocabularies and theories in casebooks like Leo Lesquereux's 1884 *Manual of the Mosses of North America*, Frank Chapman's 1895 *Handbook of Birds of Eastern North America* (to which Seton contributed), or Israel C. Russell's 1897 *Volcanoes of North America*.[46]

Academic connections between Canada and the States were especially strong. As Thomas O'Hagan explained from residence at Cornell University in the fall of 1893, 'Commendable ... as is the Canadian system of education, it is lacking in one particular – provision for carrying on special investigation, or, if you will, post-graduate work. This want drives to American universities such as Johns Hopkins, Harvard, and Cornell a large number of Canadian young men ...' (and women, as his own examples show). O'Hagan's account notwithstanding, it wasn't just Canadian graduates who sought American degrees: according to a brochure mailed to prospective Canadian students by the Canadian Club of Harvard University, by 1890 Harvard had granted 495 undergraduate and professional degrees to Canadians, almost all of them from the three existing Maritime provinces.[47] Nor were American universities content to let Canadians pay their tuition and leave. Carman's brother-in-law William Francis Ganong, a Harvard graduate, taught botany at his alma mater from 1887 to 1893 before becoming director of the Smith College Botanic Garden in Northampton. Cornell doctorate Eliza Ritchie of Halifax was associate professor of psychology and philosophy at Wellesley College throughout the 1890s. James Edward Le Rossignol, later to author five collections of short stories set in his native Quebec, taught psychology, economics, and political science at several American universities in the 1890s before settling into an administrative position at the University of Nebraska. This is just a sample: by 1906, the University of Chicago alone employed twenty-four Canadian-born professors. In 1910, American census-takers recorded 428 Canadian-born college professors and presidents.[48]

Most tangibly, family ties bound many of Canada's literary expatriates to the United States. A paternal ancestor of Craven Langstroth Betts, Thomas Betts, emigrated from England in 1639 and became a founder of Guilford and Norwalk, Connecticut. Carman's first paternal ancestor, John Carman, helped found Hempstead, Long Island, and his grandparents on both sides were among the 1783 Loyalists. Stinson Jarvis, Mary Bourchier Sanford, E.W. Thomson, and Slason Thompson all came of Loyalist stock. Marshall Saunders claimed to be descended on both sides of her family from the *Mayflower* pilgrims, and Sophie Hensley was a descendant of Cotton and Increase Mather. What the New York *Bookman* said of Carman in October of 1895 could have been said of many Canadian emigrants to America, literary or not: 'Mr. Carman's residence in the United States is, in a sense, the return of the native.'[49]

Modern Alexandria

Cultural affinities matter, but the main reason so many Canadian writers of the 1880s and 1890s moved to the United States was the obvious reason: more opportunity. Much more. The entire Canadian printing industry at the turn of the century was less than half the size of New York City's book and job business alone. Across America, publishers and printers employed over 200,000 people (including 5,136 first- and second-generation Canadians, about half the number then employed at home) and produced 347 million dollars' worth of product a year.[50] By the census of 1900, printing and publishing had become of such importance to the American economy that the Census Office commissioned a special report on the industry from William S. Rossiter, a Massachusetts publisher and statistician. Filling over eighty pages of text and tables in the *Twelfth Census*, Rossiter's report focused mostly on the periodical sectors of the industry. As his figures make abundantly clear, periodicals were the main and best market for the aspiring writer of the eighties and nineties. Simply put, American periodical publishers needed more and more copy to fill more and more pages. Between 1880 and 1900, the number of periodicals published in the United States rose by 88 per cent. By 1900, America was home to over 21,000 newspapers and magazines with an aggregate circulation of about 114 million copies per issue.[51] And it wasn't only the rising total of periodicals that increased the demand for writers: the 1890s, especially, also saw a sharp increase in the number of dailies at the expense of the weeklies and of the monthlies at the expense of the quarterlies. Advancements in printing technology had made this development possible, but the new presses couldn't write the copy to fill the pages they printed, however much their increasingly squeezed owners might wish they could.

By a curious twist of a cultural stereotype that would later work to their detriment, Canadian writers found in American periodicals not just greater opportunity, but preferential opportunity. Americans, it turned out, liked Canadians – liked them better than they liked themselves. In November of 1895, a New York journalist known only as 'An Outsider' wrote a lengthy letter to Toronto's *Week* urging Canadians to resist union with the States. Canadians, said the anonymous correspondent, are vigorous and hardy, while Americans are 'sybaritic, nervous,' and dislike 'violent athletic exercise.' Canadians love learning for its own sake; Americans love degrees and certificates. A Canadian employee is 'patient and plodding and trustworthy,' but an American 'is ever anxious not to do more than he is paid to do.' Canadians are 'quiet, sober, and amenable with regard to discipline,' while Americans are 'unreliable, impatient, unwilling to obey.' Canadians are principled, but 'Americans will not stand by any principle if another pays better.' If, predicts Outsider, Canadians can only resist the corrupting influences of America, especially greed, 'THEN YOU WILL RULE THIS CONTINENT!'[52]

Outsider may have been more enthusiastic than the average American in his assessment of the political potential of Canadians, but many shared his assessment of their character. Right up to the First World War, Americans cherished a romantic notion that Canada's unspoiled topography and more vigorous climate produced hardier, more dependable, more moral employees than those reared under relaxing southern skies. Eager to benefit from this superior gene pool, American employers habitually retained agents in Canada to ensure a steady supply of Canadian labour. Presumably motivated by the stereotype's assertion of Canadian reliability, physical health, and even cleanliness, New York hospitals of the 1890s hired Canadian nurses in disproportionately high numbers.[53] In the literary world, Canadians regularly found editorial positions on periodicals with an explicit focus on moral or physical well-being, as did Carman on the religious weekly *Independent*, Thomson on the juvenile *Youth's Companion*, and Edwyn Sandys on the sporting magazine *Outing*.

Most pervasively, the myth of the virile Canadian together with the predilection of American editors of the day for poems, stories, and articles with a robust morality in an outdoors setting created a disproportionately high acceptance rate for Canadian contributions to American periodicals. In 1899, Frank Pollock wrote home from New York that 'this is the very psychological moment for the new Canadian writer who wishes to obtain literary recognition in the United States. It is an admitted fact that it is easier just now for a Canadian to become so recognised, other things being equal, than for a mere American of the same ability.' Although Pollock ultimately gave most of the credit for this 'vogue of Canadiana' to the success of Canadian literary pioneers in the city (Roberts and Carman), his initial explanation better explains the particular success of Canadian writers with outdoors subjects: it came about, said Pollock, 'through a very logical belief on the part of publishers that artistic work coming from a young country is likely to have in it more virility and crude strength than if it had emanated from the cafés and clubs of the metropolis.'[54]

For different reasons, the demands of the American literary market also created more and better opportunities for Canadian women than existed at home. In the last decades of the nineteenth century the major urban newspaper developed from the voice of its owner's political party into its present form as a vehicle for mass entertainment and, more important, mass marketing. Overnight, women became important to American newspapers and their advertisers. To editors, women had qualities especially suited to the new domains of mass-market journalism, its society news, community affairs, human-interest stories, and of course its women's pages. To advertisers, women writers meant women readers and therefore women consumers, increasingly responsible for household purchases. To both, women added spice and sales to the manufactured stories of the period: a man travelling around the world in eighty days was one thing, but a woman beating that record, as American journalist Nellie Bly did for Pulitzer's *New York World* in 1890, was quite another.

Because Canadian papers responded to these changes more slowly than their American counterparts, women entered journalism in Canada more slowly and in proportionally fewer numbers. 'Here in Canada,' wrote Sara Jeannette Duncan in 1888, 'nothing, comparatively speaking, has been accomplished by women in journalism, partly because the Canadian newspaper world is so small as to be easily occupied by some half dozen influential journals, partly because it is a very conservative world indeed, and we know what conservatism means in relation to the scope of women's work.' For Duncan's only female predecessor in Canada's parliamentary press gallery, Eve Brodlique,

The hour and the woman finally arrived in the Canadian newspaper world, but not together – the hour was a little late in coming. There has not been in Canadian journalism, even approximately, the same influx of women that there has been in the States. There are several good reasons for this. First: that receptacle for manuscript, varied and sundry, that convenient vehicle for trundling ideas feminine, the Sunday newspaper, is not a Canadian product; it did not obtain in my day, and does not now. Nor was there then a 'Woman's Page,' nothing more than that now despised column bearing the heading: 'Things of Interest to Women.' The papers of the United States seem to have been the first to discover that there is no sex in brains, and that women could be educated to an interest as wide as that enjoyed by men. The change in American journalism, which made a place for women, came rapidly, while in Canada the taint of old-time conservatism clung persistently, and the change came slowly.

'And so,' said Brodlique, '[I] decided ... to go into the Union and cross swords, or rather pens, with the newspaper women of the States.'[55]

Brodlique exaggerated the open-mindedness of American newspapers, but census statistics support her and Duncan's account of the opportunities for women in the two countries. In 1890, women accounted for 4.1 per cent of American journalists and 4.5 per cent of Canadian journalists. But by 1900, women had increased to 7.3 per cent of the American profession (2,193 out of 30,098) while Canadian returns showed movement, if any, in the opposite direction, with women now holding 4.0 per cent of the reporting and editorial positions (52 out of 1,306). For authors the discrepancy was much greater. In Canada, women represented 21 per cent of the authors reported in the census of 1891 and 27 per cent in the census of 1901 (15 out of 56). In the United States, women accounted for 41 per cent of American authors in 1890 and 43 per cent in 1900 (2,616 out of 6,058). Even in the printing industry, jobs for women were more numerous in the States, with female printers and engravers increasing in Canada from 11 per cent of the trade in 1890 to 14 per cent by 1900, while their American counterparts increased over the same period from 14 to 18 per cent of the trade – probably less because of liberal thinking than because of the highly competitive industry's constant search for cheaper labour.[56]

Canadian women clearly responded to these differences. There is no way to determine how many emigrated of their own accord versus how many were expatriated as children, but of the 4,106 Canadian-born employees of the American printing and publishing industry in 1910, 804 were women. Of the 93 Canadian-born authors then resident in the States, 39 were women. And of the 570 Canadian-born editors and reporters, 75 were women – six more than in Canada at the time.[57] Brodlique's enthusiasm aside, most female staff on major American newspapers and magazines of her day were confined to the women's and society pages, but some few, including Canadian women, did break out into other sections or win editorial positions. Brodlique herself wrote theatre, book, and art reviews for several Chicago papers. Sophie Hensley became an associate editor of a New York magazine, *Health Culture*, in the mid-1890s. Montreal journalist Lily Barry joined the editorial staff of New York's *Collier's Weekly* in 1893, and Ontario journalist and poet Ethelwyn Wetherald served as an editorial assistant with the popular *Ladies' Home Journal* in Philadelphia over the winter of 1895–6. Hamilton-born Trinity graduate Helen Gregory Flesher covered the opening of the First Japanese Parliament for *Cosmopolitan* and, after moving to San Francisco in the early 1890s, edited a women's reform magazine called *The Search Light* and served on the editorial staff of the *Californian Illustrated Magazine*. On average, male writers left Canada in larger numbers than women and had better success finding the kind of reporting or editorial work stateside that could jumpstart a literary career. But the relatively small number of women among Canada's literary expatriates of the eighties and nineties doesn't change the fact that opportunities for women writers were more limited still in Canada.

For Canadian literary migrants to the United States, both general and preferential opportunity were greatest in the cities, especially the major centres of the northeastern states. The antimodern rebellion that fed the desire for virile, outdoor literature was an urban phenomenon, born of anxieties only a urbanite could feel and offering an escape no ruralist needed. The economic forces that brought women into late-nineteenth-century newspaper offices were also the product of cities, of rapidly growing and changing audiences for periodicals and their advertisers. And it was in the major cities that an aspiring writer stood the best chance of attracting editors of publishing houses and magazines with reputations and distribution beyond the local.

For writers as for the general population, the most popular urban destinations for the Canadian emigrant of the 1880s and 1890s were Chicago, Boston, and New York. Chicago, said the *Canadian American* in the spring of 1884, was the Mecca of ambitious young Ontario men unable to find employment in hometowns already saturated with professionals. By 1900 Chicago was home to over 29,000 first-generation English Canadians and the second-most Canadian city in America. Already renowned for its commercial activity, Chicago became a major literary centre, eclipsing Boston, with its hosting of the World's Fair in 1893. By century's end the city had thirty-seven dailies and the second largest number of book and job printers in America, almost six hundred establishments employing some twelve thousand people.[58]

For the New York correspondent of the *Prince Edward Island Magazine*, Boston was the 'promised land of Canadians in general, and P.E. Islanders in particular.' As early as 1880, Boston had more Nova Scotian residents than the combined population of Yarmouth, Sydney, and Pictou; by 1900, the Canadian-born population of Boston was over fifty thousand.[59] Most of these, of course, worked in non-literary industries, notably domestic service for young women and carpentry and mechanical trades for young men. By the mid-1880s Boston's long tenure as America's literary arbiter was passing, even past, but the city was still home to the venerable *Atlantic Monthly* and to established publishing houses such as Little, Brown, and Houghton, Mifflin. Something of its former status survived in Rossiter's survey, which shows that Massachusetts of 1900 had considerably fewer news and political periodicals than either New York or Illinois, but still housed a disproportionately large number of literary magazines.

If Chicago drew primarily young Ontarians, and Boston Maritimers, New York called to them all. New York was the flash point of the periodical explosion of the 1880s and 1890s: by 1890, the aggregate circulation per issue of New York State periodicals was three times that of its closest competitor. In stark contrast to the situation at home, a Canadian writer arriving in New York that year could choose from over 1,600 periodicals published throughout the state, including 162 dailies (55 in the city alone), 927 weeklies, and 395 monthlies. Of these, some nine hundred were devoted to news, politics, and 'family reading.' The state also published at least ninety-eight general literature magazines – more than a third of the nation's total – and two dozen of the new Sunday papers, literary catchalls that published just about anything that might hold a reader's interest.[60] Most important, New York City of the eighties and nineties was home to the most widely read magazines in North America. Even a partial list of those that had by 1900 achieved national circulation and reputation reveals the city's dominance over the various reading tastes of America: the *Century*, *Harper's*, and *Scribner's*, for instance, or *Munsey's*, *Cosmopolitan*, and the *Smart Set*, or the *Nation* and the *Outlook*, or *St. Nicholas*, or the *Critic* and the *Bookman*. Canadian expatriates worked or wrote for each of these magazines (Roberts, for one, had by 1900 contributed to them all) and dozens more, adding to, as much as benefiting from, the market they joined.

The American periodical boom of the 1880s and 1890s, concentrated in but not limited to New York, was the product of diverse and complex factors, including improvements to printing and illustrating technology, cover-price wars, the emergence of national advertising, and dramatic social changes in the readership.[61] But whatever the causes, the Canadian response was quick and sure. For Sara Jeannette Duncan, the market for Canadian writing of any sort was 'self-evidently New York.' Although he thought literary life in any major city 'apt to be neurotic and unwholesome,' Frank Pollock admitted that from a financial point of view there was 'certainly no place like New York for the struggling "free-lance," be he Canadian or otherwise.' Arthur Stringer remarked that 'You may talk a good deal about Boston being the Athens of America, and you may confess to a weakness for English-made novels, but all along you can't shake off the immovable idea that New York, after all, is the Alexandria of the modern and somewhat decadent Egypt of letters.'[62] For Pollock, Stringer, and many of their compatriots, New York offered their best chance for a literary career. The city was, as Stringer put it, their Alexandria – perhaps the most unintentionally apt of the utopian metaphors late-nineteenth-century Canadians used to represent the promise of American cities, for while it suggests the peak of a culture's literary achievements, it also calls to mind the ultimate fate of those achievements.

Chapter 2

Agents of Modernism

Edith Wharton's canonical society novels and their better-known film adaptations have now taught several generations to understand turn-of-the-century New York as the hollow core of a nation predicated upon wealth and superficial pleasures, an endless ball for the Four Hundred whose glitter barely concealed its lack of substance. It is impossible, however, to read at any depth in the popular literature of Wharton's period and not be struck by the insatiable and seemingly genuine appetite for self-improvement. In the 1890s, at about the same time Lily Bart was lamenting the gilded manacles of life in *The House of Mirth*, Americans and Canadians living outside that house were educating themselves in droves via Chautauquas, book clubs, libraries, correspondence schools, how-to books, and more generally across the media spectrum, whether through newspaper reports and specials, articles and departments in the general-interest magazines, or informative or morally improving content in children's magazines like *St. Nicholas* or the *Youth's Companion*.

Both feeding and feeding off these desires, the daily press, lecture circuit, and cheap book industry all expanded massively. But the most spectacular media boom of the period, perhaps of any period in modern history, belonged to the magazines. For their historian Frank Luther Mott, this is the golden age of mainstream magazines, an era when publishers, editors, illustrators, and writers were fumbling their way into a new medium that hadn't yet ossified into the lacquered sameness of the industry today. For the less romantic Richard Ohmann, the magazines of the 1890s worked seamlessly with the forces of capital to create the mass culture of the modern age, using journalism to tell readers what to care about, fiction to tell them what to dream for, and advertising to tell them what to buy. For the similarly minded Jackson Lears, the magazines of the day were the not-so-thin end of the modern wedge, their enthusiasm for individual and social improvement a reflection of the

'Promethean optimism of the official culture' and their emphasis on information as the route to improvement a symptom of that culture's conviction that
the answers to life, the universe, and everything were there to be found.[1]

On the numbers, the most common point of access for a writer to this print-
hungry culture was still the daily press. All journalism asked for in these pre-
professional years was a good general education (the first school of journalism
didn't open until 1908, at the University of Missouri), an ability to write,
considerable ambition, and, for most positions, testicles. According to articles
on the life of a New York reporter published in Toronto's *Week* in early 1884,
'A man who goes to New York to become a journalist, or even a literary writer,
simply starts on his career by becoming a reporter on one of the large papers
like the *Herald*, *Tribune*, *Sun*, *Times*, or *World*, and it is in that excellent school
that he learns that crisp, racy and reckless style of composition that character-
izes every American paper from Maine to California.' Breaking into the top
five New York dailies wasn't as easy as this made it sound: 'About 1,000 men
in a year,' the author cautioned, 'go up to New York to seek admittance to one
of the large offices. Very few of them ever get past the boy who runs the
elevator.'[2] But for those who did, reporting for one of the city's absurd number
of dailies (fifty-eight in 1900) offered a steady salary of fifteen to seventy
dollars a week, depending on ability and employer. If not on salary, writers still
had access to the daily press through 'specials,' sketches or articles written for
the weekend supplements and usually paid at space-rates, up to five dollars a
column by the turn of the century.

New York reporters were hardly overpaid. They worked long if loose shifts,
typically noon to midnight, and most of their work appeared without credit.
But for aspiring writers, the rewards of New York journalism were less tangible than a byline or a paycheque: the chance to write about subjects declared
off limits in fiction (sex, capital punishment, blasphemy, the criminal, the
vicious, even the poor); the doors the job opened to editors on and off Park
Row; the chance to rub shoulders in the eating-houses of Printing Square or the
cafés of Fulton Street with the city's Bohemian literati; and, perhaps most of
all, the raw experience of reporting the city itself. As Lincoln Steffens said of
his days as city editor of the *Commercial Advertiser*, 'We had use for any one
who, openly or secretly, hoped to be a poet, a novelist, or an essayist. I could
not pay them much in money, but as an offset I promised to give them
opportunities to see life as it happened in all the news varieties.'[3]

As it did for American writers from Twain to Dreiser, the daily press gave
many of Canada's literary migrants to New York their entry into letters.
Norman Duncan began on the Auburn *Bulletin* and moved to the New York
Evening Post, while Harvey O'Higgins got his start in the city on Steffens's

Advertiser. Arthur E. McFarlane, Arthur Stringer, and others began by freelancing specials to the weekend editions. For others, New York's dailies provided employment throughout much or all of their known careers. From Sophie Hensley, for instance, we know that Herbert Sinclair of Hamilton, Ontario, worked for the morning edition of the *Commercial Advertiser* in the early 1890s and had done 'a good deal of Wall street and general newspaper work.'[4] Historian Marjory Lang has discovered several Canadian women journalists of the period working in the States, including Mary Elizabeth McOuat, a University of Toronto graduate who moved to New York shortly after earning her BA in 1891 and found work on the women's pages of the *Recorder*, a new morning paper backed by tobacco millionaire J.B. Duke. McOuat returned to Canada around 1900 and took a position with the Ottawa *Evening Journal*, but within a few years she was back in New York, briefly editing a journal for the New York City Teachers' Association before joining the editorial staff of the *Tribune*.

Another Quebec native, Acton Davies of St Jean, initially found work with the New York Gas Company as a seventeen-year-old arrival in the city in 1887. Three years later, his sketches and stories landed him a reporting job on the evening edition of Charles Dana's *Sun*. In 1893, Davies became the *Evening Sun*'s drama critic, a position that gave his reviews a potential audience of over a hundred thousand readers (success had its price: Davies was later assaulted at a Broadway café by the enraged husband of an actress whose performance he had panned.) Aside from a high-profile stint as a *Sun* war correspondent during the Spanish-American War, Davies spent the rest of his life in the theatre, first as a critic and later as a scenario-writer for stage and screen. Besides his long-running *Evening Sun* column, he reviewed for the New York theatre and literature monthly *Impressionist*, wrote a fan biography of stage star Maude Adams, and contributed articles on the theatre and its celebrities to *Cosmopolitan*, *Munsey's*, and *Good Housekeeping*. In 1912-13, he published novelized versions of two popular plays, Charles Nirdlinger's *The First Lady in the Land* and Edward Sheldon's *Romance*. Davies left the *Sun* in 1914, moving briefly to the *Tribune* before resigning to join the production staff of several New York theatrical companies. When he died just two years later, the *New York Times* remembered the forty-six-year-old unmarried critic as having a 'lively, personal' writing style and a reputation for his thorough knowledge of the New York stage and its players: 'There was no dramatic critic whose judgment was accepted more readily by the world of the theatre.'[5]

Toronto printer Sydney Reid found reporting work within two years of his move to New York in 1881, initially on the *Brooklyn Union* and then on the *Brooklyn Eagle*, the *Union*'s more successful rival. The *Eagle* was an oddity among newspapers – a community paper with a national reputation, that was the first to deliver newspapers by air, that maintained its own press tent in Cuba during the war. But given the *Eagle*'s dedication to Brooklyn and Reid's membership in at least two local historical societies, it seems likely that he primarily covered local events for the paper.[6] In 1895, Reid left the *Eagle* and went freelance. His first known American periodical publication, a humorous sketch that follows dog-catchers on their Harlem rounds, had appeared in *Harper's Weekly* three years before, and in 1894 he had returned to the weekly with a series of tough-minded articles on political corruption in Coney Island, Brooklyn, and Tammany Hall. After publishing his only known short story in *Lippincott's* in 1896, Reid went silent for several years, possibly at work on an unlocated history of Brooklyn for the Long Island Historical Society. He reappeared in 1900 with the first of two books for children, a novel initially serialized in *St. Nicholas*, and in the following year began his association with the *Independent*, a former Congregationalist paper by then reborn as a general-interest weekly. Over the next decade Reid published on average an article a year in the *Independent*: parodies of over-exploited literary genres, illustrated articles on the new Public Library and Grand Central Station, a report on the America's Cup Race and another on the sinking of the *Titanic*, a sketch of a summer vacation, and so on. Having, as he said, traversed the streets of New York as a newspaper man for over forty years, Reid retired into genteel poverty in the mid-1920s.[7]

The two most well-known Canadian journalists in New York of these years left Canada for reasons other than literary. By his own account, James Creelman left his native Montreal in the early 1870s at age twelve and walked the four hundred miles to New York to be with his recently separated mother. However he got there, in the eighties and nineties Creelman was one of the city's best-known figures, a correspondent for Bennett's *Herald*, Pulitzer's *World*, and Hearst's *Journal* whose dispatches from three wars and interviews with the famous were newsworthy events in their own right. Rarely content just to report, Creelman became personally involved in his assignments: in his coverage of the Hatfield-McCoy feud in Kentucky, he managed to get himself shot at by a Hatfield. His most celebrated moment came on 1 July 1898 when he joined the charge of American troops on the Spanish-held Cuban village of El Caney, a moment preserved in paint by *Journal* artist Frederic Remington. Creelman's colleague on the *World*, the former Methodist minister Herbert Newton Casson, had left his Owen Sound church in 1893 after being found guilty of heresy and moved to Boston, where he became a well-known agitator for Christian socialism. Cured of 'all sympathy with Socialism or Communism' by a six-month stay at a Tennessee commune, Casson converted again, this time to capitalism – leadership by the 'Efficient Few,' as he called it – and moved to New York.[8] After a short period with the *Evening Journal*, he joined the *World*, eventually becoming editor of its Forum page. Like Creelman, Casson made his name from interviews with the famous, including President Grover Cleveland, retailers Edward Filene and John Wanamaker, scientists Thomas Edison and Alexander Graham Bell, and the first published interview with the Wright brothers after their flight at Kitty Hawk. In 1905, Frank Munsey hired Casson away from the *World* to write a series on the country's steel barons for *Munsey's Magazine*, collected in 1907 as *The Romance of Steel: The Story of a Thousand Millionaires*.

Dailies provided a salary and experience for many, and fame for a handful, but for most writers of the period the real market was the magazines. It wasn't that magazines paid especially well, at least for the rank and file. From the late 1880s to around the turn of the century, the standard rate of the 'quality' New York magazines (the *Century*, *Harper's*, *Scribner's*) for unknown writers was ten dollars a page, or three-quarters of a cent a word, while the new ten-cent illustrated magazines typically paid about a cent a word. *Cosmopolitan* paid half that; *Outing* only paid a quarter of a cent a word. *Harper's Weekly* paid a cent a word, and *Truth*, *Once a Week*, and *Town Topics* five dollars a column, or about half a cent a word. Piecing together a living at these rates wasn't easy. Bliss Carman, estimated by Mott to have been one of the period's three or four most prolific magazine poets, once confessed to Arthur Stringer that in his best year as a freelancer he'd made just eight hundred dollars. As a freelance humorist Peter McArthur received between fifty cents and $2.50 a joke, rarely taking home more than twenty dollars a week. They all dreamed of more, of course: of the twelve thousand dollars Sam McClure paid Kipling for serial rights to 'Captains Courageous,' or of the staggering fifty thousand dollars the *Century* reportedly paid John Hay and John G. Nicolay for their serialized life of Lincoln.[9] But more fundamentally (and more realistically), writers of the period wanted magazine publication because the magazines' surging circulations promised audiences beyond the city, into the nation and across the continent.

Almost all the known Canadian writers who moved to the States in these years wrote or worked for mass-market monthlies or weeklies, all more or less dedicated to serving the dominant culture of information. With the notable exception of Palmer Cox, the more successful among them leaned towards the antimodern side of Lears's cultural divide, contributing to, developing, and in several cases founding key subcultures within its therapeutic, outdoors, and new romantic movements. Besides the mostly anonymous Canadians who wrote for the daily press, however, a few expatriate Canadians found careers in literary cultures directly or indirectly supportive of the official culture. Two of them edited magazines explicitly devoted to education and self-improvement: Graeme Mercer Adam, who after working in New York for America's largest publisher (himself a Canadian) of the cheap reprints that were the book side of the information boom moved to Chicago to edit the home-study periodical *Self-Culture*; and Charles G.D. Roberts's younger brother William, manager for over thirty years of the information weekly *Literary Digest*.

Supplementary Adam

The seeds of Graeme Mercer Adam's expatriation were sown when he converted from protectionism to free trade while serving as business manager of Goldwin Smith's *Bystander* in the early 1880s. By 1886 Adam had become secretary of the Reciprocal Trade Movement, and two years later he edited a collection of papers for the Commercial Union Club of Toronto. Late in 1888, he voiced his own support for continental trade in a letter to his employer, C.B. Robinson's *Week*, arguing that 'the stream of commerce, like the rivers, seeks the channels which nature has cut out for it.' By this time, Adam was despairing of the literary opportunities available in Canada, writing in the *Week* of his surprise that 'the native writer remains in the field of active labour' and later contributing a sobering article in which he enumerated the causes for the 'literary exodus' to the States, causes that included indifferent readers, inadequate copyright protection, and discriminatory postal and tariff policies.[10]

Early in 1892, Adam and his new bride Frances Isabel left Toronto for New York. On their departure the city's literary and publishing elite presented him with 'an address and purse, in recognition of his long and important services to Canadian letters, and of regret at his departure from the country.'[11] Sixteen years before, in the fall of 1876, Adam had joined Montreal publisher John Lovell in a venture designed to skirt the Foreign Reprints Act by in effect becoming a foreign reprinter, operating a branch plant in nearby Rouse's Point, New York, from which Lovell could legally ship pirated British reprints back into Canada. Lovell installed his son, John Wurtele Lovell, as the plant's manager, but shortly after Adam's arrival he and John Jr left Rouse's Point and moved to New York City, where they established Lovell, Adam and Company, soon reorganized as Lovell, Adam, Wesson and Company with the acquisition of a third partner. During Adam's year with the firm it printed over sixty titles from its Broadway offices, but the partnership dissolved and in 1878 Adam returned to Toronto. Lovell remained in New York, striking out under his own name and aggressively pirating standard and newer authors, many of them in Lovell's Library, a paper reprint series he launched in 1882. By 1890 Lovell's

Library numbered almost fifteen hundred titles and the John W. Lovell Company was selling seven million books annually.

By the time the Adams arrived in New York in the spring of 1892, Lovell had embarked on his most audacious enterprise, the United States Book Company. Incorporated in July of 1890, this giant trust aimed to eliminate competition in the cheap book industry by single-handedly becoming that industry: Lovell bought the plates to more than three thousand volumes from a dozen major competitors, and soon controlled half of the industry's clothbound trade and three-quarters of its paperback market. He then proceeded to flood the market with the widest range of series in publishing history, reprinting standard fiction and non-fiction titles in libraries like the Westminster, the Seaside, the Columbus, and the Canterbury. Through U.S. Book and its many satellites Lovell also actively published titles that reflected his own interests in socialism, labour, and women's issues. As Madeleine B. Stern argues, Lovell was a pirate with a social conscience, 'a man who gave the masses the cheap paper-covered volumes that advanced their causes.'[12]

Adam went to work for his former partner at the U.S. Book Company's headquarters on Worth Street in downtown Manhattan, he and Isabel taking up residence at 55 West Seventeenth Street, between Fifth and Sixth. He served as a reader and literary advisor for the firm, and according to Sophie Hensley was soon managing its publishing branch. Early in 1893, the inevitable occurred – overextension drove U.S. Book into receivership. The directors fired Lovell in January and sheriffs occupied the firm's offices in April, effectively ending the meteoric career of 'Book-a-Day Lovell.' After an unsuccessful attempt to do the same thing to the magazine industry that he had done to cheap book printing, Lovell declared personal bankruptcy in 1900, and never again entered publishing in anything approaching his former scale. He died in 1932, 'perhaps partly out of boredom,' writes American publishing historian John Tebbel, 'because there was nothing left for him to promote.'[13]

Adam found himself out of work, though he may have stayed on with one of the surviving satellites of U.S. Book or with the American Publishers Corporation, as Lovell's creditors styled the firm they created to manage the wreckage. In 1894 the International Book Company, a U.S. Book subsidiary, reprinted a popular history of England by Justin McCarthy with supplementary chapters by Adam updating the work to William Gladstone's resignation that March. *A History of Our Own Times* was probably a U.S. Book publication that Adam completed after the firm's collapse, as other editions bear the imprint of both U.S. Book and the American Publishers Corporation. Also in 1894 appeared Adam's account of the training methods of professional strong-man Eugene Sandow, published by J. Selwin Tait and Sons, a recently formed New York house that had bought part of U.S. Book's plates and stock. Again, *Sandow on Physical Training* may have been a U.S. book title that Adam completed for its new publisher.

On 14 December 1894, the *Week* reported in its Literary and Personal column that 'our old contributor, Mr. G. Mercer Adam, has taken a position on the staff of that eminent publishing firm, Macmillan & Co., at the New York branch.' No more is known of Adam's work for Macmillan, whose offices were then opposite J.S. Tait's on lower Fifth Avenue. His next sizeable project seems to have been assisting dime novelist Edward S. Ellis with a popular history of the United States, published in 1896 by the London house of Ward, Lock, and Bowden. As with the earlier English history, Adam provided an introduction and other supplementary material.

Adam moved to Chicago in May of 1896 to assume the editorship of a new home-study magazine. Founded the year before, *Self-Culture* was published by the Werner Company, American publishers of the ninth edition of the *Encyclopædia Britannica*. Its subtitle declared it 'A Magazine Devoted to the Interests of the Home University League,' one of the many adult-education projects that sprang up in the 1890s, in this case in Chicago (Adam also served as the League's secretary). Issued semi-annually, the magazine's reading program was largely based on reprints from Werner's *Encyclopædia*, though Adam gradually introduced new material and in 1898 the magazine dropped the Home University concept altogether, while remaining what Mott calls a 'magazine of information.' Adam followed *Self-Culture* when it moved to Akron, Ohio, but was replaced as its editor in September of 1900 by William W. Hudson, who changed the name to *Modern Culture* and moved it to Cleveland, where it expired a year later.[14]

Now in his sixties, Adam returned to New York and, according to Canadian biographer Henry James Morgan, 'engaged in editorial and general literary work for the chief Eastern publishing houses.'[15] After a number of odd jobs, including an introduction for a reprint of Walter Savage Landor's *Imaginary Conversations*, Adam seems to have hired on as a house writer with the H.G. Campbell Publishing Company, a minor reprint house based out of Milwaukee. In 1903 Adam updated eight popular biographies for Campbell's Great Americans of History series, including biographies of George Washington, Daniel Webster, and Thomas Jefferson. For each biography Adam wrote a supplementary essay and probably contributed the 'Anecdotes, Characteristics, and Chronology' added to each. From 1903 to 1906 he also had a close connection with A.L. Burt of New York, a leading reprinter of popular fiction, standard authors, and home reference books. For Burt he translated a French novel, updated a history of Russia, wrote a biography of Robert E. Lee, and edited a selection of Lincoln's speeches. He also edited a history of Spain for J.D. Morris of Philadelphia (his most successful book, with nine known editions by 1939), and in 1908 returned to his Canadian origins by editing for John Lovell Sr the fourth edition of *Lovell's Gazetteer of the Dominion of Canada*.

Adam died in New York on 30 October 1912. His body was returned to Toronto and buried in Saint James Cemetery on Parliament Street, not far from a perpetually broken drinking fountain in Allen Gardens that carries his name. Some thirty years before, Adam had written a where-is-our-Shakespeare essay for the *Week* lamenting the decline of creative literature. 'The literary men of the time,' he observed, 'are, in the main, bookmakers. They are compilers, adapters, re-issuers – doing eminent service, it is to be admitted, in making literature attractive to the masses, and apt in chopping up the feed to suit the varied conditions of the mental teeth and digestion. Too often, it is to be regretted however, they put the commerce of literature before their art, and, at the instance of greedy publishers, impair their reputation by continuing to quarry in worked-out veins, or in employing their pens in scattered and ephemeral labour.'[16] Ironically, Adam's assessment of the literary failings of his information age accurately sums his own career on both sides of the border – a life spent reviewing, reprinting, rewriting, updating, and supplementing the work of others.

Will Roberts and the *Literary Digest*

William Carman Roberts was just six years old when his brother Charles published his landmark *Orion and Other Poems* in Philadelphia in the fall of 1880. Perhaps feeling the pressure of the family name, he turned to poetry at a young age, his first published poems appearing in the *Dominion Illustrated* in his sixteenth year. Like his older brother, William attended the University of New Brunswick but quit in the spring of 1896 because of health problems and went to Washington, D.C., to recover, possibly staying with his cousin Bliss Carman at Richard Hovey's family home. By early 1897 he had recuperated and was living in New York in a boarding house at 123 East Fifty-eighth Street that was already something of a Canadian colony, home to Charles, Bliss, and at least one other Canadian, actress Madge de Wolf.

Charles had come to New York in February to take a position as assistant editor of the *Illustrated American*, a general-interest weekly of which a friend from the *Youth's Companion* had just assumed the managing editorship. Within a month, he got twenty-three-year-old Will a job in the weekly's offices on East Twenty-third, about two miles south of their boarding house, between

First Avenue and the East River. As Charles remembered this period for his first biographer Elsie Pomeroy, Will's duties on the *Illustrated American* were light, not much more than the writing of an editorial a week on an assigned topic. His only signed contributions to the magazine were 'a couple of full-page poems, appropriately illustrated.'[17] Sometime before Charles quit the magazine in mid-January of 1898, William left to take a position on the *Literary Digest*.

Called by Mott 'the typical periodical of a generation which placed a high value on ordered information in many fields,' the *Literary Digest* was founded in 1890 by Isaac Kauffman Funk, co-founder of Funk and Wagnalls. Its first issue of 1904 provides a good idea of William's duties for the weekly and a window on the culture it was created to serve. Thirty-two pages long, the issue opens with Topics of the Day, featuring editorials on Democratic support for the Panama Canal Treaty reprinted from the *Atlanta Constitution*, the *New Orleans Picayune*, the *Brooklyn Citizen*, and several other American dailies. Next comes the Letters and Art section, including a feature called 'Is Mr. Yeats a Decadent?' in which the editor summarizes with extensive quotation articles on Yeats in the *Evening Post* and the *Independent*. The Science and Invention section contains articles on a new fire-fighting device and something called 'earth currents,' while the Religious World quotes from the London *Church Times*, the New York *Outlook*, and others on the subject of Herbert Spencer's religious beliefs. Next comes Foreign Topics, Notable Books of the Day, and Current Poetry, reprinting poems by Howells from *Harper's* and Stringer from *McClure's*. The issue's final pages are given over to More or Less Pungent, a department for reprinted jokes; selected gossip from the periodical press, such as 'How Grant Acquired the Cigar Habit'; a calendar of the week's events; and a lengthy chess section. Although sections came and went, the *Digest* retained the essence of this issue throughout William's tenure with the magazine. Like the Washington *Current Opinion* and the London *Review of Reviews* it was modelled after, it was a content-heavy magazine for readers who wanted to stay informed in all fields and who preferred a range of opinions to a strong editorial stance.[18]

William occupied a number of editorial positions over his almost forty years with the *Digest*. Its pages were entirely anonymous, a policy intended to emphasize its impartiality. From Frank Pollock, however, we know that by early 1899 William was editor of a *Digest* department. He spent much of the rest of that year in England on an unidentified assignment for the magazine, leaving New York with Charles in early May and remaining in London after Charles returned in November. In his letters, Charles refers to William as the *Digest*'s literary and religious editor in 1906, as the political editor in 1928, and finally as the office editor in 1932. According to William's obituary in the *New York Times*, however, for his last thirty years with the *Digest* his chief role was as its managing editor, a position for which he was evidently well suited.[19] By the mid-1920s the *Digest* had a circulation of a million and a half, second among American weeklies only to the runaway *Saturday Evening Post.*

Although Charles had remarked of one of his brother's early poems in a letter to Carman that 'It is better than either of us could do at that age, ne'est-ce pas?' William soon gave up trying to emulate his more famous relatives.[20] In the late 1890s he published a handful of poems in New York magazines, and in the fall of 1899 these and earlier efforts were collected alongside verse from brother Theodore and sister Jane in the Robertses' family volume *Northland Lyrics*, but by the turn of the century he had stopped publishing poetry altogether. He turned instead to prose, publishing articles in *Munsey's* on the North-West Mounted Police and the recently re-elected Wilfrid Laurier. Some years later he contributed a couple of political articles to the *Craftsman*, then edited by his wife, Mary Fanton, a native New Yorker and herself a noted journalist, a former staff writer for the *Herald*, *Tribune*, *Journal*, and *Sun* and an editor with several women's fashion magazines before she assumed the managing editorship of the *Craftsman.*

Will Roberts never won the literary accolades of his brother and cousin, but he achieved the financial security that eluded them for most of their careers. In fact, Charles's correspondence shows that in later years William financially supported both Charles and their youngest brother Theodore from time to time. William and Mary entertained for years in their Stuyvesant apartment at 142 East Eighteenth Street, Mary, in particular, serving as 'friend and hostess to many artistic and theatrical personalities.'[21] William became involved in business pursuits outside the *Digest*, notably organizing the Garden Tower Corporation, which in 1917 purchased Madison Square Garden for a reported 2.4 million dollars (the deal fell through because of title problems, and the Garden's owners were ordered to return William's $100,000 deposit).[22] He also served for a time as a professor of politics at New York University.

In the 1930s William's *Digest* declined, a victim of the Depression and of the new, fresher *Newsweek* and *Time*, the latter of which took it over in 1938. William left the *Digest* shortly before its final issue and he and Mary retired to an estate in Oswegatchie, near Waterford, Connecticut. Less than a year later, in early October of 1941, Mary wrote Charles in Toronto to tell him that 'Bill is quite ill, rather serious heart trouble. He is not allowed to work or drive, and is fearfully depressed. If you can spare us a few weeks, do come.' Charles didn't make it in time: on the evening of 21 November, a chauffeur found William lying on a road near his estate where he had apparently collapsed from a heart attack during his evening stroll. He died in the police car that arrived to take him to the hospital. Mary eventually returned to New York, spending her last years in the since storied Chelsea Hotel. She died in 1956, the *Times* granting her the same space it had her husband and reproducing a portrait of her by Paul Swan.[23]

Laughing It Off

As the presence of a jokes department in Will Roberts's *Literary Digest* reveals, humour wasn't incompatible with the official culture's earnest obsession with education and improvement. Then as now, humour served the dual purpose of helping its audience accept rapid social, economic, and technological changes with a world-weary smile, and teaching that audience to laugh at those who wouldn't or couldn't accept those changes – the rich, the poor, the rural, the stupid, the Irish, and always the old. It's no accident that the American publishing industry of these years experienced a comic explosion. In direct contrast to the humourless Canada that Herbert Casson complained about in *Munsey's*, more high quality humour magazines were published in America in the 1880s and 1890s than in any other period in the country's history. St Louis had its *Commodore Rollingpin's Illustrated Humorous Almanac*, Philadelphia its *Jester*, Chicago its *Figaro*, and Boston its *Harvard Lampoon*. Presiding over these and many more lesser magazines were the extremely well-illustrated New York weeklies *Life*, *Judge*, and *Puck*, with *Truth* and John W. Lovell's *Tid-Bits* not far behind. In addition to these humour-dedicated magazines, most of the new Sunday papers and some dailies featured regular 'colyums' by established humorists like Bill Nye, Opie Read, and Eugene Field.

Not every editor could afford a Nye or a Field, and even if he could, he faced another problem their columns couldn't solve. Less glamorous but more widespread than the 'colyum' was the 'paragraph' – to a cynic, the humour of available space. With newspapers increasing in length as well as number, typesetters were more pressed than ever for small blocks of text to fill out their columns, and jokes, epigrams, and snippets of verse fit the bill – and the space. To an optimist, the paragraph was less a by-product of typographic requirements than it was a quintessentially modern development. As one observer wrote in Toronto's *Saturday Night* at the beginning of the 1890s, 'In this age, when the world is rushing on at a gallop, that which is concise and pithy "catches on." Hence the rise of the paragrapher, an essentially modern phase of literature. The humor, the satire, and the wit which long ago was driven to the world in bulky volumes and slashing articles is now served up in tart, spicy dialogues, paragraphs or epigrams.' The equivalent in humour of the 'crisp, racy and reckless style of composition' that the *Week*'s newspaper insider told would-be Canadian journalists characterized American newspapers, and like that style a reflection of the fascination with speed and newness that Modris Eksteins and others have argued typifies the modern consciousness, the paragraph spread like a virus through the periodicals of North America. Dailies and weeklies printed them by the dozen, and some monthlies began to carry them as well. Each reprinted from the others, so that it wasn't unusual for a joke, epigram, or bit of verse to travel farther and live longer than its author.[24]

Apart from Palmer Cox, before his reinvention as a children's author, at least two other Canadians launched these jokes into the American press: secretary by day Mary Bourchier Sanford, and *Truth* editor Peter McArthur. Like McArthur, Sanford began her literary career in the pages of J.W. Bengough's *Grip*. Born and educated in Barrie, Ontario, she debuted in the Toronto humour weekly in the late 1870s with some paragraphs in which one Bridget O'Flannagan, who would become a recurring character of hers, visited a regatta. Apparently Bengough liked what he read, for Sanford became a *Grip* regular, contributing two columns a week for the next several years. In August of 1882, Sanford moved to Cleveland and took a position as secretary of the International Institute for Preserving and Perfecting Weights and Measures, a job that involved writing reports and reviews for its journal, the *International Standard*. She remained with the Institute for seven years, quitting in July of 1889 upon the death of her employer and moving briefly to Baltimore before arriving in New York in 1890.

In New York, Sanford settled in at an address off lower Broadway and found work as the private secretary of a civil engineer. While in Cleveland she had written little for publication other than her work for the *Standard*, but shortly after her move to New York she began writing again in the evenings. Little of what she wrote over the next decade has been recorded, but her nightly labours are known to have been published in a wide range of venues, including general-interest magazines, many of the established and newer women's magazines, juveniles, religious periodicals, literary magazines, and most of New York's leading dailies. Her work spanned as many genres as it did periodicals, ranging from essays on anti-Semitism and homes for fallen women to juvenile verse and fiction, but her standby was humour. She revived Bridget O'Flannagan for *Puck*, wrote humorous articles for *Kate Field's Washington*, the *New York Tribune*, and others, and 'contributed squibs innumerable to the comic press, and to the comic departments of other periodicals.'[25]

In the summer of 1897 Sanford published her first novel, a Parkmanian romance set during the martyrdom of the seventeenth-century Jesuit missionaries Brébeuf and Lalemant. Although minor points of doctrine in *The Romance of a Jesuit Mission* offended some Catholic readers, the New York *Bookman* reported that the novel had attained a 'considerable sale.'[26] Sanford's next novel, *The Wandering Twins: A Story of Labrador* (1904), returned to a Canadian setting but aimed at a younger audience. It too sold well, earning the recommendation of several reviewers for public and Sunday schools and eventually adoption as a reader by schools in Kansas. But despite their sales, these novels didn't earn enough to release Sanford from her secretarial job, in part because she had signed contracts with both their publishers that would pay her royalties only on sales after the first thousand.

Sanford continued in the engineer's employ for at least the first decade of the new century, but by about 1905 she seems to have mostly given up on her off-duty literary work – perhaps because of failing health (the strain of maintaining two careers had resulted in a breakdown shortly after the publication of her first novel), perhaps because the rewards were incommensurate with the effort. In 1909, she declined the offer of a North Dakota minister to collaborate on a romance, citing the demands of work and when the minister pressed the issue her exhaustion and age. All she had time and energy for these days, she said, were the jokes with which she had begun her career thirty years before. 'I do that occasionally even now, for it does not require concentration of thought, and the little stories can be jotted down at odd moments. I should prefer to write a dignified romance; but a saintly deaconess, a dear friend of mine, thinks that harmless jokes have a useful place, and that I need not regard the writing of them as a folly.'[27]

Mary Sanford's contributions to the form notwithstanding, a handful of male writers dominated the 'paragraph' market. 'It is a well-known fact,' wrote Sophie Hensley in the spring of 1893, 'that in spite of the hundreds of comic newspapers printed all over the United States, the work required to fill the pages of these periodicals is done by five or six men. Mr. McArthur is one of these.' Peter McArthur was every bit as prolific a jokester as Hensley claimed. The editor of *Life* once remarked that McArthur had 'a joke output equalled only by two other practitioners of this exacting vocation; one of whom went mad and the other of whom committed suicide.'[28]

McArthur began his career as a humorist while a student at the University of Toronto, where to help pay his expenses he wrote a weekly page of jokes for *Grip*. The $2.50 a page wasn't enough: early in 1889, his debts forced him to leave university for a reporting job on the *Toronto Mail*. Encouraged by the reappearance of some of his jokes in American periodicals, he began sending his paragraphs to various New York papers and magazines, including Dana's *Sun*, H.C. Bunner's *Puck*, John Ames Mitchell's *Life*, and Julian Ralph's

Chatter. Enough of these were accepted to satisfy him that, as his first biographer William Arthur Deacon put it, 'his facility in joke-making would always provide food,' and in May of 1890, at age twenty-four, McArthur moved to New York.[29]

Upon or shortly after his arrival McArthur moved into a Brooklyn boarding house at 15 Cranberry Street, apparently taking the attic flat Bliss Carman had recently vacated for quarters across the river. By September, he was sharing that flat with a young American writer, Harold Hall, and with the ever nomadic Carman, who stayed with them for a few weeks before leaving for a writing holiday with Roberts in Nova Scotia. In 1891 he gained another Canadian roommate, illustrator Duncan McKellar. McKellar was born in Middlesex, Ontario, and like McArthur attended Strathroy Collegiate Institute, where the two had met and become close friends. Shortly after leaving school McKellar joined the staff of the *Toronto News*, but when its editor Edmund E. Sheppard left the paper in 1887 to launch *Saturday Night*, McKellar went with him as the new weekly's first literary editor, drama critic, and illustrator. He remained with *Saturday Night* for three years, publishing several stories in the magazine in addition to his editorial work and accepting for its pages some of McArthur's light verse. Sometime in 1891, McKellar left Toronto to study like many other young Canadian artists of his day at the Art Students League of New York, then still on East Twenty-third.

From their home on Cranberry Street, a five-minute walk from the Brooklyn Bridge, McKellar and McArthur set to work. McKellar submitted illustrations and written work to the city's editors while attending classes at the Art Students League, and by 1893 his name had spread sufficiently for Hensley to take notice and report back to Canadians that 'in spite of his limited time, Mr. McKellar manages to keep up his literary tastes, besides contributing with pen and pencil to all the leading comic papers; he writes both in prose and verse for many of the well-known city publications.' McArthur, who had a year's head-start on his friend, had already made an arrangement with *Harper's* for first refusal of all his jokes; if their editor wasn't interested, he would pass them along to the editors of several other periodicals. As McArthur told *Saturday Night* in an interview conducted seven months after his move to New York, 'Those that are left when all the editors have selected come back to me and I try to dispose of them to other papers until they have been all around.' The system worked: by his first Christmas in New York, McArthur's paragraphs had appeared in *Puck*, *Judge*, *Life*, *Town Topics*, *Chatter*, *Drake's Magazine*, the *Epoch*, the *New York Racket*, the *Sun*, and the *Herald*, as well as *Harper's Monthly*, *Harper's Bazaar*, and *Harper's Weekly*.[30]

During this first year as a freelancer McArthur claimed to be writing twenty-five to fifty jokes a day, and had had days of over a hundred. 'I do not depend so much now on what I see or hear for my ideas,' he told *Saturday Night*. 'I go upon the principle that every possible thought can be treated in a manner to make it humorous or pointed ... I have my characters, though, into whose mouths I put different sentiments, and they are as real to me as any novelist's are to him or her.' As his last comment implies, most of McArthur's jokes are dialogues that employ a straight man to set up the punch line; he liked ethnic jokes, especially Irish, English, and 'nigger' jokes. Rarely more than mildly satiric, his paragraphs consistently avoid lewd or even suggestive humour. Alec Lucas, who some years ago examined almost a thousand of McArthur's jokes, remarked that 'frequently the humor derives entirely from verbal play – puns, ambiguities, dialect, bad grammar, bad spelling, misapplied metaphors and similes.'[31] The samples selected from McArthur's work for his *Saturday Night* interview are typical:

LESSENS THEIR NUMBER.

Cynic – I am always happy when two fools marry.
Binnick – Why?
Cynic – Because they are made one.

THE CITY CHILD'S IDEA OF IT.

Teacher – How many of you can tell me something about grass? Well, Johnny, what do you know about it?
Johnny – Please, ma'am, it's something you've allus got to ke'p off'n.

THE DEAR GIRLS.

Ethel – My papa always gives me a book as a birthday gift.
Maud – How nice! What a fine library you must have.

GAVE HIMSELF AWAY.

Wife – John, did I hear you swearing?
Husband – I trust not. I didn't intend you to.

'THE GLORY AND THE NOTHING OF A NAME.'

I met a poet once, a worthy man,
  Who after years had won the fame he sought;
I wished him joy; he blushed and wrung my hand
  And borrowed dollars from me on the spot.

Now more tedious than humorous, the genre (and many of its jokes) survives today, if nowhere else than in the pages of the *Reader's Digest*.

By the mid-1890s, after five years of freelancing, McArthur was earning something under twenty dollars a week from jokes like these, a living wage but not much more than he could have made as a police reporter for one of the dailies and not enough to keep fears of poverty at bay. In March of 1895, he received an invitation to become an associate editor of *Truth* from his friend Tom Hall, who had just been appointed the magazine's editor. After some behind-the-scene negotiations, McArthur began work at the *Truth* offices at 203 Broadway on 9 April. Three months later he was promoted to editor-in-chief at a salary of a hundred dollars a week, apparently replacing the very man who had secured his initial appointment. On 11 September, emboldened by his new position and salary, McArthur married Mabel C. Waters in her home town of Niagara-on-the-Lake, with Duncan McKellar as his best man.[32]

Mott calls *Truth* of the 1890s a brilliant weekly, one that at its best was 'lively, enterprising, and beautiful.' Founded in 1881, the magazine went through some growing pains until it reorganized ten years later with enough capital to add colour covers and attract leading writers and illustrators. From its start a chronicler of high society, the reinvented *Truth* retained this focus but under its new editor Blakely Hall added a dose of social satire and some spice to its illustrations – not quite one of the 'nudes in art' magazines, but plenty of actresses in tights and girls at the beach. By the time McArthur joined the magazine it had a circulation of fifty thousand and was the leading competitor of Colonel Mann's high-society weekly, *Town Topics*. Despite its success, McArthur promised readers a 'new TRUTH,' declaring that henceforth the magazine 'will be clean, bright and entertaining. It will be filled from cover to cover with beautiful pictures, jokes, sketches, poems and stories; in short, it will in every way be the most interesting and readable publication in America.'[33] Given that all these things were already true, or at least claimed to be true, of the magazine, it's possible that McArthur's promise of a 'new' *Truth* was a reference to the departure of Blakely Hall, and that the key word in his announcement is 'clean,' an editorial direction consistent with McArthur's aversion to salacious humour.

McArthur did make some content changes to *Truth*, including reducing its pictorial emphasis, reintroducing its former interest in New York theatre via a column with himself as critic, and adding 'A Department for Deserving Domestic Animals' comprised of anecdotes about readers' pets. He also contributed at least two poems, seven short stories, and a satirical series of 'Tales of Millionaires' under his own name, and undoubtedly wrote much unsigned material. Perhaps the largest change he made, however, was to increase the magazine's already significant Canadian content – 'those were,' recalled Arthur Stringer a few years later, 'the palmy days of *Truth*, when its columns bristled week by week, with good Canadian copy.'[34] Ontario artist Jay Hambidge, another Canadian at the Art Students League and a *Truth* regular since its refinancing in 1891, contributed no fewer than nine covers and two dozen centrefold illustrations during McArthur's editorship. Duncan McKellar's artwork appeared regularly. Stephen Leacock, then virtually unknown, contributed some eighteen pieces. Charles G.D. Roberts weighed in with eleven poems, Duncan Campbell Scott with four (including 'The Piper of Arll,' published in a two-page spread in the 1895 Christmas number with illustrations by Hambidge), Archibald Lampman with three, and Carman with at least one.

In July of 1897 McArthur resigned from *Truth* after an argument with its publishers, probably over the magazine's persistent financial difficulties (its beauty didn't come cheap). After spending the rest of the summer at his wife's family home, he returned to New York and spent the next few years freelancing. Among other projects, he reviewed for the American edition of *Literature* and wrote short stories for a newspaper syndicate and essays on police practices and big business for *Everybody's* and *Ainslee's*. In 1899, he moved to Amityville, Long Island, where he and Jay Hambidge were to work on a series of illustrated humorous sketches on mathematics commissioned by *Life*. Their research led them away from the original assignment into what Hambidge would later call 'dynamic symmetry,' a theory of art that used Greek architecture and sculpture to formulate laws of natural proportion.[35] Three years later, McArthur and his family moved to England to start a magazine with Hambidge devoted to their new philosophy. The two quarrelled and the magazine never got beyond its prospectus. McArthur published some satirical sketches in *Punch* and worked briefly for William T. Stead on his *Review of Reviews* and *Daily Paper*, but it was evident that England wasn't working out even before Stead fired him, apparently on the advice of a California clairvoyant.

In April of 1904 McArthur returned to New York, settled his family in Montclair, New Jersey, and with a friend opened the McArthur and Ryder Publicity Agency out of a Broadway office. Not so far from humour as it might appear, the relatively new field of advertising was merely the most overtly commercial agent of modern America's management of mass culture. Like the periodical boom it helped to create, it generated hundreds of new writing and illustrating jobs. Because of this demand, and because of the industry's relatively high pay, many Canadian writers who moved to the States wrote advertising copy at one time or another: even Vagabondian Bliss Carman took a position after the First World War with Alfred Erickson, future co-founder of the giant McCann-Erickson advertising agency.[36] Intended to profit from this market by using McArthur's experience as advertising manager of Stead's *Daily Paper*, McArthur and Ryder instead produced McArthur's most widely read short stories in the form of three booklets of fiction he wrote to puff the products of a lock company, a door-check manufacturer, and a life-insurance agency. The business also gave him time to prepare his first volume of poetry, *The Prodigal and Other Poems*, brought out by Mitchell Kennerley in the summer of 1907. Throughout his years as a paragrapher McArthur had published the occasional piece of serious verse in the *Independent*, *Frank Leslie's*, the *New England Magazine*, the *Youth's Companion*, *Harper's Weekly* and other magazines, and at least twice in privately printed chapbooks. According to Hensley he thought more of his poetry than he did of his humour. The critics thought differently: reviews of *The Prodigal* in the *New York Times* and the Chicago *Dial* were lukewarm, with the one objecting that McArthur's sonnets were too much copies of their Shakespearean originals and the other finding his inspiration 'a little tame.'[37] No more successful, McArthur and Ryder closed its doors, and the McArthurs gave up on New York and moved home to Ontario.

McArthur's career was far from over: in 1909 he started a column on farm life for the *Toronto Globe* that would run for fifteen years and produce several very popular books. But his career as a paragrapher and to a large extent as a humorist had come to an end. In his *Globe* column humour took second place to the ardour of his new-found antimodern agrarianism, and he rarely made use of his old talent for churning out jokes and epigrams. For the rest of his life he was the Sage of Ekfrid, the genial narrator of the adventures of Fenceviewer the cow, Beatrice the Pig, and other inhabitants of the McArthur family farm. There was a time, though, when his life was more Bohemian than bucolic, a time and a place when he had wondered 'who would pipe on oaten straws / When he might suck mint-juleps through them!'[38]

Palmer Cox, the Brownie Man

Palmer Cox took, quite literally, the roundabout route to New York. Born in 1840 on a small farm near Granby, Quebec, and educated at the local academy, Cox worked as a finish carpenter on railroad cars in Springfield, Massachusetts, and later as a barn framer around Lucknow, Ontario. On 29 December 1862, he left Canada for the American West, sailing via pre-canal Panama.[39] Settling in San Francisco, he ran his own contracting business out of Oakland for the rail industry. A gifted sketcher and natural versifier since childhood, he also took night classes at the San Francisco Graphic Arts Club and began submitting humorous illustrations and verse to the San Francisco papers. He published his first book in 1874, an illustrated diary based on his journals and probably modelled after Mark Twain's *Roughing It*, a copy of which he acquired soon after its publication two years before. Like *Roughing It*, *Squibs of California* is a rambling, at times genial, at times cynical, account of Western types and incidents. 'For launching this Book adrift upon the great sea of letters,' wrote Cox in a prefatory note, 'I have no apology to offer. Having carried the manuscript with me for a year, adding to its pages daily, it has grown too heavy for my pocket and I now saddle the public with the burden.'

Sometime before the publication of *Squibs of California*, Cox travelled east to meet with its publisher, Mutual Publishing of Hartford, Connecticut. Prompted by this trip and by the sale of a cover cartoon to the New York *Daily Graphic*, he considered chancing a full-time writing and illustrating career in New York. After a year's indecision he made the leap late in 1875, arriving in New York 'with nothing but a pencil to make my living with.'[40] For the next three years he worked for the satiric weekly *Wild Oats*, contributing cartoons to it and like-minded periodicals and supplementing his income with advertising work and several illustrated paperbacks for the railway bookstall trade: *Hans Von Pelter's Trip to Gotham* (1876), a picaresque tale of a Hoboken bumpkin's adventures in New York; the comic-book-like *How Columbus Found America* (1877); and *That Stanley!* (1878), a burlesque of Stanley's expedition in search of Livingstone. But Cox's publisher, the engraver Frederick Juengling, closed his business in 1879 to attend art school, and *Wild Oats* was showing the signs of its own impending demise. Tired of having to 'beg and skirmish' for their pay, Cox and a friend at *Wild Oats*, Richard Munkittrick, quit the magazine and together rented two small rooms in a boarding house on Bond Street.[41]

Years later, Cox explained that around this time he became dissatisfied with the broad humour of the satiric papers, and at Juengling's suggestion, decided to try his hand at children's humour. He wrote his first children's poem while sitting in Brooklyn's Prospect Park one summer day in 1878, sent it off to the New York children's monthly *St. Nicholas*, and was rewarded with four times the pay he would have received from the adult weeklies and a request from the magazine's famous editor, Mary Mapes Dodge, for more of the same. 'From that time on,' said Cox, 'I did all my work for the children.'[42] In fact, Cox continued to write for adults, including political cartoons for *Life* and a stint as chief artist for the short-lived *Uncle Sam: The American Journal of Wit and Humor*. But by the early 1880s, the childless Cox had reinvented himself as a children's author, contributing sketches, cartoons, and verses of 'everything that could be dressed up in odd costumes and talk like human beings' to children's magazines the likes of *St. Nicholas* and *Harper's Young People* in New York and the *Youth's Companion* and *Wide Awake* in Boston.[43]

In February of 1883, *St. Nicholas* published a short illustrated poem by Cox called 'The Brownies' Ride.' Poem and pictures told the story of a band of small nocturnal creatures taking a horse and cart for an evening ride. Over the next thirty-five years these creatures would multiply through eighty-eight periodical appearances, thirteen books, a two-act cantata, and a three-act stage play. Their likeness would adorn everything from children's toys to china dinnerware. They would ride the first bicycles, drive the first automobiles, fly the first airplanes. They would visit the Philippines, the Suez Canal, the Columbian Exposition, and the White House. And they would make Palmer Cox the best-known American children's author of their day: 'It is doubtful,' remarked a *New York Times* editorial on Cox's death, 'whether any fashion in children's literature has ever swept the country so completely as Palmer Cox's Brownies took possession of American childhood in the early '80s.'[44]

Cox based his Brownies on childhood memories of the legends recounted in the primarily Scottish-settled community in which he was born. His genius, however, was to transform the Brownies of legend from individual sprites who served only fortunate families into a roving band motivated as much by curiosity as by their desire to serve humans. Over time, Cox separated some of his Brownies from the band, giving them a limited but distinct set of attributes that children could easily identify – a key principle of modern toy marketing, and not the only time Cox anticipated twentieth-century marketing strategies. Some fifty distinct Brownies eventually emerged from the band, including social types of the period, like the Wheelman and the Dude, professionals, like the Policeman, Sailor, and Jockey Brownies, and particular races and nationalities, such as the Canadian, Irish, Indian, and Chinese Brownies. One of the last to be added was the Rough Rider Brownie, created (or so children were told) at the suggestion of President Roosevelt himself.[45] Clearly individualized, the Brownies were nonetheless completely egalitarian, the melting pot epitomized. When they need to build a vessel to carry them across the Atlantic in *The Brownies Around the World*, they scorn a ship with staterooms 'Wherein a favored few can hide' and opt instead for a raft, on which 'all alike, through storm or wreck, / Must take their chances on the deck.'[46]

As Cox scholar Wayne Morgan has shown, the Brownies eagerly explored the technological and social changes that were altering the face of America. Most children's literature of the period offered a romantic escape to a world outside the reader's experience or a nostalgic return to a sentimentalized past; the Brownies, Morgan argues, were 'almost alone' in their enthusiastic embrace of the here and now.[47] In story after story, they scrambled around, over, or through virtually every major technological innovation of late-nineteenth-century America: the Corliss steam engine, the automobile, the airplane, the

Brooklyn Bridge, and the new national canal, rail, and telegraph systems, among many others. In one characteristic story, they visit a science academy, marvelling at 'electric currents,' phrenology, microscopes, and a stereopticon machine.[48] They also helped middle-class families adapt to the modern concept of leisure time, official culture's cagey recompense for another technological innovation of the period, the time-clock that by the 1880s governed the lives of many Americans. In 1886 alone, they went tobogganing in January, strapped on roller skates in May, toured a menagerie in July, played tennis in September and baseball in October, and visited a gymnasium in November. Their stories provided a moral as much as a social education for the times, enacting a model of democratic philanthropy whose principal ethic was to 'do good to all the world,' whether repairing city streets, setting up a hospital, or ensuring a pure milk supply. But as Cox explained the philosophy that had much to do with his success, 'the moral must not be so strongly emphasized in any picture or story that it will frighten the children away.' That way, he said, children would read for pleasure, and 'get the moral lesson without knowing that they are getting it.'[49]

By July of 1887, twenty-four Brownie stories had appeared in St. Nicholas; all were collected that fall and published as The Brownies: Their Book by the magazine's publisher, the Century Company. The Times greeted the first Brownie book with a ringing endorsement of its difference from Old World fairy tales: 'long live the American elfkinship, the Palmer Cox Brownie.'[50] In 1890, Another Brownie Book collected a second series of St. Nicholas stories together with thirteen previously unpublished. In the fall of 1891, the Brownies found a new home for a time: Edward Bok, the new editor of the Ladies' Home Journal, signed Cox to an exclusive two-year contract that produced two dozen new stories, collected as The Brownies at Home (1893) and The Brownies Around the World (1894). The first depicts the Brownies at appropriately seasonal activities for each month; in the second, they become tourists, visiting first Canada and then rafting across the Atlantic to Europe, Asia, and the Polar regions. St. Nicholas responded with its own Brownie travel series, this time taking the diminutive tourists Through the Union, a series collected in 1895. Again, the Brownies reflected modern social developments, their travels at home and abroad coinciding with the increase in travel for pleasure (once the privilege of the upper class) to the new middle-class resorts in such places as Newport and Saratoga Springs, to historic American cities and the parks in Yellowstone and Yosemite, and to Europe and other overseas destinations.

On 12 November 1894, The Brownies, a three-act musical by Cox and fellow St. Nicholas writer Malcolm Douglas, opened at New York's Fourteenth Street Theatre. The play ran in New York for over a hundred performances, then went on tour for four years through the States and Canada. Cox took a break from his Brownie stories (he'd been in print every month since 1874) and toured with the play throughout its run, appearing on stage each night to greet the audience. Capitalizing on what was by now a full-blown Brownie craze, the musical required five railroad cars pulled by a special locomotive to transport its twelve sets and cast of more than seventy-five Brownies, fairies, and demons. When it came to Toronto's Grand Opera House in March of 1896, the *Week* called it 'one of the most notable attractions of the present theatrical season,' promising readers that the play would be 'witnessed here exactly as it was produced in the metropolis.'[51]

Cox also had his hands full with another side of the Brownie craze: Brownie products. By this time, the Brownies adorned toys, card games, clocks, stationery, stamps, handkerchiefs, Christmas ornaments, gold jewellery, silver and china tableware, humidors, candlesticks, and many other products. Many of these were imitations, but some were made with Cox's permission, and to his profit. On 1 April 1890, the Library of Congress awarded the first patent for a doll based on a fictional character with the author's permission to Myra Whitney of Bradford, Pennsylvania, for her Brownie dolls of leather and cloth over a wire frame. The McLoughlin Brothers' Brownie products were the first toys made from an author's characters with his direct involvement and profit (the Whitney dolls were a cottage industry, and it's not known if Cox ever received any money from their sale). Cox also designed and created advertisements for several products in the new national market, including Procter and Gamble's Ivory Soap, and licensed (a concept he developed) his Brownies to the manufacturers of over forty other commercial products, from toys to coffee. The National Biscuit Company's (later Nabisco) Brownie Biscuits were the first character-based food product, the progenitor of Spice Girls gum and Harry Potter chocolate bars.[52] Most successfully, though not for Cox, the Brownies helped sell Eastman Kodak's Brownie camera, introduced to dealers in February of 1900 in boxes decorated with drawings of Brownies and supported with full-page ads in which the technology-loving creatures showed consumers that photography was accessible to 'any School Boy or Girl.' Although no letter of permission has been found and Eastman replaced the Brownie look-alikes with their own 'Brownie Boy' once the camera had become a hit, the source of both its name and its initial campaign was clearly Cox's Brownies. With their unpaid help, the Brownie camera sold just under a quarter-million units in its first year of production.[53]

In September 1898, the Brownies returned from a three-year print hiatus to a new series of stories for the Sunday edition of the Chicago *Inter-Ocean*. The series (very nearly a modern comic strip, but without speech balloons) ran for twenty weeks, collected the following year as *The Brownies Abroad*. Two colour strips followed, one for the New York and Los Angeles *Herald* that became *The Brownies in the Philippines* (1904), in which the Rough Rider Brownie made his debut, and one syndicated strip that reappeared in *Brownie Clown of Brownie Town* (1908). After a fifteen-year absence, the Brownies returned to the pages of *St. Nicholas* for a series of stories collected as *The Brownies' Latest Adventures* (1910) and *The Brownies Many More Nights* (1913). In 1918, Cox published his thirteenth and final Brownie book, *The Brownies and Prince Florimel*, a prose story based on the Brownie musical.

In their print, product, and stage appearances the Brownies made Palmer Cox a wealthy man – the books alone sold more than a million copies in his lifetime. The Bond Street boarding house gave way to a Broadway studio, its walls crowded with portraits sent by fans, and in 1902–3 Cox built a seventeen-room 'Brownie Castle' in his hometown of Granby, complete with a Brownie turret topped with a Brownie flag overlooking a Brownie weathervane. In later years Cox summered in Quebec and wintered at a hotel in East Quogue, Long Island: 'I have never liked the severe Canadian winters,' he told the *Times*.[54] After a short illness, Cox died at Brownie Castle on 24 July 1924; he was buried in Granby's St George's Cemetery under a tombstone paid for by a collection taken among New York State school children. 'Palmer Cox is dead; the Brownies have lost their father,' the New York *Nation* reported. 'Eleven of his thirteen Brownie books are still in print: and hardly a year passes without a reissue of one or another of them ... that their popularity survives his death at eighty-four is eloquent tribute to his genius.'[55]

So far as I know, Palmer Cox didn't leave Canada for the same reason he left California, to further a literary career. I have included him here with a younger, more purposeful generation of Canadian literary emigrants because he more than any of them found fame in their America. It's possible, of course, that had Canada possessed a culture of children's letters that could have fostered and supported his talents, Cox would never have left at all. Although he became an American citizen while in California, he remained attached to his homeland, writing in *Squibs of California* that 'ten years ago I turned my back upon all I loved,' and he returned to Canada to build his dream home, Brownie Castle.[56] But the necessary culture manifestly didn't exist in Canada: although Canadian children seem to have followed the Brownies' adventures as avidly as their American counterparts, they did so exclusively in American magazines and American books.[57] Cox's work never appeared in a Canadian periodical, and the only known Canadian edition of his books is Rose of Toronto's *Queer People and Their Kweer Kapers* (1888), an amalgam of previously published work. And so Palmer Cox became an American, and his Brownies icons for a modern America – 'almost as authentic and universal a part of American childhood,' the *Nation* eulogized, 'as Cooper's red Indians.' Perhaps atypical in children's literature of the period for their enthusiastic embrace of new technologies, the Brownies were nonetheless completely typical of their age's dedication to learning more and living better, and Americans loved them for it.

Chapter 3

Living the Significant Life

In August of 1892 a new publishing house and bookstore opened for business in the first floor and basement of 125 East Twenty-third Street. Advertising a complete stock of 'Occult, Metaphysical and Christian Science publications,' Lovell, Gestefeld and Company was the ideological love child of expatriate Canadian publisher John W. Lovell and one of his several protofeminist authors, Ursula N. Gestefeld. Designed as an outlet for Lovell's interests in socialism, progressive labour, and the single tax (whose champion, Henry George, was a Lovell author) and Gestefeld's in women's rights, the firm also published books on mental science, theosophy, palmistry, astrology, and mesmerism, giving it 'the most exotic list in New York.'[1]

Eleven blocks south of Lovell and Gestefeld's bookstore, Italian immigrant Maria del Prato opened one of the new Italian restaurants born of the city's introduction to spaghetti. By mid-decade, Maria's spaghetti hour had become the favourite rendezvous of New York's Bohemian set, a diverse group of writers, actors, and artists united less by their generation than by their social habits, including a fondness for Maria's Chianti. Nathaniel Hawthorne's son Julian was a regular, as were magazinists James L. Ford and Theodore Dreiser, Julius Chambers and William Walsh from the *New York Herald*, James Huneker and Richard Harding Davis from the *Sun*, humorists Oliver Herford and Charles Battell Loomis, artists George Luks and Archie Gunn, and poets Henry Tyrell, Richard Le Gallienne, Richard Hovey, Bliss Carman, and Charles G.D. Roberts. Guests were encouraged to sing, tell a story, or recite original verse: Henry Collins Brown remembers Mickey Finn performing 'Slattery's Baby,' and Frank Pollock records that Carman 'enraptured the house' with his reciting of 'The Unsainting of Kavin.' Henry Tyrell contributed a sonnet in Maria's honour:

How oft, Marie, hostess debonair,
Have we, gay wanderers in Bohemia's way,
Gathered at closing of a weary day
To feast on thy minastra past compare!
Thou makest spaghetti and ambrosial fare,
And oh, thy ravioli! Hence we say
Salute! and as staunch admirers may
Pledge thee in Tuscan rose Chianti rare.
The storms of fate and weather beat in vain
Around the walls that comradeship enclose,
Who haply entereth in thy domain,
Dulness resigneth, care to the four winds throws.
For hid in cold Manhattan though it be,
The place is part of sunny Italy.

Sometime early in the new century, the 'chartered colony of Bohemia' closed its doors, Maria retiring to Italy and her patrons to the offices and studios of the modern professional. By 1914, even the word 'Bohemian' had become 'quaintly obsolete.'[2]

Lovell and Gestefeld's metaphysical bookstore and Maria's spaghetti hour served a common impulse. Towards the end of the nineteenth century, as Jackson Lears has shown, many Americans recoiled from the modern world so eagerly explored by Cox's Brownies. Lovell and Gestefeld's bookstore catered to Christian Scientists, theosophists, and other factions of a broad-based therapeutic movement that sought to counter the rationalizing scientism of the age by making science subservient to moral and spiritual ends. Maria's restaurant provided a haven for those who sought respite from 'cold Manhattan' in the simple, authentic pleasures of camaraderie and an unassuming cuisine, as well as an opportunity for those who wanted to live, if only briefly, beyond the bounds of social conventions, 'to live life,' as Le Gallienne ended his biography of the decade, 'significantly – keenly and beautifully, personally and, if need be, daringly.'[3] Elsewhere on the antimodern map, aesthetes and reformers advocated replacing the numbing routine of the modern factory or office worker with the satisfying life of the medieval craftsman. Militarists and hunters, reacting against an increasingly domesticated culture, urged a more strenuous life. Religious enthusiasts, dissatisfied with the softness of late-century liberal Protestantism, yearned for the conviction and ecstasy of more ancient religions, especially Eastern and mystical ones. Uniting these movements, says Lears, was their reaction against the overcivilization of modern existence and their search for more intense, more authentic means of experience.

Expatriate Canadians played leading roles in this antimodern rebellion. New York of the 1890s was the epitome of the modern, and for all that Canadian writers recognized and sought the opportunities of the city, recent arrivals struggled with their transition from Canada's smaller centres to the world's fastest growing metropolis. Most worked out this struggle in bouts of nostalgia, such as Pollock's 'The Lost Trail,' published in the *Atlantic Monthly* of May 1901:

> While the drizzle falls on the slimy pavement, swelling
>   The yellow gutters' flow,
> And the ways are dense with the hosts of buying, selling,
>   And hurrying to and fro,
> I know that out in the North the winds are crying
> Round the willowed shores of the long white lakes outlying,
> And the black pine woods where my old lost friends are dwelling,
>   And the splendor of the snow.[4]

Many, however, threw themselves into the projects of antimodernism, whether the revolt against urban complexity that animated Bliss Carman's *Vagabondia* series, the retreat from the modern West into the ancient East that produced Craven Langstroth Betts's *The Perfume-Holder*, or the rescue of the primal self from the banality of modern culture that motivated the forays into mesmerism, theosophy, mental healing, and early psychiatry of Carman, Stinson Jarvis, John and Ella McLean, Charles Brodie Patterson, and Sophie Hensley.

The Apostle of the Vagabonds

Bliss Carman never liked New York. In the city for less than two months, he wrote his Boston friend Maude Mosher that 'New York is so beastly big it makes me tired ... Cosmopolitan be damned! ... I want a decent handy town like Boston where you can get around and know people, and find what you want – not a great big barn of hideousness! Yes sir, New York is too big for any use.' After a few years in the city he was complaining to another New England friend that 'New York will never give the world any great artist; but will kill everyone who goes into it,' and arguing in print that while living in Canada cut poets off from the intellectual currents of London, it also insulated them from 'the deadly blight of New York, that center of American letters, that gangrene of politics on the body of democracy.' But for all Carman's aversion to New York, he knew the limits of a literary career in Canada, writing to his cousin that Fredericton was 'not much of a place to get ahead in,' and to his sister

Muriel that 'Boston is one of the few places where my critical education and tastes could be of any use to me in earning money. New York and London are about the only other places.' By the end of the 1880s Carman's graduate studies in England together with disparaging English reviews of a recent poem had soured him on London, and repeated attempts to find work in Boston had come to nothing. In January of 1890, he answered an advertisement in the New York *Independent* for an office editor and literary assistant to the editor.[5]

'Mr. Carman,' reported the Toronto *Week* in early March, is 'to be congratu-lated upon his appointment to the editorship or assistant editorship, it is not clear which, of so distinguished a publication as the N.Y. *Independent*.'[6] Actually hired as an editorial assistant at twenty dollars a week, Carman soon emerged as the weekly's literary editor, responsible for screening submissions and writing the Literary Notes section. Then still a religious paper, the *Inde-pendent* had a large general readership and a history of literary publication, especially poetry. Elizabeth Barrett Browning, Sidney Lanier, Henry Wadsworth Longfellow, and Richard Henry Stoddard had appeared in its pages, and dur-ing Carman's tenure its contributors included Thomas Hardy, A.C. Swinburne, James Whitcomb Riley, John Greenleaf Whittier, and William Butler Yeats. Like McArthur on *Truth* a few years later, Carman used his position to advance his friends and countrymen, soliciting, promoting, and publishing the work of Boston friends Louise Imogen Guiney and Richard Hovey and Canadians Wilfred Campbell, Archibald Lampman, Duncan Campbell Scott, Charles G.D. Roberts, and Gilbert Parker.

Carman slept under many roofs during his New York years, few of them his (Arthur Stringer called him 'a sort of intellectualized hobo'). After leaving his first New York address, the Brooklyn boarding house Peter McArthur would shortly call home, he and New Brunswicker Tappan Adney moved in May of 1890 to a fifth-floor flat in the University Building on Washington Square.[7] By September, Carman was back in Brooklyn with McArthur and Harold Hall, but by November he had moved to a flat at 1244 Broadway with the Newfound-land writer Edmund Collins, a close friend of Roberts who had given up on a literary career in Toronto and moved to New York, where he edited the weekly *Epoch*. The new address had the advantage of being the closest yet to the *Independent* offices, located in Carman's time across from City Hall Park at Broadway and Murray, but the disadvantage of life with a troublesome room-mate who would drink himself to death a little over a year later.[8]

The following November, Carman signed an improved contract with the *Independent*, but by the spring of 1892 he was finding the six-day work week draining, and in May he wrote his sister that he was worn out and planning to leave the magazine. In reality, Carman was being pushed out of his job by owner and publisher Henry Chandler Bowen, who wanted to rearrange his staff to make room for a new denominational editor and had already presented Carman with a letter asking him to preside over his own discharge. Bowen's restructuring and Carman's exhaustion coincided, and it must have been with some relief that Carman agreed to his own termination at the end of May.

Shortly after receiving Bowen's letter, Carman made a quick job-hunting trip to Boston, again without success, though he did collect requests for poems and articles from the editors he visited. Within days of his return to New York he had several offers of editorial positions, all at better pay than his *Independent* job. After spending June with Roberts in Windsor, Nova Scotia, and visiting family in Fredericton, Carman took up the editorship of *Current Literature*, an eclectic monthly with offices at 52 Lafayette Place that, like Will Roberts's *Literary Digest*, reprinted literary gossip, humour, news, and poetry from current magazines. He soon found his new job as confining as his last, writing to one friend that he had a 'lot of responsibility' and longed for 'home and rest,' and to another that 'the wilding heart has been kicking against grind-work and says it wants to get out of doors.'[9]

That hot summer of 1892 Carman made a chance discovery in a New York library that would shape much of his work over the next decade and win him his place in American letters. Flipping through an old law text, he came across an English statute on 'Vagabonds and Vagrants' – those who, the preamble declared, 'wake on the night and sleep on the day, and haunt customable taverns and alehouses and routs about, and no man wot from whence they came, nor whither they go.' According to biographer Muriel Miller, Carman 'seized pencil and paper' and began writing 'The Vagabonds,' published in the *Independent* that December. As much inspired by the 'grind-work' of editing as by the English statute, the poem gives lyric vent to the feelings of confinement Carman had been expressing since his arrival in New York: 'We are the vagabonds of time,' declares his plural speaker, 'Willing to let the world go by / ... / We have forgotten where we slept, / And guess not where we sleep to night.'[10]

Rusticity and wanderlust were by no means new notes in Carman's poetry, but 'The Vagabonds' is the earliest sustained expression of an antimodern poetic that would find full voice in the *Vagabondia* series produced over the next eight years with American poet Richard Hovey. Carman had met Hovey in Boston in the fall of 1887, and the two became friends on a walking tour down the New England coast that November. Years later, Roberts wrote that the young theology student had a 'broadening and emancipating influence' upon Carman. 'He had the effect,' said Roberts, 'of liberating those robuster elements in Carman's character ... which had hitherto lain dormant.'[11] By 1890

Hovey had abandoned his theological studies and was in New York, writing and acting. He twice accompanied Carman on his annual visits with Roberts in Windsor, and when Carman finally left *Current Literature* at the end of October it was to the Hovey family home in Washington that he retreated, there to spend the next seven months working on the Boston articles promised the previous spring and sorting his poems into volumes for future publication. The first of those volumes, *Low Tide on Grand Pré*, appeared the following November, but Carman's second book departed from the Washington grouping, drawing instead upon material gathered and much of it written during a third writing camp in Windsor with Roberts and Hovey in the fall of 1893. Originally intended to include Roberts, *Songs from Vagabondia* bore only Hovey's and Carman's names when it was published in September of 1894; fittingly, the designs were by Thomas Buford Meteyard, the Boston artist who had introduced its authors.

Songs from Vagabondia is a rejection of the superficial constraints of urban civilization in favour of the more authentic experiences of the vagabond, whether represented as a care-free vagrant (Carman's 'The Joys of the Road'), a world-weary companion of dryads and naiads (Hovey's 'The Faun'), a daring pirate (Hovey's 'The Buccaneers'), or even a roving bee (Carman's 'A More Ancient Mariner'). Hovey's 'Vagabondia' opens the book and sets its tone: 'Off with the fetters / That chafe and restrain!' it demands, for 'Here we are free ...'

> Free as the whim of a spook on a spree, –
> Free to be oddities,
> Not mere commodities,
> Stupid and salable,
> Wholly available,
> Ranged upon shelves;
> Each with his puny form
> In the same uniform,
> Cramped and disabled;
> We are not labelled,
> We are ourselves.
>
> Here is the real,
> Here the ideal ...

Carman's contributions are a trifle less eager than his younger partner's, but ideologically of a piece. He too rejects the commodification of the modern self, mocking in one poem, 'Let him wear brand-new garments still, / Who has a threadbare soul,' and pleading in another for April to 'Make me over in the morning / From the rag-bag of the world!' Pervaded with a robust masculinity, soaked in wine and beer, *Songs from Vagabondia* was a virtual guidebook for the disenchanted modern male, an escape from overcivilization into a place where 'strong men,' as Hovey says in the final poem, 'drink together,' 'roam together,' and 'die together.'[12]

Low Tide on Grand Pré had been well received for a first book of poetry, but *Songs from Vagabondia* won the hearts of readers. The first printing sold out by Christmas; the book would become Carman's most popular work, with at least fifteen printings in his lifetime. Carman himself expressed doubts about its merits, writing to a friend that 'it too often approaches the boisterous to be really very good, I fear' and to his former teacher, George Parkin, that there were 'only one or two things in it worth while,' and some of the more sober critics confirmed his fears. In Toronto, the *Week* admired the volume's youthful energy, but noted that it was 'an old cry.' In New York, Thomas Wentworth Higginson found merit in its 'tuneful' rhythms, but thought it 'an undergraduate book, and this to a degree rather surprising from two authors who have already done maturer work.' 'On the whole,' he continued, 'there is a sensation ... of young gentlemen who only play at vagabondism, and have no real objection to a bath-tub and clean linen ...'[13] As Lears points out, Higginson's review illuminates an unlooked-for consequence of American antimodernism, namely that its quest for authenticity helped ease the nineteenth century into a modern culture of consumption. Far from inspiring an actual revolt, or even actual vagabondism, *Songs from Vagabondia* allowed the harassed modern businessman to return from its pages with his spirit rejuvenated – 'made over,' in Carman's words. Henrietta Hovey's anger when a London paper reported that her husband's book had been written by two American hobos confirms both Higginson's suspicions and Lears's analysis. 'I am still raging,' she wrote her mother-in-law. 'To think of their taking Richard for a vagabond! ... Only an aristocrat would write nonsense and play the vagabond ...'[14]

After leaving the writing camp that produced *Songs from Vagabondia* in early December of 1893, Carman had returned to New York and found a temporary editorial position on John Brisben Walker's *Cosmopolitan*. That spring the magazine offered him a permanent job, but Carman chose instead to go into 'friendly slavery' with his new publishers, Stone and Kimball of Cambridge.[15] Both seniors at Harvard, Herbert Stone and Ingalls Kimball brought Carman on board as a literary advisor for their fledgling publishing firm and to help edit their new house organ, the *Chap-Book*. Carman was overjoyed to be back in Boston, but within a fortnight he had again begun to resent editorial work. He took August off for a holiday, and when Stone and Kimball moved their publishing firm and their magazine to Chicago that fall, they did so without Carman. After spending the winter in Washington, Carman returned to Boston in June of 1895 to fill in for an absent editor on the *Atlantic Monthly*. The following spring, Herbert Small, another Harvard student with publishing aspirations, sent Carman to London and Paris to develop contacts with European writers and publishers, especially those connected with the Symbolist movement.

Carman's work on the French-flavoured *Chap-Book*, together with his own *Behind the Arras*, published in December of 1895, had already attached the Symbolist label to his work, and in early 1896 the *New York World* went a step further, calling him 'The American High Priest of Symbolism.' The *World* article offended some of Carman's friends, especially Peter McArthur, but they needn't have worried, for privately Carman thought the *Chap-Book* 'pretty juvenile,' and although he continued to appear in its pages, he used it more often than not as a home for material he could not or would not publish elsewhere.[16] In fact, that very spring Carman published in a Canadian magazine a sweeping verse indictment of decadence and all else modern, from the cycling craze to the New Woman. 'I'm sick of all these Yellow Books, / And all these Bodley Heads,' Carman raged,

> I'm sick of all this taking on
>   Under a foreign name;
> For when you call it decadent,
>   It's rotten just the same.
>
>   .....
>
> I'm sick of all this poppycock
>   In bilious green and blue;
> I'm tired to death of taking stock
>   In everything that's 'New.'
>
>   .....
>
> I want to find a warm beech wood,
>   And lie down; and keep still;
> And swear a little; and feel good
>   Then loaf on up the hill.

And let the spring house-clean my brain
   Where all this stuff is crammed;
And let my heart grow sweet again;
   And let the Age be damned.[17]

Carman may have dallied with the decadents, but his heart stayed in Vagabondia. In January of 1897 Carman's Boston interregnum came to an end when he received a letter from Roberts saying he had found editorial work in New York and asking his cousin to find quarters in the city for them both. Chosen for its proximity to the Hoveys' rooms in the Carnegie Hall Studios, the resulting flat on East Fifty-eighth was home to Carman, Roberts, and later Roberts's brothers William and Theodore. That winter Carman, Roberts, and Hovey 'went around much together' with Richard Le Gallienne, recently arrived from England. They must have made quite a sight, even among Maria's Bohemians. Carman invariably wore a wide-brimmed black hat, soon 'as marked on the Avenue as Mark Twain's over-arresting suits of white,' over his long, meticulously shampooed light-brown hair, his six-foot-three figure clothed in grey, his pale 'Emersonian countenance now brooding, now quizzical.' Hovey's hair was 'as wild a mop as Carman's but of an inky blackness and usually surmounted by an old slouch felt.' Le Gallienne affected a black silk top-hat perched on long, raven-black hair parted in the middle à la Oscar Wilde, a black Inverness coat-and-cape, and a flowing black Byronic tie beneath his 'cameo-like' features: 'Dick Le Gallienne isn't a poet,' Stringer once overheard a 'fluttered female' say of him, 'he's a poem!' Feeling a little invisible in such company, Roberts began letting his own hair grow until the *New York Sun* dubbed the foursome 'The Angora School of Poets.' 'Forthwith,' recalled Roberts, 'I betook myself to the barber and acquired a close haircut; but at the same time, in self-defence, I adopted a broad black ribbon to my eye-glasses as my one mark of distinction.' These were the days, Stringer noted in the Angora School's defence, when 'a successful poet was supposed to be a bit of a showman,' but it was more than that, for through their conspicuous appearance the foursome were living the significant life Le Gallienne urged upon the decade as the only response to modernity.[18]

   Carman and Hovey published two more *Vagabondia* books together, *More Songs* in November of 1896 and *Last Songs* in the fall of 1900, after Hovey's untimely death in February. Both went through almost as many printings as their predecessor, but with the advent of the new century the public taste for vagabondism wore thin. Early in 1901, the *New York Sun* ridiculed *Last Songs from Vagabondia* as a product of 'the tea-table school of poetry,' and another

New York paper, reporting Carman's presence at a dinner in honour of socialist editor Elbert Hubbard, remarked that the 'apostle of Vagabondia' looked 'more than ever like a caricature of a chrysanthemum.'[19] By the winter of 1902–3 much of Maria's crowd had moved two blocks south to the Griffin, a French restaurant on West Tenth, and though Carman was still welcome in the new circle he was also, as even his most devoted apologist admits, 'the butt of much of their wit.' A few years later Carman found himself out of the lime-light, struggling to make ends meet. When, early in 1906, he was unable to meet a bank note that had come due, the *Halifax Chronicle* gleefully com-mented that 'For a man of Bliss Carman's cast of mind this is the height of Vagabondia, the quintessence of Bohemianism, and we have no doubt that he feels prouder of being presented at the Bankruptcy Court than he would be in being presented at the Court of St. James ... if he came down from his high Pegasus to the common Shank's Mare of newspaper work, Bliss Carman could make a good honest living, pay his debts and perhaps find some time to worship his muse, occasionally in private; but that wouldn't be art with a big A ... Come home to Canada, Bliss, and start again at fifteen a week and let art rip.'[20]

Two years later Carman moved to New Canaan. He never again lived in New York, though he did visit from time to time, and on one such trip in 1916 the American writer Hamlin Garland spotted him and recorded his impressions for his diary: 'As I was walking up Fifth Avenue this afternoon, I met Bliss Carman swinging along in stately promenade like a figure out of the past. He was dressed in a long, dark coat with a high-pointed linen collar and black stock, and on his head was a wide-brimmed black hat. He was a poet of the time of Emerson's day rather than of ours – entirely alien to the crowds and commerce of the avenue ... I carried away an impression of serenity and nobility which comforted me.'[21] Like Bohemianism, the apostle of Vagabondia had become quaintly obsolete.

Saint Craven of Harlem

In July of 1900, while Carman was in the Catskills preparing *Last Songs from Vagabondia* for the press, the young American poet Edwin Arlington Robinson moved into a friend's house at 450 Manhattan Avenue in Harlem. 'I came home in the evening,' he wrote on 5 August, 'and found Betts – of whom it is my duty to sing.'

> I have had a chance to find out what he is like [as a] housemate and I hasten to say that no orthodox heaven could give him any more than he deserves. Almost the

whole of his life has been given up to others and he is now well along on the road to fifty years old. When I think of what he has done and the spirit in which he has done it, I feel as if I had no real right to exist. The active and supposedly successful fellow who makes a lot of money and cuts his figure in Wall Street does not embarrass me in the least, but the fellow who knows in his heart that he is looked upon by his friends as one condemned to mediocrity and yet goes on as Betts goes, trying to make life a little pleasanter for all the hungry-looking victims who come his way – to say nothing of actual financial self-sacrifice in favor of those who would never think of doing as much for him – I feel that I have received not only, as you say, 'what I deserve,' but a great deal more.

Craven Langstroth Betts, Robinson's host and benefactor, was born in 1853 in Saint John, New Brunswick. The son of a sea captain at the end of the era of sail, Betts earned a teaching diploma from the Provincial Normal School in Fredericton and taught for a year at a country school in Nova Scotia. The next year found him clerking for a Saint John merchant, and in August of 1879 he moved to New York 'to pursue the literary calling.'[22] Like many other writers before and since he secured his income with a day job, working for the next decade as a salesman for a manufacturer of chromolithography equipment.

Betts began writing in earnest soon after moving to New York. His earliest known published poems appeared in the Toronto *Week* in 1886–7, but according to Sophie Hensley, his first American publication was a poem in Bunner's *Puck* in the early 1880s that 'won the special commendation of the editor.' In 1888 Betts published his first book, a translation of the *Chansons* of French poet Pierre-Jean de Béranger that he dedicated to Edmund Clarence Stedman, an influential New York poet, critic, and anthologist who had taken Betts under his wing several years after his arrival in the city. Betts sent a copy of *Songs from Béranger* to another Stedman protégé, Charles G.D. Roberts, who wrote back praising the fidelity of Betts's translations.[23]

In 1890 Betts edited a small New York magazine, and the following year he and a partner, J.K. Hoyt, established the Literary Bureau in Newark, New Jersey. Neither the magazine nor the partnership have been otherwise identified, but the latter was likely some sort of bookselling and perhaps publishing concern that Betts, at least, continued to operate into the new century. By the spring of 1893, Betts was editing another unidentified magazine in Orange, New Jersey, and a year or so later serving on the editorial staff of the Boston *Youth's Companion*. Although he may have relocated for these positions, his only known address in the 1890s is in New York, at 65 West Twelfth Street, not far from Maria's restaurant. Throughout these years Betts stayed active in the city's clubs, especially those with a literary association, and earned a reputation for 'the devotion of time he gave to the encouragement of young writers and artists of all kinds.' He was a member of the prestigious Salmagundi Club, secretary of the American Authors' Guild, and a member of the Poetry Society and Authors' Club, the last founded by Brander Matthews and others in 1882 at Richard Watson Gilder's home on East Fifteenth. By his own account 'An Annexationist, a Free Trader, a Populist and a Unitarian,' Betts also belonged to the free trade sympathetic Canadian Club of New York and later the English-Speaking Union of the United States.[24]

Betts's second book appeared in 1891, in time for Christmas. Published by Saalfield and Fitch, a small New York house that had just opened in August, *The Perfume-Holder: A Persian Love Poem* retold in verse a short story from the English *Temple Bar* of two years before. The borrowed narrative recounts the misfortunes of a poor brass-worker who has fallen in love with a princess, but for most of the poem's 1,050 lines its exotic setting dominates its tragic plot. Coffee merchants and pomegranate vendors hawk their wares against a backdrop of white minarets and purple-roofed mosques; the air is redolent of spices, incense, hookahs, and, of course, perfume. To light the perfume-holder's brazier is

To lie awake in one bliss-haunted dream
Where leaves are rustling and where fountains gleam,
Within a cool and lustrous colonnade,
While near, some large-eyed, love-enchanted maid
Leans, lily crowned, against a marble jar,
Caressing languidly her light guitar ...

In its escapist setting *The Perfume-Holder* was the poetic equivalent of the Turkish Corner, a section of one's apartment draped off with thick red fabrics and decorated with vaguely Eastern curios that was then *de rigueur* among New York's smart set. It must have made ideal reading for an afternoon in the corner, smoking the newly fashionable Turkish or Egyptian cigarettes to rid the air of the distracting odours of all too modern Manhattan. As Hensley said of it, 'The warm breath of eastern winds is there, and it is with a gasp of something like dismay that one finds oneself, after reading the poem, back in the cold work-a-day atmosphere of an unromantic Western world.'[25] The Halifax setting of Betts's next book, a collection of melodramatic tales co-authored with another Maritimer in New York, Arthur Wentworth Eaton, earned Betts his only mention in the literary history of his native country, but *The Perfume-Holder* was the best and most successful of his works.[26]

By the mid-1890s Betts had joined a group of New York writers clustered around Titus M. Coan, a former doctor who ran a Bureau of Criticism and Revision for hopeful authors. The son of a prominent clergyman and a friend of Charles G.D. Roberts, Coan was an avaricious collector of the pornographic photographs that crowded the walls of his apartment. Another member of the so-called Coan Clan was Alfred Hyman Louis, a Jewish poet whom Edith Brower, one of Coan's staffers, remembered as 'the most utterly perfect specimen of the ragged Bohemian variety of high intellectual I've ever known.'[27] Mrs Henry Guy Carleton, divorced wife of a playwright, made up an occasional fourth, and in 1897 the group accepted Edwin Arlington Robinson into their circle after he answered Coan's invitation to visit the city. Of them all, Betts seems to have been the closest to the shy young poet from Maine; one of Robinson's biographers recounts that Betts's 'enthusiasm for poetry, which he could recite endlessly, won Robinson's heart.' From Robinson's correspondence it's evident the two were much together in the late 1890s and early 1900s, with the elder poet helping the younger move, putting him up at his Harlem apartment, inviting him to dinner, lending him money, and so on. Betts even found his way into Robinson's work: according to Brower, the minor poet Killigrew in Robinson's long poem 'Captain Craig' is a slightly exaggerated version of Betts.[28]

Whatever his opinion of Betts's work, Robinson appreciated his generosity and friendship. 'I am trying to think up a way in which to get Betts calendered,' he wrote Brower in the fall of 1900. 'Saint Craven of Harlem is nothing to what he deserves. The more I find out about his past and the farther I see into him, the more do I feel like tying a grindstone to my neck and jumping into North River.' A year later, with plans afoot to bring out an illustrated edition of *The Perfume-Holder*, Robinson confessed to Brower that despite his own 'poisonous dislike' for 'this romantic story-poem writing,' he was glad for Betts's sake that the poem was to be republished.[29] The illustrated edition of *The Perfume-Holder* never materialized; ironically, when a subsequent edition came out in 1910, Betts rededicated the book to Robinson.

On 10 February 1906 Betts married Elizabeth Cushing Colby, herself the daughter of a sea captain. That same year he took a sales job in the New York office of the West Publishing Company, a Minnesota law book publisher. Betts stayed with West until his retirement in 1923 but continued to write and publish poetry, including a long poem in blank verse, *The Promise*, in 1911, and a large selection from his books and fugitive verse in 1916. After his retirement Betts took an interest in Canadian literature, renewing his correspondence with Roberts after a quarter-century lapse to solicit contributions and advice for a projected anthology of Canadian verse, and on Roberts's suggestion becoming a founding member of the New Brunswick branch of the Canadian Authors' Association.

In 1931 the Betts family moved to California, where, judging from a letter from Robinson three years later, they fell on hard times. 'In spite of all you say,' Robinson wrote after hearing Elizabeth had taken ill, 'I suspect that you haven't any too much to go on just now. So I'm sending another enclosure – not a very large one – to meet any immediate convalescent requirements. She may want a guinea-hen or something – or a bottle of fizzy wine, or perchance a bottle of good whiskey, if such a thing is to be had.' Robinson died the following spring, his place in American letters secured as the first recipient of the Pulitzer Prize for poetry; Betts followed him six years later, passing away at age eighty-eight in Santa Cruz on 30 July 1941. His Canadian anthology was believed at his death to be with a publisher, but it never surfaced, and Betts slipped into the footnotes of literary history – condemned, as Robinson had said of him years before, to mediocrity. He had rejected the age, retreating from modernism into the ancient East and the past masters of his 'beloved Sonnet,' and the age, not surprisingly, rejected him.[30]

The Ascent and Fall of Stinson Jarvis

The expatriation of Thomas Stinson Jarvis demonstrates that proximity to literary centres was a more fundamental cause of Canada's literary exodus than financial security. The eldest son of prominent Toronto lawyer Stephen Jarvis and Mary Stinson of Hamilton's wealthiest family, Jarvis grew up in the centre of Toronto society. His parents enrolled him at Upper Canada College at age nine and after his graduation in 1871 sent him for a year's travel in Europe and Asia. While Carman and Betts were schoolboys in Fredericton, Jarvis, two provinces to the east, was captaining his cricket team at UCC, dancing at society balls, fox-hunting with the Thirteenth Hussars, and yachting with the Royal Canadian Yacht Club. In 1875 he published – probably at his family's expense – his first book, a compilation of letters home to his parents from his year abroad that he dedicated to his sometime yachting companion the Earl of Dufferin, then governor general. That same year Jarvis entered Osgoode Hall to study in his father's profession, and after articling with Premier Oliver Mowat, passed his bar exams in 1879. He set up practice in Niagara Falls and for the next eight years worked as a criminal attorney and as extradition counsel to the province.

In August of 1890 Jarvis published his first novel, a sensationalist detective story about a Toronto bank clerk who 'ruins' his best friend's fiancée and frames the friend for a robbery he himself committed. Published by Appleton of New York in their cheap Town and Country Library (fifty cents in paper), *Geoffrey Hampstead* sold well in both the States and Canada, though hardly well enough to become 'the most widely reviewed novel of its year in the U.S.,' as Jarvis later claimed. The *Nation* found much of the novel choked with 'pages of puerile talk and platitudinous reflection,' but conceded that it was a distinct gain on the so far mediocre Canadian novel, while the *New Haven Morning News* called it a 'book of rare fascination,' complaining only that its hero's 'end is so ignominious that the poetic equilibrium of the work is disturbed.' In Toronto, E.W. Thomson recommended *Geoffrey Hampstead* in a letter to the *Globe* as the work of 'a novelist who, if he goes on and produces a considerable body of such fiction as that with which he has begun, will take high rank by reason of his astonishingly brilliant and accurate descriptive work, his well-knit plot, and his convincing presentation of the terrible as well as the cheerful in human nature.' Less than a year away from his own move south, Thomson hoped that 'the countrymen of Mr. Jarvis will not wait till they find him acclaimed in England and the States before substantially testifying to the force of his work,' but in Montreal the *Dominion Illustrated* testified instead that although 'eminently readable and entertaining,' the novel was flawed by its crude opening chapters and by its author's 'elaborate straining after effect.'[31]

'The success of my first novel,' Jarvis later wrote, 'lured me towards the life of a writer. I sold my law library at a good figure and also the house furniture, excepting sufficient for two rooms, and in 1891 left Canada and took apartments at 23 Washington Place in New York City.'[32] Jarvis arrived in New York at exactly the right moment to take advantage of the sporting experiences of his privileged youth. Sports in general acquired a new popularity among Americans of the 1890s, but the way to the sports' page of the modern paper was paved by the pastimes of the wealthy, including horse-racing, cricket, tennis, golf, and yachting. Yachting, in particular, enjoyed a wave of patriotic appeal in the wake of the international yacht races of the late 1880s, in which the *America*'s cup was successfully defended in race after race. An eastern yacht dealer founded the *American Yachtsman* in 1887, and the year before Jarvis's arrival the monthly *Rudder* was established in New York. Most dailies covered yachting news or carried specials when the occasion warranted, and several magazines, notably *Outing*, devoted a department to 'Aquatics.'

Jarvis's first known appearance in an American periodical was an article about a Philadelphia cricket match for *Frank Leslie's Illustrated Newspaper* of October 1891, but it was his yachting background that facilitated his entrance into New York letters. In the spring of 1892 he served as aquatics editor for

Sport, Music and Drama, contributing seven signed articles and (after leaving the magazine) a poem in July lampooning Canadian expatriate publisher and yachtsman George Munro. By 1900 Jarvis had published some twenty yachting articles and anecdotes in *Leslie's*, four in Denver's *Sports Afield*, three in *Rudder*, and a half-dozen boating adventure stories in Boston's *Youth's Companion*, by then employing his Toronto booster, E.W. Thomson. His longest association was with the *New York Tribune,* for which he was yachting editor from about 1893 to 1904.

In February of 1893 Jarvis published the sequel to *Geoffrey Hampstead, Dr. Perdue,* which finds our hero living under an assumed name in Paris, follows him through a loveless marriage, a move to England, and true love in the arms of an old sweetheart, and like its predecessor uses yachting for setting and adventure. The novel won a thousand-dollar prize from its publisher, Laird and Lee of Chicago, but was dismissed by most papers but the *Toronto Mail,* whose superbly flattering review – 'very near perfection ... true to life ... a keen psychological study' – was almost certainly authored by Jarvis himself.[33] The following spring, Jarvis himself donned the reviewer's hat, debuting as a drama critic in *Leslie's* in March of 1894. By June, around the time of his second marriage (the first ended in divorce) to Emily Little of Boston, Jarvis was calling himself *Leslie's* dramatic editor. In 1899, he started a drama column in *Leslie's* under the pseudonym 'Jason' (a portmanteau of Stinson Jarvis, the name with which he had been signing his publications since June of 1892). The column ran for the next four years, producing over a hundred short articles and reviews on the New York theatre.

Throughout his years in New York Jarvis cultivated a position as a chronicler of the public recreations of his class, but his real interests lay in one of their more private pastimes. In December of 1893 Benjamin Flower's *Arena,* a Boston monthly hospitable to articles on free silver, the single tax, agrarian reform, dress reform, suffrage, and just about anything else it could find to rail against, published the first instalment of Jarvis's 'The Ascent of Life; or, Psychic Laws and Forces in Nature.' Billed in a lengthy editorial announcement as a 'monumental contribution to modern thought,' Jarvis's essay endeavoured to improve upon Darwin by demonstrating that life was still 'ascending' through the evolution of the human soul. Key to Jarvis's argument are the operations of clairvoyance and mesmerism, both of which he claims to have experienced as early as his school days in Toronto, but kept secret because of the prejudice against such subjects. The first instalments recount his experiments in psychic phenomena, including mentally ordering another law clerk to stop writing, hypnotizing a lady friend into identifying the date of a wrapped coin, and taking patients on 'mind voyages' to Europe; later chapters address such subjects as the correlation between the 'vibrations' of the soul and music and the effects of these same vibrations upon sexual intercourse. Endorsed by the American Theosophical Society of New York when it was published in book form in the fall of 1894, *The Ascent of Life* is antimodern both in its spiritualist thesis and in its insistence that science must extend its methods into immaterial regions. Clearly concerned to avoid imputations of mysteriousness, Jarvis strives to present his findings as natural rather than supernatural, the product of simple observation and reason, and later wrote in the *Arena* against those moderns who would cloud metaphysics with art, such as the artist Aubrey Beardsley, actress Sarah Bernhardt, and all those female decadents who 'fribble with a paint-brush as the home excuse for not making beds and washing dishes.'[34]

Jarvis's third and last novel reads moderns an equally stern lesson. Published in early December of 1894 while Jarvis and his new wife were honeymooning in Europe, *She Lived in New York* pretends to have been written at the request of its upper-class heroine, Estelle Crosby, who has fallen into poverty and drug abuse and asks her lover to novelize her downfall to show other women the perils of 'what they think of as a gay life.' 'Show them how with all my advantages I failed. Tell them how the life necessitates liquor and the drugs that kill. Lure them to read. Make it interesting. Tell them of my beauty. Tell them of our first kiss; and then perhaps they will patiently read on to the disgraceful end. That is my wish, and I ask you to carry it out.' A page later, Estelle throws herself from the balcony of her New York apartment, a victim of the city's modernity. Shortly after Jarvis returned from Europe he removed the novel from sale, possibly because of the poor reception of the book he said it was written to illustrate. The *Montreal Gazette* found *The Ascent of Life* interesting, but the *Toronto Globe* and the *New York Sun* ripped it apart. The Toronto *Week* thought it superficial, sarcastically concluding upon the evidence of an appended photograph that at least Mr. Jarvis 'is a very good-looking man.'[35]

In 1904 Jarvis abandoned New York and moved permanently to California. On the eve of his departure he burned nine large scrapbooks of his newspaper work, symbolically severing his connection with the city that had killed the heroine of his last novel. Two years later he edited and published in four instalments in the *Canadian Magazine* the memoirs of his great-grandfather, Colonel Stephen Jarvis, but his main project for the rest of his life was the product of what his only critic, New Yorker Jeffrey Wollock, calls possibly 'a full blown paranoid delusional system and ... certainly a grand eccentricity.'[36] Developing ideas broached in his previous work, Jarvis came to believe that an ancient Druid priesthood had been controlling history since the dawn of civilization, secretly writing all the great religious texts, setting up kings, introducing and fostering war to serve their own ends (including the First World War), and using mass hypnosis to, among other things, persuade humanity of the existence of an afterlife.

Jarvis died in 1926 while visiting a daughter in Los Angeles from his home in Balboa, a yachting resort south of the city. Like Betts, who followed him to California, he has all but disappeared from the literary memory of his home country, remembered only in a brief summary in the *Literary History of Canada* as 'one of Canada's more sophisticated authors in the early 1890's.' Unlike Betts, though, Jarvis separated himself not only from Canada, but also from other Canadians. Responding to a query from Henry Morgan in early 1895 about other Canadians living in the States, Jarvis could or would only identify 'my good friend E.W. Thomson' in Boston, whom he understandably called 'the best literary critic that Canada ever possessed.'[37] Nor do the other expatriates seem to have known Jarvis: Hensley, Pollock, and Stringer all passed him over in their surveys of Canadian writers in New York of the 1890s, while naming other, less established writers. Perhaps Jarvis just moved in different circles, preferring lunch at the Waldorf-Astoria to spaghetti at Maria's.

Thinking New Thoughts

Although his editor thought Jarvis had 'avoided with care any alliance with any sect or cult,' *The Ascent of Life* was unmistakably a product of the therapeutic cult that would come to be known as the New Thought. A blithe cocktail of religious liberalism, transcendentalism, mysticism, theosophy, Christian Science, and early psychiatry, New Thought was mostly a reaction against old thought: what it saw as the materialism of the expiring century. As cult leader Horatio W. Dresser put it, 'We have lost interest in science not explicitly employed for moral ends.' Dresser might better have said 'spiritual ends,' for the central tenet of New Thought was the divinity of the inner person and therefore that 'all real development is from within outward' – or as Jarvis preferred, from within upward.[38] The cult had its roots in the mid-century demonstrations of the New England mental healer Phineas Parkhurst Quimby and the subsequent interest in what believers called 'mental science' and the unconvinced the 'Boston craze.' As mental science developed into New Thought, mental healing remained central to the cult's beliefs, though increasingly the mesmerist vocabulary of its healers gave way to a lexicon drawn from early psychology, replete with terms like 'transference,' the 'inner force-world,' negative and positive 'thought-pictures,' and so on (patients could be cured in

the healer's presence or at distance, through synchronized 'absent treatments').
New Thought declared itself anti-doctrinal, anti-institutional, and anti-sectar-
ian – the last two of which it argued set it apart from Mary Baker Eddy's more
structured Christian Science – but it inevitably organized, founding the first of
many societies, the Church of the Higher Life, in Boston in 1894, and holding
its first national convention five years later, also in Boston. By the turn of the
century at least twenty New Thought magazines served 'perhaps a million'
believers in the United States alone.[39]

As D.M.R. Bentley has argued, Bliss Carman's post-exile poetry increasingly reflected the influence of the mental healing movement, especially that
written after his fateful meeting with 'personal harmonizing' lecturer Mary
Perry King in late 1896 or early 1897. Carman himself explained in a 1910
letter to an enquiring graduate student that 'you will find in all [my] poems
written in the past ten or fifteen years a very definite philosophy (to give it a
large name!), the same that is elaborated in *The Making of Personality*.'
Introduced as co-written with King and based on her lectures, this 1908
collection of essays was actually rewritten by Carman at its publisher's insistence. Although it never identifies itself as New Thought and is careful to
distance itself from the mesmerism of the cult's formative years, *The Making
of Personality* draws liberally upon two of New Thought's main sources,
Hellenistic ethics and early psychology, and is recognizably enough a New
Thought publication to have been so catalogued by the Library of Congress.
Arguing that intellectual and spiritual development are inseparably connected
to physical well-being, the book's loosely connected essays offer advice on
everything from developing an aesthetic sense and 'personal vibrancy' to
cultivating one's poise, walk, and speaking voice. Along the way it suggests
the reformative benefits to naughty children and criminals of enforced gym-
nastics, argues for the liberation of the foot from the 'fashionable bondage' of
modern footwear, and urges the return of a simpler, more graceful form of
dance than its 'stiffened relic,' modern ballet. Like the *Vagabondia* series of
the previous decade, it imagines a more strenuous physical life as a counter to
the 'distorted demands,' 'crazy haste,' and 'foolish absorption in affairs' of
modern life, but has learned from New Thought to incorporate modern methods into its project, arguing the necessity of a physical education that would be
'as scientific as engineering, as ethical as religion, and as artistic as the best
sculpture.'[40]

According to Muriel Miller, Roberts saw his cousin's rewriting of King's
lectures as a 'flagrant waste of talent,' but *The Making of Personality* was
probably the best reviewed book of Carman's career, earning accolades in the
Chicago *Dial*, the *New York Times*, the *Literary Digest*, and the *Independent*.[41]

Both Carman's biographer and his literary executor have downplayed the importance of the book by emphasizing that he just rewrote King's work for the editorial fee and to get her published, but Carman himself evidently thought otherwise, writing to an appreciative reader, 'your generous liking for *The Making of Personality* is meat and drink to my spirit. Poetry goes without saying and gets itself done "involuntarily" by the grace of God and the pure joy of being alive. But a prose book is a work, an *opus*, if you please; and this one is my pet.'[42] Both his private letters and his published poetry demonstrate that Carman's allegiance to his and King's brand of New Thought was more serious than a paycheque or a favour. He was, however, neither as committed nor as important to the cult as three other Canadian expatriates, all of whom found their way separately to New York but were drawn together in marriage and career by their common interest in the therapeutic movement of the 1880s and 1890s.

John Emery McLean was born in Alton, Ontario, on 7 March 1865. His family later moved to Orangeville, where McLean was educated and at age fourteen apprenticed to a local printer. Sometime after 1882 – probably closer to the end than the beginning of the decade – McLean moved to New York and became head proofreader of the American Bible Society, a New York–based organization that had monopolized Bible printing in the States almost since its founding in 1816. According to Henry Morgan, after a few years 'the burdensome routine of this position ... became too irksome for Mr. McLean,' and he instead became associate editor of a New York banking magazine, the *Financier*.[43]

McLean's next known position, the first to indicate an interest in mental science and perhaps the source of that interest, was as managing editor of *The Metaphysical Magazine: A Monthly Review of the Occult Sciences and Metaphysical Philosophy*. Founded and edited by Leander Edmund Whipple, a mental healer who had moved to New York from Hartford, Connecticut, the *Metaphysical Magazine* was published by the Metaphysical Publishing Company, which in 1896 bought the entire stock of Lovell and Gestefeld's publishing house and bookstore. Its offices were at 465 Fifth Avenue, well uptown from McLean's more modest address at 233 East Twelfth. Advertising itself as 'a strictly first-class scientific and philosophic monthly, devoted to the best and most reliable information and advanced thought-teaching, in occult lines,'[44] McLean's new employer provided a venue for articles on metaphysics, mental healing, astrology, the occult, and theosophy, the last a mystical cult with Eastern roots founded by Russian immigrant Helena Blavatsky and others in New York in 1875. McLean remained with the *Metaphysical Magazine* for two

THE BROWNIES IN THE STUDIO.

BY PALMER COX.

THE Brownies once approached in glee
A slumbering city by the sea.
When one remarked, "On every side
Now round us stretches in her pride
The greatest city, far or near,
Upon the Western Hemisphere."
"And in this town," a second cried,
"I hear the artist does reside

Who pictures out, with patient hand,
The doings of the Brownie band.
Who draws our portraits, sings our praise,
And tells the world our cunning ways."

Palmer Cox's Brownies visit their creator's studio at 658 Broadway. From 'The Brownies in the Studio,' *St. Nicholas*, January 1890.

'Only an aristocrat would write nonsense and play the vagabond.'
Richard Hovey and Bliss Carman, by Thomas Buford Meteyard, 1896.

Stinson Jarvis, as pictured opposite the first instalment of his *Ascent of Life* in the Boston *Arena*, December 1893.

'If you know Mr. Thompson – I do prefer the old way – you must be a somebody in New York just at present, for he is the vogue. His stories and drawings are the fashion, and editors are falling over one another trying to get hold of his copy.'
Ernest Thompson Seton, photographed in his Fifth Avenue studio for the New York Critic, October 1901.

'He has been two years in New York and bears the confinement of city life well.'
Edwyn Sandys, as featured in Sophie Hensley's 'Canadian Writers in New York,'
Dominion Illustrated Monthly, May 1893.

'*We reproduce herewith a recent photograph of Mr. Stringer.*'
Arthur Stringer in the New York *Bookman*, December 1899.

Harvey O'Higgins in the New York *Bookman*, August 1908.

The 'chief' of New York's 'flourishing Canadian artistic colony.'
Charles G.D. Roberts, as pictured in Jessie B. Rittenhouse's *The Younger American Poets*, 1904.

and a half years, from its first issue in January of 1895 until the summer of 1897.

In 1898, McLean married the Countess Norraikow, a 'writer and metaphysician' of New York City. The 'Countess' was actually Ella Walton, a twice-widowed orphan from Toronto twelve years her new husband's senior, and among the most mysterious of Canada's literary expatriates of the period. Born in Toronto on 9 November 1853, Ella was adopted by one William Walton of Saint John, New Brunswick, and educated in her adoptive parent's city. When quite young she married the son of a former member of the provincial legislature and with her husband spent 'many years in foreign travel,' living in most of the European capitals. She returned to North America a widow, and in 1887 moved to New York. Later that year, Ella married her second husband, an exiled Russian nobleman calling himself Count Adolphus Norraikow. Born in Warsaw in 1844, the Count claimed to have studied law at the University of Moscow but ran afoul of the government during the Polish revolution of 1863 and was arrested several times, spending eight years in convict colonies in Archangel and Siberia. In 1876 he joined a nihilistic society in St Petersburg and was forced to flee Russia, coming to the United States with two Rembrandts valued at fifty thousand dollars and settling in New York, where he found work as a canvasser for scientific books. Neither the Rembrandts nor the job lasted: in July of 1890, the *New York Times*, under the headline 'A "Nobleman" in Poor Business,' reported that Registry Clerk Norraikow had been suspended from duty at the Barge Office after he was discovered sending Russian immigrants to an East Side peddler who found them work at wages below those offered by the Labour Bureau.[45]

About this time the couple turned to writing to support themselves. Ella had published her first literary work, a story, while she was in her teens, and the Count had taught Russian law and literature while in exile in Archangel and was something of a poet himself, his work appearing in several anthologies of Russian verse 'of the revolutionary sort.' In 1891 a collection of Leo Tolstoy's stories bearing Count Norraikow's name as translator appeared under Mark Twain's C.L. Webster imprint (two years later to publish Carman's first book), and a second collection followed from the same house the next year. Although only her husband's name appears on these collections, the Count's obituary reveals that Ella 'revised for him translations which he made of some of Tolstoï's writings and of other Russian works.' At the same time, Ella began contributing articles on the situation in Russia to American magazines. She signed her first known publication, an article on Russian women nihilists in *Cosmopolitan* of September 1891, Ella Norraikow, but within a few months she had also adopted her husband's title, appearing in *Harper's Weekly* in January 1892 as 'Countess Norraikow.' In an article in *Lippincott's* later that year on the Russian famine the Countess left her readers with the impression that she was herself a Russian, appealing 'on behalf of the myriads of the Russian peasantry who are suffering for the very necessaries of life' to 'the warm-hearted American public for aid in this dire extremity.'[46]

In March of 1892, just after completing the first English translation of Tolstoy's play *The Powers of Darkness*, the Count entered the Home for Incurables, partially paralysed from a late form of syphilis. In September Ella was forced to have his sanity tested, and on 13 October the Count died at Bellevue Hospital. Again a widow, Ella cannot have been left too well off, as her husband's obituary noted that the mortician had asked the Count's Polish friends for help with funeral expenses. With the exception of a story in a popular British juvenile adventure series in 1897, nothing more is known of Ella between the Count's death and her third marriage to John Emery McLean in 1898. Given her profession as a 'metaphysician,' it's possible the couple met through the *Metaphysical Magazine* or its publisher.

After leaving the *Metaphysical Magazine* McLean had joined the staff of a new magazine devoted to the New Thought. Subtitled 'A Monthly Magazine of Liberal and Advanced Thought,' *Mind* was published by Canadian expatriate Charles Brodie Patterson, the most prominent of the Canadian members of the therapeutic movement. Born in Nova Scotia in 1854 and educated at Pictou Academy, Patterson worked after leaving school in 'mercantile pursuits.'[47] At age thirty-one, health problems forced a consequential career change: moving to Hartford, Connecticut, he sought solace in mental healing, studying and later teaching at the city's Mental Science Institute and at the Alliance of Divine Unity, a spiritual study group with beliefs similar to mental science. In 1888, he privately printed his first book, a collection of his Sunday evening talks for the Mental Science Institute that he called *Seeking the Kingdom*. Around this time Patterson established the Metaphysical Alliance of Hartford, serving as its president until at least 1904.

In 1893 Patterson moved to New York, taking the Alliance name with him for a bookselling and publishing business he established in the new *Life* building at 19 West Thirty-first Street. Calling itself 'Metaphysical Headquarters,' the Alliance Publishing Company carried occult, philosophic, and scientific literature 'relating to Progressive Thought and Psychic Phenomena, Metaphysical Healing and Mental Philosophy, Astrology and Palmistry,' and boasted a periodical department containing 'the latest numbers of the leading New Thought magazines issued throughout the world.'[48] Its own list read like the cast of an Agatha Christie novel: Sydney Barrington Elliot, the doctor whose work on prenatal influence Stinson Jarvis admired enough to append to the book version of his *Ascent of Life*; spiritual psychologist Horatio W. Dresser; Lovell's former publishing partner, feminist turned metaphysician Ursula N. Gestefeld; Atlantis theorist Dr Augustus Le Plongeon; poet Agnes Proctor, the medium of 'clairaudient impressions received from Adah Isaacs Menken, deceased'; Henry Wood's 'Idealistic Metaphysical' novels, and so on. Patterson's own *New Thought Essays* of 1898 was the first book published under the Alliance imprint, and he followed it with several others from his own hand, including the three-volume *Library of Health* (1898–1900) and *The Will to Be Well* (1901), a collection of New Thought essays on spiritual healing that became his most reprinted work, appearing in at least ten editions in his lifetime. By the end of 1901 (then in new quarters at 569 Fifth Avenue), the Alliance catalogue ran to fifty pages, and Patterson had replaced Lovell and Gestefeld as New York's most exotic publisher.

Although the record is uncertain and at times conflicting, Patterson probably hired McLean away from the *Metaphysical Magazine* to serve as editor of his Alliance-published *Mind*, launched in October of 1897. Promising subscribers 'Health! Harmony! Happiness!' and contributions from the 'best known writers' on science, psychology, philosophy, metaphysics, religion, and occultism,[49] *Mind* published many articles by its publisher (including those collected in 1898 in *New Thought Essays*) besides the work of its editor and perhaps his new wife, now calling herself Mrs Ella N. McLean, the Countess Norraikow.

In early May of 1899, Patterson became a director of Paul Tyner's Arena Company, formed to raise capital during Tyner's brief ownership of the Boston monthly. Struggling since illness had forced founding editor Benjamin Orange Flower to withdraw from the magazine two years before, the *Arena* did no better under Tyner's management, and that fall ownership of America's periodical of protest passed into the hands of Patterson's Alliance Company.[50] It was an appropriate takeover: the *Arena* had recently absorbed four New Thought magazines, and had always been receptive to spiritual and quasi-scientific investigations like Jarvis's *Ascent of Life*. Patterson moved the *Arena* to New York and, with McLean as editor, attempted to revive the monthly's reputation for social activism. Standard *Arena* topics reappeared, including opposition to the war in the Philippines, the currency debate, the 'Mormon problem,' divorce, criminology, and so on. If, as Mott says, the contributors were not as distinguished during Patterson's ownership, the sentiments were no less sincere and the crusades no less vigorous than under Flower. Patterson also used the magazine to promote the Alliance list and the new Alliance School of Applied Metaphysics, which under 'Principal Patterson' began offering elementary and advanced classes at the Royalton building on West Forty-fourth in November of 1899. Patterson's own books were favourably reviewed, and he himself appeared repeatedly in the magazine, contributing articles on mental healing, New Thought, and the problems with organized religion, as well as one short story in which the 'very much of a materialist' narrator becomes a believer after listening to a friend recount his experiences with psychic dreams, visitations, and flight.[51]

McLean seems to have left the *Arena* for several months in 1900, during which time the magazine's cover announced that it was being 'Conducted by N.O. Fanning.' Under Fanning's stewardship advertising in the *Arena* dropped to almost nothing, which may explain why the November issue seems to be without an editor, and why the December issue bears the names of three former editors: Patterson, Flower, and McLean. These three edited the magazine together for the next two and a half years. Flower lent his old magazine some of his famous fury and revived its book review section. Patterson contributed New Thought and related pieces, while McLean wrote the announcements and edited the Symposia section, 'Where Master Brains Discuss Vital Issues.' By 1902 the magazine had reached its highest circulation, just under thirty thousand, but Mott doubts it was making much money. McLean resigned the following spring, and in October Charles A. Montgomery assumed the management of Alliance and its two magazines, a change of power that has the ring of a creditor's takeover. Patterson and Flower continued to edit the *Arena* together until April of 1904, when Flower informed readers that the magazine had been purchased by a New Jersey printer who had restored him to sole editor.[52] Like McLean the year before, Patterson left the *Arena* in silence. His money had saved the magazine in 1899, and the transfer of Alliance to Montgomery suggests that he exhausted his resources on it, but he left without so much as an editorial goodbye.

After leaving the *Arena* the McLeans and Patterson went their separate ways, at least as far as the public record indicates. According to a biographical entry published in 1912, in addition to her writing Ella 'now conducts a successful practice in metaphysical healing, and is regarded as one of the noted women of the American metropolis.'[53] John became a representative for Brentano's, a well-known New York bookstore and sometime publisher, and later joined the American Real Estate Company, becoming metropolitan sales manager before the company's bankruptcy in the spring of 1916. He also became involved with the second incarnation of the Canadian Club of New York, serving as president from 1914 to 1916 and the following year chairing the committee that found the club its first permanent home at the Hotel Biltmore, one of several New York hotels owned by Canadian expatriate and club member John McEntee Bowman. In 1926 the Henry George Foundation published McLean's *Spiritual Economics: A Plea for Christianity in Action*, a monograph on Christian socialism that is both his only known book and his last known record of any kind.

The Alliance Company continued to publish *Mind* until the magazine's demise in April 1906, but it's unlikely Patterson had any interest in the company after 1903. By 1904, Patterson's own books were being published by Funk and Wagnalls and later by Thomas Crowell, both established New York publishers that by their reputation provide an indication of just how seriously New Thought was still being taken. In all, Patterson published fifteen books on mental healing and New Thought over his life, nine of them after leaving the *Arena*. His later titles include *The Measure of a Man* (1904), *The New Way to Educate Children* (1909), and his last book, *The Rhythm of Life* (1915), a collection of essays on the healing effects of music and colour. In October of 1899 Patterson had been elected first president of the International Metaphysical League at its national convention in Boston, and he continued as president until the 1903 convention, with later terms as treasurer and vice-president. In demand as a lecturer in the States and Europe, he also conducted his own mental and spiritual healing practice. Among other affiliations, he was a member of the English Society for Physical Research and the American Academy of Political and Social Science, a fellow of the American Geographical Society, and an honorary member of the Contemporary Authors' Society of Europe.

Patterson died at age sixty-three at his Fifth Avenue home on 22 June 1917. The next day, the *New York Times* announced his passing, reporting that with his wife Louise Lippincott, 'Dr. Patterson was the founder of the "New Thought" movement in this country.' Two years later, former Alliance author Horatio Dresser took exception to this claim in his *History of the New Thought Movement*. Conceding that Patterson was among the first to use the phrase 'New Thought' in the pages of *Mind*, Dresser objected to New York papers describing Patterson at his death as the movement's American founder, arguing that he didn't begin work in mental healing until 1887 and that he 'shared with several others his pioneer work in Hartford and New York.' Dresser seems too dismissive of his former publisher's contribution; it's odd that in correcting the record he doesn't mention that Patterson himself had publicly stated (in an essay Dresser elsewhere cites) that New Thought's 'first great apostle' was Phineas Parkhurst Quimby, followed by Julius A. Dresser of Boston and the Reverend Warren Felt Evans of New Hampshire, an identical lineage to that claimed by Dresser.[54]

Dresser's crankiness aside, Patterson clearly played a leading role in the establishment of probably the single most popular challenge to modernism in turn-of-the-century America. Many of his books went into multiple printings, and several were translated into other languages, including Italian and Dutch. (A copy of his *New Thought Essays* found its way into the library of another, more famous champion of the individual over and against the innovations of the new century, the escape artist Harry Houdini.)[55] As late as 1913, Patterson's books were still being sincerely and generally positively reviewed by such papers as the *New York Times*, the *Boston Transcript*, and the *Review of Reviews*. Fiction styles change, but the promise of 'Health! Harmony! Happiness!' never goes out of style: six of Patterson's books are in print today, a century later.

The Making of Almon Hensley

A month after Patterson moved the *Arena* to New York, a symposium appeared in its lead pages on the city's recently founded Society for the Study of Life. Charged with outlining the aims of the society, the symposium's first contributor opens by acknowledging the debt modern women owed to the Suffragists who 'hewed and hacked their way through the solid phalanx of social opprobrium,' but argues that with the close of the century, American women now recognized the need to turn their efforts from improving their position in society to improving society as a whole. Since motherhood is the 'first rung of the ladder of all permanent social reform,' the National Congress of Mothers helped mothers provide an ideal environment for their children. And since an ideal domestic environment requires an ideal marriage, the Society for the Study of Life provided a forum in which 'vital sex questions could be fully and honestly dealt with; where the truths of life could be scientifically studied, and the ideal of marriage raised to the level where it belongs.' Its founding, notes the contributor in closing, 'marks the cultivation and final expression of woman's thought of the last half century – marks possibly, also, the dawn of a new era in woman's work.'[56]

This outspoken advocate of American motherhood was Canadian expatriate Almon Hensley: secretary of the New York State Assembly of Mothers, co-founder and vice-president of the New York City Mothers' Club, and founding president of the Society for the Study of Life. Born Sophia Margaretta Almon in Bridgetown, Nova Scotia, on the last day of May in 1866, the Almon Hensley who opened the *Arena*'s symposium was a different woman from the young bride who had arrived in New York a decade before, different in more than name. The daughter of socially prominent parents, Sophia (or Sophie, as she generally preferred) was educated by governesses and at private schools in

England and France. While living at the family home in Windsor she became a protégée of Charles G.D. Roberts, then on the faculty of nearby King's College. According to Roberts's official biographer, Sophie was a regular member of the poet's Kingscroft circle, and Roberts seems to have encouraged her first published verse, in the *King's College Record*, the Toronto *Week*, and the Montreal *Dominion Illustrated*.[57] In April of 1889 she had her first collection of poems privately printed by J.J. Anslow, a Windsor printer who did work that year for both Roberts and Carman. The *Portland Transcript* thought *Poems* 'worthy of an extensive circulation,' while at home in Canada the *Week* also wondered why the work should have been printed for private circulation, but contrarily complained that it didn't contain 'a single poem strong enough to float a volume of verse.'[58]

The same month that *Poems* appeared Sophie Almon married Hubert Arthur Hensley, a barrister from Stellarton, Nova Scotia. According to a letter from Hensley to Montreal writer William Douw Lighthall, the Hensleys planned to sail the world and earn their living as writers, but by 1890, the couple had instead moved to New York.[59] As far as the record has preserved, Hensley's literary efforts for her first few years in New York were confined to occasional verse for her usual Canadian venues, the *Week* and the *Dominion Illustrated*. In the spring of 1892 she turned to prose, contributing the first of two illustrated articles on Canadians working in New York to the *Dominion Illustrated* and the first in an intermittent series of New York Letters to the *Week*.

In 1895, Hensley published *A Woman's Love Letters* with the New York house of J. Selwin Tait and Sons. A prominent banker, Tait had turned his private passion for books into a public venture just three years before; the two may have been introduced by Hensley's friend Graeme Mercer Adam, whose book on Eugene Sandow Tait had just published. *Love Letters* consists of a dozen lengthy poems interspersed with shorter lyrics, most, as its title says, in the voice of a woman very much in love. The only known review, a brief notice in the *Week*, seemed genuinely interested, calling Hensley's public debut 'real poetry, the outcome of personal thought and emotion, not the mere echo of what other people have sung.' According to a puzzling note by the expatriate Canadian critic Thomas O'Hagan in the Chicago *Catholic World*, at about this time Hensley was 'giving her time chiefly to story-writing, and is meeting with much success.' O'Hagan refers to Hensley as 'both poet and novelist,' but neither a novel nor any short fiction by Hensley have been located for this period.[60]

The mid-1890s marked an important transition for Hensley, a turning point signalled in the political tones of her letters to the *Week*. Largely love lyrics, Hensley's poetry up to *A Woman's Love Letters* displays little or no social, let alone feminist, consciousness: it's slightly better than average magazine fare that dips into the sentimental as often as it rises to the 'personal thought and emotion' admired by the *Week*'s reviewer. Her articles on Canadians in New York for the *Dominion Illustrated* are informative but similarly inconsequential, though the latter is as much an index of the magazine's as of Hensley's limitations (Roberts's Modern Instances column, which ran in the monthly at the same time, was by his own admission 'frivolous,' and he generally only used the magazine as a home for work that had been rejected by American editors).[61] But the edgier editorial policies of the *Week* allowed Hensley more latitude, and her letters to the weekly reveal a developing political consciousness. Alongside reports on the Health and Food Exposition at the Lenox Lyceum and the premier of Tennyson's *The Foresters* at Daly's appear comments on the currency debate, the Behring Sea dispute, and the Lexow investigation; in particular, Hensley's political senses seem to have been awakened by her perception of inequalities of class (and later, gender) in the metropolis, inequalities that the location and circumstances of her upbringing had previously sheltered her from. At the end of her first letter to the *Week*, Hensley tells her readers that she is thinking of writing an article about 'the two great pictures of New York life: the one viewed by the miserable inmates of tenement houses, and that seen by the petted denizens of the large hotels and handsome houses of the city.' 'There is no luxury,' she continues, 'that cannot be obtained in New York, only *money* is needed to purchase it; no depth of misery and wretchedness into which it is not possible to fall, only the lack of *money* is needed to bring it about. Money is the one great cry that makes itself heard above the roar of the stock exchange, and the piteous cries of women and little children.' In a later letter, Hensley takes the looming destruction of Edgar Allan Poe's cottage to make way for the new elevated railroad as evidence that 'New York city is notoriously dead to reverential and aesthetic instincts ... The greed of gold and a love of the beautiful have never been known to go hand in hand.'[62] Hensley had found her literary culture: to steal a line from Auden, mad New York hurt her into activism.

Hensley did more than write about the destruction of Poe's cottage: she helped lead the campaign to save it, occupying the mayor's office with other members of the Poe Memorial Association until he agreed to move the landmark out of harm's way. She also became a member of the Society for Political Study, the New York Press Club, and possibly the American Authors' Guild, of which expatriates Craven Langstroth Betts and Edwyn Sandys were then members.[63] Increasingly, however, Hensley began to focus her activism on women's issues, a development adumbrated in one of the longer poems, 'Misunderstanding,' in *A Woman's Love Letters*. 'I am no saint,' the speaker tells her lover,

niched in a hallowed wall
For men to worship, but I would compel
A level gaze. You teachers who would tell
A woman's place I do defy you all!
While justice lives, and love with joy is crowned
Woman and man must meet on equal ground.[64]

Not surprisingly given her concern with economic disparities, Hensley's feminism initially took a more social form than these lines would indicate, concerning itself rather precisely with teaching other women 'woman's place.'

According to her *Arena* article, the central impetus of the several mothers'
associations in which Hensley became active in the latter half of the decade
was the recognition that the time had come for women to organize for 'altruis-
tic' rather than 'egoistic' purposes. In particular, says Hensley, these organizations aimed to improve social conditions by teaching women how to produce
and raise better children and therefore better citizens – to 'strive with the
mighty lever of motherhood to effect the regeneration of the race.' Here,
Hensley reveals the affinities of the mothers' organizations she helped to lead
with the antimodern quest for more authentic experience, or in this case a more
authentic 'race': her project of racial regeneration depends upon a reactionism
that is in ironic (and unnoticed) conflict with the progressive education she
advocates. Clearly, too, this regeneration was to be achieved not only through
education, but through not-so-natural principles of selection. As Hensley saw
it, a 'mighty problem' confronted the mothers' movement: 'The child was not
a piece of white paper on which might be inscribed the thought of the parent;
not a lump of putty to be pressed this way and that until it assumed the desired
shape. It came stamped, at times indelibly, with inherited tendencies and
predispositions – the outcome of generations of wise or unwise thinking: the
result, to a large extent, of the circumstances of conception. 'Grapes,' as she
more succinctly states the problem, 'do not grow upon thorns.'[65] And so she
helped organize the Society for the Study of Life to teach women the 'grand
laws governing reproduction,' lectured at mothers' clubs and other venues
throughout the city on such subjects as heredity, child culture, and tenement
children, and eventually published a full-length work on the 'mighty problem'
of eugenics, *Woman and the Race*, printed under the pseudonym Gordon Hart
by Ariel Press of Westwood, Massachusetts.

From the evidence of Hensley's New York Letters the city itself appears
most responsible for the transformation of Sophie M. Almon, provincial poet,
into Almon Hensley (a name she first used in print for the *Arena* symposium),
social activist. But just as Carman's frustrations with 'beastly' New York found

literary form through a fortuitous textual encounter, so too Hensley seems to have been provoked into activism by her reading of certain texts within the *fin de siècle* Anglo-American culture of protest. Perhaps most important, one of her letters to the *Week* makes clear that she has read and is in sympathy with Edward Bellamy's Christian-socialist utopian novel *Looking Backward*, an international best-seller from its publication in 1888 to the century's end. 'Did they but understand and appreciate the significance of it,' she writes of New York's economically divided citizenry, 'Bellamy's world would be a paradise of joy and bliss, after which rich and poor alike would long with a yearning unspeakable.' A later letter takes favourable notice of the *Philistine*, the icono-clastic monthly of American socialist Elbert Hubbard: it is 'new and auda-cious,' says Hensley; 'we wish it all success.'[66] Her *Arena* article quotes at length from English reformer Edward Carpenter, sex psychologist Havelock Ellis, and American feminist Charlotte Perkins Gilman. Finally, Hensley's allegiance with the New Thought of the *Arena*'s publisher and editor is evident in the article's emphasis on a psycho-scientific approach to 'the truths of life'; in particular, her argument about the importance of controlling the circum-stances of conception parallels the work of Alliance author Dr Sydney Barrington Elliot on prenatal influences.

By 1904 Hensley had become well known enough in the city to appear in the first edition of *Who's Who in New York* as 'a radical and fearless speaker and thinker.' She and Hubert and their three children maintained a city address at the Hotel Balmoral on Lenox Avenue and a summer home in Barton, Nova Scotia. In 1906 she published her third collection of verse, *The Heart of a Woman*, to indifferent reviews. A few years later she moved to London, where she wrote the most overtly feminist of her works, *Love and the Woman of Tomorrow*, which argues against marriage (a favourite target of the *Philistine*) and for social support of unmarried mothers. Sometime before its publication in 1913 Hensley returned to New York, taking up residence at another hotel, the Somerset on West Forty-seventh. Bibliographic evidence suggests she remained in New York at least through the war years but later moved west, where in 1928 she published her last book, *The Way of a Woman and Other Poems*.

In January 1934 Hensley's last known work, the lyric 'Repatriated,' ap-peared in the *Dalhousie Review*. Forty years before, Hensley had concluded her article on Canadian writers in New York with an expression of collective gratitude for 'the cordial welcome and kind encouragement that are always accorded us in this great busy, pushing, hard-working city'; now, she writes that in her years spent in the 'clamour of great cities,'

always was I alien, nationless,
With voices calling from St. Mary's Bay
From little sleepy towns of Gaspereaux.
I have come home from world-wracked troublous climes
To the calm haven of the Maritimes ...[67]

For both 'Repatriated' and her last book *The Way of a Woman* Hensley returned to her pre-*Arena* signature, signing the first Sophia M. Hensley and the second Sophia Margaretta Hensley. Sophie Hensley always called the Maritimes home; Almon Hensley was a creation and a resident of New York City.

Chapter 4

The New Romantics

In November of 1894, Bliss Carman gave the *Chap-Book* a belated review of expatriate Canadian author Gilbert Parker's *Pierre and His People*. In these stories of the Canadian North-West, says Carman, Parker found 'a background well suited to his purpose, a canvas large enough for the elemental scenes he wished to portray.' 'For "Pierre" is not a drawing-room product – that daring, reckless, gambling, adorable half-breed. He has morals of his own, and is not amenable to our strait code of petty conventions. A sinner he may be, a *man* he certainly is, and a distinct creation in our contemporary letters.' Rarely a good critic of his own work, Carman here discerns a literary phenomenon that would dominate publishers' lists for well into the next century. For Carman, the main features of what he called the new romance movement were its 'strong, self-assured, manly outlook upon life'; the adventurous spirit of its authors, to whom 'a day of sport is better than a night of study'; and most of all, its preference for the thrilling incident over careful study or charming manner: 'Not analysis, but story-telling, pure and simple, is the aim of the school. To be life-like concerns them less than to be moving, enthralling, and vivid.' Having learned from realism to avoid 'palpable falsity and childish exaggeration,' the new romantic still prefers the dramatic to the commonplace, and especially rejects what Carman perceives as the feminine influence of realism upon the literary sensibility: 'We had become so over-nice in our feelings, so restrained and formal, so bound by habit and use in our devotion to the effeminate realists, that one side of our nature was starved. We must have a revolt at any cost.' The revolt wasn't long in coming: four years later, the New York *Bookman* informed its readers that 'a bookseller is reported as saying the other day that "the sex novel is dead, and the women who did things are at a discount." Evidently the novel of adventure is the live novel of the present, and it is the men who did things who are wanted.'[1]

Later critics have since clarified some of the cultural influences on the revolt Carman describes. For Larzer Ziff, its principal target was overcivilization, and its most prominent leaders – Senator Henry Cabot Lodge, historian Brooks Adams, and President Theodore Roosevelt – accordingly advocated a return to a more manly conduct in American life and politics. For Ann Douglas, the feminization that Carman deplores resulted less from the advent of realism than from the triumph of anti-intellectual sentimentalism over the Calvinist values of the founding colonists. For Jackson Lears, who uses Carman's review to help make his case, the late-nineteenth-century fashion for romantic adventure stories was yet another face of the antimodern movement, the product of longings for spontaneity, vitality, and rejuvenation.

By the late 1890s the romantic revolt had produced a clearly defined literary culture. Roosevelt preached and lived *The Strenuous Life*, the title of his 1900 collection of essays and addresses. Owen Wister, Roosevelt's author-champion, romanced his patron's favourite hunting ground in *The Virginian*, becoming the Kipling of the west and the father of the modern western. Jack London and Zane Grey, the darlings of a periodical press suddenly intent on vigorous, brawny tales of outdoor life, inspired hundreds of imitators. Hunters, fishermen, and naturalists returned urban Americans to the outdoors in new magazines like *Recreation* and *Field and Stream*, teaching them everything from how to build a better camp fire to how to identify, track, and kill animals. At once the prey and the ideal of antimodern longings, the animal became the hero of its own romances at the same time that it was being hunted across the pages of others, giving rise to a subgenre of the romantic adventure story – the romance, to paraphrase the *Bookman*, of the animal who did things.

In Carman's judgment, Parker belonged in company with such leaders of the new romantic movement as Rudyard Kipling, Robert Louis Stevenson, and Richard Harding Davis. It's perhaps hard to realize this now, with Parker's books crumbling away in libraries, but Carman didn't exaggerate: Parker's *The Seats of the Mighty*, for instance, entered the *Bookman*'s best-seller lists in August of 1896 at number three uptown and number four downtown, and reached number one in Toronto, Montreal, Albany, Boston, Buffalo, Pittsburgh, and Portland, Oregon. Nor was Parker the only Canadian to succeed in the movement: not surprisingly given the preconceptions of American editors, Canadians abroad and at home fared especially well at placing work with an outdoors setting with American magazines and publishers. E.W. Thomson in Boston published over a hundred outdoor adventure stories in American (and British) juvenile magazines between 1885 and 1912. Frank Pollock wrote at least fifty outdoor stories and sketches and some twenty serialized novels of outdoor adventure between the late 1890s and the 1940s. Ernest Thompson

Seton dominated the new genre of the animal story, with Charles G.D. Roberts not far behind. Ontario hunter-journalist Edwyn Sandys served on the editorial staff of *Outing*, a New York monthly devoted to outdoor life to which he and many other Canadians contributed poems, stories, and sketches. Arthur E. McFarlane wrote dozens of juvenile adventure stories for the *Youth's Companion* and other periodicals before switching to exposés of corruption in the fire insurance business. Less predictably, two Canadian expatriates built successful careers on fast-paced adventure stories with an urban setting: Arthur Stringer turned to crime, and Harvey O'Higgins launched his long career with stories of the New York fire department. The Canadian North-West may have furnished Parker with a ideal background, but ultimately the particular setting didn't matter to Carman's new romantics. What mattered, he said, was having a story to tell.

Wolf Thompson, Wilderness Prophet

So far as I know, Ernest Thompson Seton is the only Canadian writer whose expatriation to New York was divinely ordained. In 1879–81, young Ernest was in London, studying art at the Royal Academy, reading in natural history at the British Museum, and struggling, as he later recalled in *Trail of an Artist-Naturalist*, with a late and particularly nasty case of puberty. Convinced that he had been possessed by 'a demon of sensuality,' Seton fought his demon by reading the lives of the saints, bathing in cold water several times a day, sleeping on a hard board, avoiding store windows with suggestive pictures, and eliminating all meat from his already meagre student diet. Eventually, this stern regime yielded 'the peace that passeth all understanding,' and with it a daily visitation of increasingly insistent Voices. In the summer of 1881, then twenty years old, Seton received his longest message from the Voices. He had assumed that his career lay in London, as an artist –

> But my Voice said: 'No. A year from now you will be living on the Plains of western Canada. You will there regain your health ... Your future will be, not in Canada or London, but in New York, where, as an illustrator and writer, you will make your fortune. Go to Canada, and rejoice in life on the Plains. But do not stay too long. Go soon to New York, and there you will find your way.'

A few months later, the by now seriously ill Seton fortuitously (or providentially) received a letter from his mother ordering him home to Toronto. On 26 October 1881, he sailed for Canada, 'sick, weak and white,' but persuaded of his destiny.[2]

Back in Toronto, Seton resumed his childhood investigations of the wildlife in and around the city. Pressed less by his Voice's decree to go west than by his father's insistence that he contribute something more tangible to their large family than an abandoned education and a mounting pile of bird carcasses, he resolved the following spring to join his brother Arthur at his farm in Carberry, Manitoba. Here, on the prairies and sandhills of Manitoba, Seton matured his talents for field naturalism. He also made important connections via letter with leading American ornithologists Elliott Coues, founding member of the American Ornithologists' Union and the editor of its journal, the *Auk*, and Spencer F. Baird, secretary of the Smithsonian Institution, and published his first natural history articles in Canadian government and scientific journals. In the fall of 1883, threatened with a second winter on the prairies, Seton again heard his Voice urging him on to New York, and a few days after the first snowfall, he left Carberry for the East.

Arriving in New York in late November, Seton rented a room on lower Lexington and went looking for an old art-school friend from Toronto, Charles Broughton. After a weekend spent rationing a bread roll, drinking water from the Madison Square fountain, and fending off the advances of a Central Park 'sex pervert,' he found Broughton at his employer's, a lithographer on Vesey Street. The two decided to live together, taking two rooms at 34 Clinton Place. Seton looked for work and soon had his first New York sale, a sketch for a cigar advertisement he sold for five dollars to lithographers Sacket, Wilhelms and Betzig, who subsequently took him on salary at fifteen and later twenty dollars a week. In January, encouraged by Broughton, he began taking night classes at the Art Students League, where he met artist-naturalist Dan Beard and other New York illustrators. Then, in March, a letter arrived from Arthur reminding him that unless he returned to Carberry to help with the spring planting, he shouldn't expect any help with his own land claim. After a stop in Toronto to address the Natural History Society, Seton returned to Manitoba, bringing to an end 'my first contact with New York, the beginning of all my most important work in the world of story-writing and illustrating.'[3]

In Carberry for the rest of the year helping Arthur and collecting specimens, Seton returned to Toronto early in 1885 to spend the next seven months working on the manuscript of *The Birds of Manitoba*, his first book-length work of natural history. In September, his welcome worn out with the 'home government,' he put the manuscript aside and again left for New York. On his first stay in the city Seton had sold an illustration to W. Lewis Fraser, art manager of the *Century Magazine*, so after renting a garret on East Ninth, he drew a sketch of a mule deer in the Central Park menagerie and took it to Fraser's office. Fraser bought the drawing and several others, and, on the condition that their mutual friend Elliott Coues would edit its biological entries, gave Seton a commission for a thousand illustrations at five dollars each for the new *Century Dictionary*. 'After that,' said Seton, 'I had little to complain of; for in one day I could make more than enough to keep me for a week.'[4]

In June of 1886, two months before returning to Toronto to look after an ailing brother, Seton's 'A Carberry Deer Hunt' appeared in *Forest and Stream*, a New York weekly owned and edited by naturalist George Bird Grinnell. The first of Seton's many publications in the magazine, 'A Carberry Deer Hunt' was also, he later claimed, the first realistic animal story ever published.[5] Inherently continental, the animal story has been claimed as both a Canadian and an American invention: the *Literary History of Canada*, for instance, awards the laurel to Charles G.D. Roberts's 'Do Seek Their Meat from God' of 1892, while for American naturalist John Burroughs the first modern animal story was Charles Dudley Warner's 'A-Hunting of the Deer' of 1888, which 'forever killed all taste for venison in many of his readers.'[6] As Burroughs's comment suggests, it wasn't just the continental range of the animal stories' models that made the genre accessible to authors and readers on both sides of the border; of equal importance, their sympathy for their animal heroes served a growing and necessarily continental concern about the disappearance of animals and their habitat. For Seton, North America consisted of two spaces: the prairie where he did his work, and the city where he sold it. It was as irrelevant to him whether the soil of that prairie was Canadian or American as it was to the animals he studied. As John Henry Wadland puts it in his study of Seton the naturalist, 'Seton's political perspective, such as it was, grew naturally out of his biological insights ... Although most of his original work prior to 1915 was based upon his Canadian experience, he always spoke in continental terms – not because he was a Goldwin Smith liberal, but because [C. Hart] Merriam's Life Zone Theory acknowledged no man-made boundaries.'[7] With due respect, however, for Seton's sincerity as a naturalist, what would later attract him to animal fiction (despite his retroactive claim for the nature sketch 'A Carberry Deer Hunt,' his first real animal story was still eight years away) was less its conservationist than its literary potential, its ability to realize the fortune his Voice had promised.

Apart from several visits, from 1886 to 1896 Seton's story isn't a story of New York. He managed another brother's farm on Lake Ontario for several years, spent a summer in Manitoba doing fieldwork, and went twice to Paris to study art, in 1891 and 1894–6. Working mostly in Toronto, he completed the *Century* drawings and the manuscript of *Birds of Manitoba* and contributed regular natural history sketches and articles to *Auk*, *Forest and Stream*, and *St.*

Nicholas. In September of 1893, motivated partly by his anger at the Canadian art establishment for their refusal to accept his painting of a wolf gnawing on a human skull for that summer's Chicago Exposition, Seton took a job as a wolf killer on a New Mexico cattle ranch. At the urging of his friend Professor James Mavor of the University of Toronto, Seton wrote up his fight with one especially tenacious wolf and sent the story off to *Scribner's Magazine*, giving him his first and best-known animal story: 'The King of Currumpaw,' published with Seton's illustrations in *Scribner's* of November 1894.[8]

In April of 1896, Seton returned from Paris to New York in company with Grace Gallatin, daughter of a wealthy Chicago divorcée. Grace had helped Seton in Paris with his *Studies in the Art Anatomy of Animals*, and two months after their return the couple married and with help from Grace's mother bought Sloat Hall, a thirty-room country home on 235 acres near Tappan, New Jersey. From this point on, New York City, a half-hour train ride away, was the centre of Seton's social and working world. With Grace and her mother providing the social introductions and *Art Anatomy of Animals* opening doors into New York's artistic circles, Seton found himself keeping company with the likes of Hamlin Garland, Mark Twain, Theodore Roosevelt, Frederic Remington, John Burroughs, William Dean Howells, and others of the city's cultural elite. In November, Sloat Hall proving impossible to heat, the Setons moved into the city to a small studio apartment on lower Fifth Avenue. The following March, a showing of Seton's artwork at a nearby gallery arranged by Grace and her mother caught the attention of George O. Shields, owner-editor of *Recreation*. In return for stories and illustrations for his magazine, Shields offered to help fund an expedition to Yellowstone Park, and in June Ernest and Grace left the city for the first of many wildlife trips together.

The next year saw the publication of the book that made 'Wolf' Thompson (a nickname acquired from his paintings) a household name. In Seton's version of the story, in the spring of 1898 he gathered up eight of his animal stories and took them to the offices of Charles Scribner's Sons. The firm's readers approved the collection, and on 1 July Seton signed a contract that forgave all royalties on the first two thousand copies but paid 20 per cent, double the usual, on any copies sold thereafter – a deal forged at Seton's insistence, who planned to promote the book on his own through lectures and exhibits.[9] It was the right decision: the first two thousand copies of *Wild Animals I Have Known* sold in three weeks, and by Christmas the book was in its fourth printing, partly because of Seton's talents at the lectern, but also because of the enthusiasm of his reviewers. The London *Athenæum* said Seton's book 'should be put with Kipling and Hans Christian Andersen as a classic,' while in Detroit the *Free Press* thought it 'ought to make any boy happy' and in Iowa the *Muscatine Tribune* called the story of Lobo 'the best wolf story ever told.' At home in New York, the *Nation* judged Seton a master at both pen and pencil, while the *Times* described his work as 'a better attempt than Kipling's to restore the kinship of man and the animals.' An especially important review in the influential *Bookman* by assistant editor James MacArthur ran to four pages, included two of Seton's illustrations, and concluded that 'no more entertaining stories of wild animals have ever been written.'[10] Wolf Thompson had arrived.

By 1904, *Wild Animals I Have Known* had sold a hundred thousand copies. According to Seton, it was more than a best-seller: 'There can be no doubt,' he later wrote, 'that this book founded the modern school of animal stories, that is, giving in fiction form the actual facts of an animal's life and modes of thought.' Seton's often repeated claim that his animals were true to life has since become entrenched in the generic label 'realistic animal story.' But however carefully qualified, this label obscures the central point that although Seton's stories are not beast fables, they are also not examples of literary realism or 'scientific' (Seton's word) in the implied sense of rejecting literary models of representation. In fact, virtually all of Seton's animal stories employ a blatantly romantic literary model: the model of the hero, popularized in the mid-nineteenth century by Thomas Carlyle's homage to the 'great man.' Key lines in Seton's introduction to *Wild Animals I Have Known* could have been lifted verbatim from Carlyle's *On Heroes, Hero-Worship, and the Heroic in History*: 'What satisfaction,' asks Seton, 'would be derived from a ten-page sketch of the habits and customs of Man? How much more profitable it would be to devote that space to the life of some one great man. This is the principal I have endeavored to apply to my animals.'[11] And apply it he does, chronicling in the stories that follow the exploits of the noblest wolf, the smartest crow, the fastest horse, and so on.

Readers of the day noticed, even if latter-day critics have not, that these were the superlatives of romance, not the metonymies of realism: the London *Zoölogist* called Seton 'the Carlyle of the animal world,' and for every reviewer who noted the realism of *Wild Animals* there were a hundred readers like 'D.J.', an eleven-year-old girl who wrote Seton to say, 'I think it is the saddest book I have ever read. It is just the kind of book I cannot talk about ... Please excuse the spots on your book – tears made them.' Seton did strive to depict his animals accurately (with some liberties), but a realistic method wasn't incompatible with the new romanticism: the novel of the future, said Carman, 'must bear the impress of truth and conscientiousness given it under the tutorship of realism' even as it rejected its exaltation of the commonplace. In sum, despite Seton's claim to have founded a modern school of animal stories, his stories and others in the genre participated in the same late-century revolt *against* the modern that fuelled Carman's *Vagabondia* series and Betts's *Perfume-Holder*. Seton always saw himself, says Wadland, as the 'radical antithesis' of his technological age.[12] Whether writing about animals or, later, preaching the 'gospel of the Redman,' the synthesis he repeatedly sought was not the modern union of man and science, but the antimodern reconciliation of man and nature.

In May of 1900 Seton's animal answer to urban exhaustion paid for six old farms totalling a hundred acres off the Cos Cob highway near Greenwich, Connecticut. Over the next few years Seton transformed the land into an artificial wilderness he called Wyndygoul, complete with a large house of rough stone and heavy timbers, an eleven-acre lake dug from a swamp, a veritable menagerie of ducks, geese, peacocks, muskrats, squirrels, and rabbits, and a ten-foot barbed fence to keep the wilderness in and the world out. The Setons also maintained a large apartment on West Fortieth overlooking Bryant Park, where they hosted weekly gatherings for the city's literati and, as at Wyndygoul, received the inquisitive press. Fashionable *Harper's Bazar* sent a writer and photographer to report on their apartment's decor ('a model of tasteful arrangement'); the *Ladies' Home Journal* countered by sending its reporter out 'With Ernest Seton-Thompson in the Woods.' *Everybody's Magazine* dispatched author Hutchins Hapgood, while the *Critic* sent poet William Wallace Whitelock, one of several to whom Seton told the story of his first visit to 'the city that is now madly anxious to pour money into his lap.' That same year, a *Times* interviewer felt it superfluous to describe Seton's appearance, since 'it is probable that Kipling alone as often enjoys the pleasure of gazing upon his own counterfeit presentment in magazines and newspapers.' At least two Canadians were enlisted in the cause, Charles G.D. Roberts describing Wyndygoul for *Country Life in America* and Arthur Stringer telling readers of the *Montreal Herald* that 'if you know Mr. Thompson – I do prefer the old way – you must be a somebody in New York just at present, for he is the vogue. His stories and drawings are the fashion, and editors are falling over one another trying to get hold of his copy.'[13]

Other books followed *Wild Animals I Have Known*, all designed by Grace and supported with lectures by Ernest: *The Trail of the Sandhill Stag*, called by the *Bookman* the best story in the best magazine of the month when it first appeared in a *Scribner's* fiction number; *The Biography of a Grizzly*, reviewed by the *Times* as 'so captivating and so interesting, that we read of Wahb with bated breath and an interest that could not be intensified were he a human being';[14] *Lives of the Hunted*, which made a pop icon of a Yellowstone garbage bear after Bryn Mawr's graduating class adopted the ailing cub; and *Two Little*

Savages, after *Wild Animals* Seton's most enduring work, appearing in at least twenty editions to date, eight since his death. Seton was also increasingly occupied with his Woodcraft League of America, an outdoors organization for boys he started at Wyndygoul to win over some local youths who had vandalized his new property. As Black Wolf, medicine man and head chief of the Woodcraft Indians, Seton held annual retreats for the League at Wyndygoul and promoted its message though lectures, a column on woodcraft in the widely read *Ladies' Home Journal*, and his own adventures at 'playing Injun' in *Two Little Savages*, also serialized in the *Journal*.

By 1903 cracks had begun to appear in the animal-fiction trough. The previous February, the *Independent* had printed a parody of the genre called 'Trouble in the Jungle' by Canadian expatriate Sydney Reid, to my knowledge a stranger to Seton. In Reid's sketch, characters from animal stories assemble to discuss a common problem: as Kipling's Mowgli puts it for his delegation, 'The man-pack are ceasing to read the books about us ... Two rains ago we jungle-folk were most popular of any in the world, now we don't sell a hundred copies a month.' Each character blames the others for the decline – a rhinoceros objecting, for example, that 'I'm sure there was no occasion for an Autobiography of a Grizzly' – and after Kipling's Baloo attacks Seton's Wahb's Nephew the assembly degenerates into a pitched battle.

Much better known than Reid's piece is American naturalist John Burroughs's attack on the genre in the *Atlantic Monthly* of March 1903. Burroughs claimed in this and later articles that the animal stories of Seton, Roberts, and others were fundamentally inaccurate, but, sidestepping the scientific debate behind his prolonged attack (in essence, whether animal behaviour was instinctive or rational), it's enough to note that his complaints were as symptomatic of consumer exhaustion with the genre as Reid's light-hearted parody. As Reid's animals tell us, readers grew tired of animal stories, and they used Burroughs's considerable authority to justify their boredom. At least on the Canadian side, Seton and Roberts have typically received joint credit for founding the modern animal story; what's less often acknowledged is that the stories with which they then flooded the market were also responsible for killing the genre. Like a thousand fashions before and since, the animal story was a victim of its own success: by 1903, just five years after *Wild Animals I Have Known* sent New York editors scrambling for more of the same, writers could of course still write animal fiction, and publishers could publish it, 'but,' as one of Reid's animals asks, 'who's to buy it? That's the main question nowadays.'[15]

Although Seton claims in his autobiography to have publicly defeated Burroughs's argument, his career after this and other attacks on the 'nature fakers' became increasingly removed from both the genre and the scene of the controversy.[16] For financial reasons he continued to publish animal stories based on older notes and drafts, but after 1903 he returned from fiction to his naturalist roots, beginning work the following year on his *Life-Histories of Northern Animals*, for which he made fieldtrips to Manitoba, Ontario, Idaho, Norway, and the Canadian north, and in 1910 joining with others to launch the Boy Scouts of America. As Seton intended, *Life-Histories* vindicated his credentials as a naturalist, earning respectful reviews and the Camp Fire Club's Gold Medal after its publication in 1909. Less successful, Seton's role in the Boy Scouts of America (for which he wrote the first handbook) effectively came to an end three months after its founding when the executive decided that his Indian model was incompatible with British founder Sir Robert Baden-Powell's militaristic ideals: smeared privately and publicly as a pacifist, an anarchist, and a socialist, Seton was given the figurehead title of Chief Scout to retain the prestige of his name but cut off from real power.

By 1915, the year Seton bitterly resigned from the Boy Scouts altogether, most of New York's elite had abandoned him to his Indians. Three years before, he had sold Wyndygoul and bought an estate closer to Greenwich where he continued to hold annual retreats for his Woodcraft League, now reconstituted to admit girls. About this time Seton claimed to have first met Julie Buttree, a young teacher he hired to help with the League and with his current project, the massive *Lives of Game Animals*. Over the years of their marriage, Seton later wrote, he and Grace had developed 'divergent interests,' and it was with Julie, not Grace, that he embarked on the final stage in his life-long celebration of nature's way.[17] Eight years in the making, *Lives of Game Animals* (1925–8) was even better received than its predecessor, winning medals from the National Academy of Sciences and, ironically, the John Burroughs Memorial Association, but despite his pleasure at its success it was to something much less scientific that the ageing Seton was now being drawn.

Back in 1905, while lecturing in Los Angeles, Seton had answered an invitation to visit a woman at her cottage in the Beverly Hills. When he rose to leave, the woman, a Mahatma East Indian born in Iowa, stopped him: 'Her eyes blazed as she said, in tones of authority: "Don't you know who you are? ... You are a Red Indian Chief, reincarnated to give the message of the Redman to the White race, so much in need of it. Why don't you get busy? Why don't you set about your job?"' From his earliest years Seton had thought of himself as an anointed prophet of outdoor life; now, his destiny had again received supernatural sanction. With his reputation as a naturalist secured, it was finally time to deliver the Redman's message. In 1930 Seton and Julie moved to a two-thousand-acre tract near Santa Fé, New Mexico, where they opened the College of Indian Wisdom, described at Seton's death as a 'cult devoted to nature, Indian lore and Indian dancing.' As defiantly antimodern as Patterson's School of Applied Metaphysics or Carman and King's School of Personal Harmonizing, Seton's college shared with these and other products of the therapeutic movement a desire to counter the civilizing forces of modernity by reuniting its students with a more authentic form of experience, in this case through the vehicle of the American Indian, happily reincarnated as the college's president. In 1936, Seton finally delivered the Redman's message as ordered in *The Gospel of the Redman*, at nine printings to date the most successful of his books written after his move from New York. He died ten years later at his New Mexico home at age eighty-six. Wolf Thompson had gone, *Time* magazine couldn't resist titling its obituary, to his 'Happy Hunting Ground.'[18]

Now for the Killing: Edwyn Sandys

Even more so than Seton, Edwyn William Sandys fit Carman's description of the new romantic as one to whom 'a day of sport is better than a night of study.' The second son of Francis W. Sandys, Archdeacon of Huron, Sandys was born in 1860 in Chatham, Ontario, and educated mostly by his father. If we're to believe a later hunting sketch, Sandys worked in a bank before one eventful day on which he 'fired the confounded books into their places in the vault, and vowed most solemnly that a bank or banking business should know me no more.' Telling his horrified family he was 'going shooting,' he left on a summer-long journey by rail through the American west. Sandys intended to repeat the trip the following year but 'unforseen circumstances interfered.'[19]

Although the dates are uncertain, these circumstances were likely new responsibilities as an associate editor of the *Canadian Sportsman*, a Toronto weekly that called itself the only sporting paper published in Canada. Sandys joined the *Sportsman* sometime before the completion of the Canadian Pacific Railway in 1885, upon which the railway hired him to promote fishing and hunting opportunities along its western route. As Sophie Hensley, who later met Sandys in New York, described this development, 'when the Directors of the Canadian Pacific Railway invited him to make the tour and do their literary work for them Mr. Sandys and his employers were mutually satisfied with the arrangement. Mr. Sandys scaled the Rockies, hunted the deer, and captured the salmon to his heart's content and furnished the C.P.R. with their beautiful books of western scenery and guides to the sport and travel "westward to the far east."' More often ephemeral pamphlets than 'beautiful books,' the only surviving CPR publication to which Sandys is known to have contributed is a variously titled free guide to *Fishing and Shooting by the Canadian Pacific Railway*. Sandys wrote the third edition of this guide, and probably parts of its earlier editions as well, at least the first of which is credited to 'Commissioners of *The Canadian Sportsman*.'[20] In the late 1880s he also began contributing short hunting and fishing sketches under the pseudonym 'Nomad' to the fledgling *Saturday Night*, then or soon to become the employer of his sister, Grace Denison.

According to Hensley, Sandys' reputation as a sportsman won him an invitation from the owners of the New York sporting monthly *Outing* to join their editorial staff, and in the early spring of 1891 Sandys moved to New York, arriving within a year of *Saturday Night* regulars Peter McArthur, Duncan McKellar, and Graeme Mercer Adam. Founded in 1882, *Outing* was owned and edited for most of Sandys' tenure by James Henry Worman, a journalist and educator connected with the Chautauqua movement. The magazine ran a short story or two each issue based on travel or sport, and occasionally some serial fiction, but its more numerous and important serials were non-fiction, many of them bicycle travel articles with titles like 'World Tour Awheel' (which ran for five years before its author went missing in Kurdistan), 'Through Erin Awheel,' and 'Five Weeks Awheel in France.' It was also known for its monthly review of amateur sports, which by 1893 included seven departments: college athletics, amateur photography, cycling, aquatics, Rod and Gun, Kennel and Loft (for dog and pigeon fanciers), and Equestrian Sports. Its offices were at 239 Fifth Avenue, where Sandys hung the walls of his own 'little sanctum' with sketches of hunting and fishing scenes.[21]

Over his life Sandys contributed well over a hundred articles, stories, and even the odd poem to *Outing*. One of his earliest pieces, an illustrated article on woodcock shooting published in the October 1890 issue, gives a general idea of his work in the hunting and fishing genre. The article has three basic elements: detailed but non-technical observations on the habits and habitat of the quarry; advice on guns, ammunition, dogs, and other equipment; and finally a narrative of the hunt itself. The tone is casual, personal, with frequent use of what is by today's standards a rather grim humour. After describing in respectful detail, for instance, the touching display of a mother woodcock protecting its young, Sandys ends by yanking the rug out from under the sympathy he's created over the last two paragraphs: 'But enough of random notes about this bird for the present; now for the killing.'[22]

As this passage suggests, Sandys operated on the other side of the outdoor culture that gave rise to Seton's animal stories: Seton was always more of a naturalist than a hunter and eventually gave up the gun entirely for the camera, while Sandys favours the drama of the hunt and a wry humour over science or even observation. As he characteristically remarked in a later article, 'I do not purpose introducing scientific terms into this sketch, being satisfied that dead game is more important than dead languages.' Sandys also harboured other differences with the nature fakers: a late animal story, one of the few he seems to have written, includes an interjected paragraph on the impossibility of authors knowing the minds of animals that is clearly meant as a light rebuke to Seton and company. 'It is all very fine,' he writes in part, 'for a few peculiarly gifted, or otherwise, folk to minutely describe the joys, sorrows, hopes, fears and aspirations of young wild things, but the important fact remains that, at least, one-half of such statements is either sheer tommy-rot or mere guess-work.'[23]

Of more importance than these family quarrels, Sandys' career in the animal-killing industry served the same antimodern revolt that generated Seton's and Roberts's animal-worship, like them modelling a more vital, more authentic, more heroic experience in answer to modern culture's attenuation of existence. Like them, too, and like Betts's and Carman's brands of antimodernism, Sandys' work helped reconcile his audience with the very world it ostensibly rejected. Just as animal stories provided a woodsy vacation for world-weary urbanites, so too Sandys' hunting articles offered a temporary respite (both imaginative and actual) for the urban businessman, 'compelled,' as he wrote in one, 'like a chained dog, to nose around within the length of his business tether.' To alleviate (but not alter) this bondage, Sandys and others like him prescribed a day of hunting or fishing – 'no bad medicine,' as he put it, 'for a hard-worked man.'[24]

Whether because of Sandys' intervention or because their origins authenticated their outdoor experiences, Canadians found favour in *Outing*. Sandys' sister Grace contributed several cycling articles, including the above-mentioned serial 'Through Erin Awheel.' Other Canadians in *Outing* over the 1890s included E. Pauline Johnson and E.W. Thomson, as well as the now forgotten names Matthew Richey Knight, Charles Gordon Rogers, Eugene McCarthy, and S.R. Clarke. In one especially Canadian-heavy issue, that of October 1893, Toronto's *Week* proudly noted the appearance of no fewer than four Canadian contributors. Canadians continued to appear regularly in *Outing* under its next editor, explorer Caspar Whitney, in charge from 1900 to 1909. Norman Duncan contributed several sea stories; Agnes C. Laut, who became an *Outing* staffer, wrote about Indians; Arthur E. McFarlane provided a half-dozen outdoor adventure stories, and Frank Pollock and Bliss Carman a poem apiece. Charles G.D. Roberts, a friend of Whitney's, contributed a dozen or so animal stories, including the serialized novel *Red Fox* in 1905 (by which time his son Lloyd was the monthly's assistant editor).[25] Seton published two poems in *Outing*, both in 1900, but none of his animal stories ever appeared in the magazine – perhaps because its new editor publicly sided with Burroughs in the nature faker controversy, but perhaps also because he didn't want to share space with Roberts.

By 1905 Whitney had brought *Outing* to its largest circulation ever, giving Sandys' sketches a monthly audience of something over a hundred thousand. Already a member of the American Authors' Guild, in 1902 Sandys lived up to his membership by publishing his first book, a guide to *Upland Game Birds* co-authored with *Outing* contributor Theodore Strong Van Dyke and illustrated by some of the best names in the business, including bird artist Louis Agassiz Fuertes, a friend of Seton's; Arthur Burdett Frost, illustrator of the *Uncle Remus* stories; and Charles Livingston Bull, an illustrator for both *Outing* and the *Saturday Evening Post* and by this time Roberts's regular illustrator. As evidence that the budding conservationist movement was having its effect, the only known review of *Upland Game Birds* praised its predecessor in the series for its condemnation of the 'game butcher' but took Sandys to task for his 'sadly warped' ethics: 'It is interesting reading, but it leaves one with a better opinion of Bob White [a bird] than of some of his persecutors.'[26] Undeterred, Sandys published three more books in the next three years, all, like his first, with New York's Macmillan Company: *Trapper 'Jim'*, an outdoor boys' adventure novel; *Sportsman 'Joe'*, a *Two Little Savages* on wheels in which the sickly son of a New York stockbroker is sent to the Canadian Rockies to spend the summer hunting by car with a friend of his father; and *Sporting Sketches*, mostly reprinted work from *Outing*.

Sandys died at just forty-six of heart disease in New York City on 23 October 1906. That same year, his magazine ran its most successful serial and one of the most popular celebrations of the new romantic ethos, Jack London's *White Fang*, whose half wild canine hero escapes civilization to find his rightful place in the wilderness. Himself always susceptible to the call of the wild, Sandys by the end of his life seems to have been won over with many Americans to the side of the outdoors movement that advocated observing over hunting. His last article, published in *Outing* four months after his death, is not a hunting but a nature sketch in which the narrator wanders through a winter forest noting the passage of its birds and animals. 'I have shot much on upland and marsh, in wood and copse, on mount and plain,' says Sandys, 'yet I am not sure that even the cream of the actual shooting has more enduring charm than the silent, lonely, bloodless raids through the almost spectral white-gray silences of snowy forests.'[27] Perhaps as much the result of disappearing game as a changing heart, Sandys' new-found sensitivity is further suggested by the titles of some of his last articles for *Outing*, including 'Scarcity of Game Birds' in 1904 and 'How to Offset Winter Depletion of Game' in 1905 – a far cry from older titles like 'A River of Geese' in 1892, or even 1901's 'Skirmish with the Squirrels.'

'Three Musketeers of the Pen'

Late in the summer of 1900, three young friends from Ontario moved into the attic of a rundown old brownstone at 140 Fifth Avenue, a former private residence whose lower floors housed, among other tenants, the American branch of English publisher John Lane (managed by Carman's friend Mitchell Kennerley) and the working studio of Ernest Thompson Seton. University of Toronto students all, the three had come to New York determined to make a living from their writing, a goal the oldest among them, twenty-six-year-old Arthur Stringer, later said 'made migration to New York or Boston or London almost obligatory.'[28]

Stringer, like Sandys a native of Chatham, had the most writing experience of the three, with poetry and prose in some half-dozen Canadian and English magazines, three privately printed collections of poems, and a job on the *Montreal Herald* before being hired away to New York in the summer of 1898 by the American Press Association, a rewrite firm that put him to work transplanting a Maupassant peasant to a New England farm on one day and posing as a 'special correspondent in four different parts of the world' on the next.[29] London-born Harvey O'Higgins, at twenty-three the trio's youngest member, had contributed to *Saturday Night* and the *Canadian Magazine* and worked for the *Toronto Star* before he too went to New York to see if he could 'catch on.' Arthur E. McFarlane of Islington turned to writing after graduation, shopping stories and specials around to Toronto editors. 'Most of the editors,' *Saturday Night* later reported, 'printed his copy but sent him no cheques in return, so McFarlane cursed Canadian newspapers and magazines and editors, all and sundry, with a mighty curse, and left the country.' By the time O'Higgins and McFarlane arrived in New York Stringer had already published his first stateside book, a collection of stories about New York slum children called *The Loom of Destiny* brought out by Carman's publisher H.S. Small. When the three decided a year later to live together, he quit the American Press Association and with them set out to make his way freelance.[30]

At first, said Stringer's friend and biographer Victor Lauriston, 'poverty dwelt with the three adventurers in the attic.' They bought cots left over from the Spanish-American War, had frequent dietary recourse to oatmeal porridge and something called tomato slush, and when winter arrived avoided coal bills by reopening a bricked-up fireplace and using the staves from an old rooftop wooden water tank as fuel. When money ran especially short, they would pawn McFarlane's cherished dress suit until 'Stringer could write a Saturday special on the goats of Harlem or O'Higgins produce something cashable on the beer-halls of the Bowery.' Specials provided the mainstay of their income, but as time offered the three also sent fiction and verse off to the more discriminating weeklies and monthlies – most of which, says Lauriston, brought only rejection letters, so many that they began to paper the walls with their growing collection of 'regrets' and 'come-backs,' a decorating tactic that gave the attic its bittersweet name of 'The Chamber of a Thousand Sorrows.' Their rooms became a gathering place for other Canadians in the city, largely, said Stringer, because of his ability to procure the ingredients for milk-punch on credit from a Greenwich Village bartender a cousin of his had luckily married. Carman visited regularly, the punch sometimes inspiring a 'garret recital' of his latest work, as did Charles G.D. Roberts, Peter McArthur, and James Shotwell, the last a student and lecturer at Columbia University.[31]

Somewhere between the tomato slush and milk-punches, between the regrets and come-backs, all three members of what Lauriston called the 'Three Musketeers of the Pen' emerged from their attic to recognition and even fame. More than journalistic puffery, Lauriston's phrase was entirely apt, for the initial vehicle of the trio's success was in each case fast-paced, male-centred adventure stories that championed the new romantics' fondness for the thrilling incident at the same time that they expressed more than a little antimodern nostalgia for the days of Athos, Porthos, and Aramis.

Stringer's *Loom of Destiny* had met with kind reviews, at least two of which noticed its obvious debt to Kipling's child characters, and he'd been equally successful with the verse he would continue to write throughout his career, regularly placing his trademark epigrams with the *Bookman* and *Harper's Weekly* and in early 1899 selling three short lyrics to *Harper's Magazine* for the atypically high sum of sixty dollars.[32] In 1900–5, he expanded his periodical repertoire to include short fiction, poetry, and the occasional article in the *Canadian Magazine, Munsey's, Collier's Weekly*, the *Century*, the *Atlantic Monthly*, the *Youth's Companion*, the *Valley Magazine, Everybody's, McClure's, Macmillan's*, and the *National Monthly of Canada*, as well as Mary Fanton Roberts's *Craftsman* and Mitchell Kennerley's *Reader*. During this period he also did a stint as literary editor of *Success Magazine*, a New York monthly aimed at the growing business class.

In the summer of 1903 Stringer published his first novel with the Fifth Avenue house of D. Appleton and Company, publishers of Jarvis's *Geoffrey Hampstead*, Roberts's *Canadian Guide Book*, and Parker's *The Seats of the Mighty*, as well as better-remembered books like Stephen Crane's *The Red Badge of Courage* and Joseph Conrad's *An Outcast of the Islands*. The sometimes autobiographical story of a struggling English writer in New York, *The Silver Poppy* enjoyed a brief vogue in the city as something of a *roman à clef*, its novel-plagiarizing heroine believed to be a prominent writer of the period.[33] Two years later, Boston's Houghton, Mifflin brought out Stringer's less successful second novel, *Lonely O'Malley*, a Tom Sawyerish story set in Ontario about a young boy with a vivid imagination and a talent for trouble.

Boiler-plate journalist, freelance poet and fictionist, magazine editor, author of three books within, successively, the genres of tenement literature, the novel of Bohemian manners, and the juvenile *Bildungsroman* – as the variety of Stringer's literary activities in New York indicates, by 1905, his seventh year in the city, he had not yet found his literary culture. Like Carman the decade before, he finally found that culture quite by chance.

According to Lauriston, Stringer got the idea for his next novel from his dentist, who complained to him between drillings how he had been conned out of half a year's earnings by a gang of 'wire tappers.' Published in May of 1906 by Little, Brown, *The Wire Tappers* is the story of a pair of reluctant criminals, the English Frances Candler and the vaguely Canadian Jim Durkin, who run various confidences on New York gamblers and bookies before reforming and quitting the city to live honest lives in quiet old England. Fast-paced and a little salacious, it probably would have sold well even without the help of several morally offended reviews. A pre-digital *Neuromancer*, the novel depicts a shadowy world of 'lightning-slingers' and 'overhead guerillas' who tap into New York's nascent network of electrical, telegraph, and telephone wires. Like William Gibson's cyber-cowboys, Stringer's characters speak the language of their technology. They understand, even if their reader doesn't, what a 'Tesla current' is, and can tell the difference between a rheostat and a graduated pointer. When in trouble, they can communicate with each other by tapping out Morse code on a beer glass, a table, even their own teeth. Armed with a telegrapher's key, a fishing pole, and a length of wire, they can distinguish one rooftop or subterranean wire from dozens of others, tap into it, and listen in on the telephones of the rich or steal enough electricity to power their equipment or melt through a safe door. Stringer, being Stringer, overdoes it, as for instance in this passage, in which Frances is having one of her recurring fits of guilt: 'we were both initiated into wrong-doing so quietly and so insidiously that the current caught us before we knew it. Yet I feel that I have none of the traits of the Female Offender, though in my anxiety and crazy search for causes and excuses I have even taken my cephalic index and tested my chromatic perception and my tactile sensitiveness and made sure that I responded normally to a Faraday current!' Like Seton's animal romances (equally prone to documentary excess), *The Wire Tappers* used the formula of a dramatic plot buttressed with realistic detail that Carman urged upon the new romantics. It worked: just as Seton's animal stories gave thousands of young Americans their notions of animal behaviour, so too Stringer's depiction of the electrical underworld was accepted by many as gospel, even by the New York City police department, which for years ordered its new detectives to read Stringer's books 'for their authentic portrayal of criminals and criminal life.'[34]

Although the technological realism of *The Wire Tappers* attracted critical interest, most reviewers accepted and enjoyed the novel for what it was: a romance. Some of the more highbrow among them condemned its immorality, but they all loved its plot. The *New York Times* called it 'a frankly sensational story, literally packed with incidents'; the *Arena* thought it 'one of the most original, interesting and suggestive romances of the year'; the *Literary Digest* said that 'the book is at once action and life, virile and alluring'; and others weighed in with similar praise for what the *Bookman* called 'Arthur Stringer's unique and strongly handled story.'[35] As the *Digest's* string of adjectives suggests, the novel struck a chord with antimodern concerns about the loss of authentic experience: its moral and physical riskiness was precisely the antidote moderns sought for their overcivilized lives. Stringer had found his culture, a culture, like Carman's Vagabondism, that masked modern accommodation with antimodern dissent. The next year Little, Brown brought out the sequel to *The Wire Tappers*, and by the early 1920s Stringer had added another eight novels and dozens of magazine stories to his catalogue of crime.

For his first year in the city Harvey O'Higgins seems to have managed just unsigned specials for dailies like the *Evening Post*, the *Sun*, and the *Commercial Advertiser*. Sometime in 1901, he found regular work as a telegraph editor for the *Advertiser*, then run by a maverick team of writers and editors from the *Evening Post*, including Norman Hapgood as drama editor and Lincoln Steffens as city editor. As staff writer Carl Hovey later recalled O'Higgins's appointment, 'We didn't think he was any good' (possibly because he lacked the Ivy League degree the reinvented *Advertiser* looked for in its reporters), 'so we allowed him to work on the telegraph desk, but he practiced writing on our Saturday supplement.' Probably more important to O'Higgins than the practice were the ties to Hapgood and Steffens, both soon to be associated with magazines that would regularly publish his work: Hapgood was editor of *Collier's Weekly* when O'Higgins later won one of the magazine's thousand-dollar quarterly fiction prizes, and Steffens moved to *McClure's* in 1902, the year O'Higgins debuted in the monthly with one of the New York City fire department stories that were his first taste of literary success.[36]

O'Higgins's first fire-fighting story appeared in *Scribner's* in May of 1902, dramatically illustrated by George Wright. That November, *McClure's* fell to

O'Higgins's superheated version of the new romanticism, and the *Century*, *Everybody's*, and *Collier's* soon followed. (The *McClure's* debut, in which O'Higgins's story ran alongside the first instalment of Ida M. Tarbell's indictment of Standard Oil as well as fiction by Conan Doyle, Hamlin Garland, and Robert Barr, was especially auspicious.) In 1905, the Century Company collected under the title *The Smoke-Eaters* ten of O'Higgins's stories of a Lower East Side Hook and Ladder Company, reworked from their magazine appearances to create a developing narrative about one set of characters. Fast, well-told adventures populated by rough, swearing men (more scared than heroic), most of the stories thrive on psychological as much as physical conflict, especially between the new civil service breed of firefighter and their older 'unlettered' colleagues. O'Higgins rarely intrudes, preferring to let action and dialogue speak for itself. The opening paragraph of 'Private Morphy's Romance,' in which a rookie fireman struggles to save a jealous girlfriend from a fire, is typical of his pacing and style:

> The hook-and-ladder truck of Company No. 0, with plunging horses and a furious bell, came struggling through the frozen slush of the dark side street, shot out into the cleaner avenue, and slewed and slid wildly on the icy asphalt as it turned the circle of the corner light. 'Skatin's good,' Sergeant Pim observed.

All the hallmarks of O'Higgins's fire department stories are in this short paragraph: his tendency to begin in the middle of the action; his love of speed; the authentic details; and the brief touch of tough, laconic humour. As New York columnist Heywood Broun later said in praise of O'Higgins's style, 'Up to and including the boiling point, Harvey O'Higgins remains the great precisian.'[37]

Like Stringer's crime novels, O'Higgins's stories combined romantic adventure with realistic detail. According to the *Book Review Digest* for 1905, O'Higgins acquired his knowledge of fire-fighting through his experience on a New York newspaper, possibly the *World*, which one source has him working for sometime before 1905. O'Higgins himself said in his dedication to *The Smoke-Eaters* that he was indebted for 'whatever there is in it of truth to life, of accuracy in detail, of honesty in point of view' to 'Lieutenant E. D. F. of the New York Fire Department,' a move that while no doubt genuine also helped to authenticate the stories that follow. However educated, his stories demonstrate their authority on every page through a detailed fire-fighting lexicon, much of it new enough to require quotation marks: scaling ladders, 'back draft,' 'fire-proofed' buildings, helmets and rubber 'turnout' coats, and so on. As openly racist as any popular fiction of the period (O'Higgins's Italian firemen are sure to panic, his arsonists invariably Jewish), the stories are more canny than most about the power politics behind the ethnic divisions of their underworld setting. As the gruff Sergeant Pim tells a new recruit in one story, 'There's more things to be learned on th' East Side ... than comes out'n a civil service exam.'[38]

Reviewers responded even more positively to O'Higgins's technical realism than they had to his roommate's more exaggerated environment. An especially lengthy review in the *New York Times* called *The Smoke-Eaters* 'one of those rare good treats that fall to the reviewer's lot just about often enough to prevent him from becoming a full-fledged pessimist': 'These stories ... all bear witness that their author knows whereof he speaks. It is not too much to say that he has written the epic of the New York firemen, and not only are they the best sort of stories about firemen, but some of them would stand as models of all that any short story should be – so compact, so restrained, and yet possessed of a vigor and force that keep expectation keyed to the highest tension.' For its part, the *Critic* thought the stories were 'told with extraordinary simplicity' but carried 'complete conviction,' while the *Dial* enthused that 'At last the American fireman has had something like justice done him in our literature.' Will Roberts's *Literary Digest*, in a review that suggests as well as anything the compatibility of the modern thirst for information with the antimodern quest for authentic experience, praised the book's 'mass of information,' but also its 'healthful excitement' and 'many lessons in manliness.'[39] So encouraged, O'Higgins went on to write a second series of fire-fighting stories, collected in 1909 as *Old Clinkers*, and around mid-1905 made a natural transition from the largely Irish cast of his fire department stories to the local colour stories of New York's East Side Irish for which he was best known.

Like O'Higgins, Arthur E. McFarlane began his stateside career with unsigned specials and stories for the *Evening Post* and the *Commercial Advertiser*. Also like O'Higgins, he found his literary culture relatively quickly, within two years of his arrival in the city: in fact, his first known American publication is in both the genre and the magazine that would be his main support for the next decade. Serialized in Boston's *Youth's Companion* between January and March of 1902, 'Tales of a Deep-Sea Diver' recounts the undersea adventures of an old American diver, one of the first of his profession, while unobtrusively passing on a great deal of information about diving and the sea. Intentionally or not, McFarlane had written the ideal *Companion* story, a blend of adventure and instruction, and the serial's first instalment ran as the lead story in a magazine that regularly published established authors like Edith Wharton, Hamlin Garland, Gilbert Parker, Jack London, and Willa Cather, and that by this time had a circulation of around a half-million readers.

Over the next nine years MacFarlane published three more serialized novels and nine short stories in the well-paying *Companion*. Most were boys' adventure stories, but he also created female heroines, including 'Cissy Make-Believe,' an imaginative bookworm from Ohio who has only a 'burning contempt' for girls' books, preferring instead the adventure stories in her brothers' library. After Cissy survives being swarmed by bees by pretending she's a spy saving Cuba, her uncle rewards her courage by paying her way through college, where she learns both to be thankful for being a woman and to use her imagination for other things: 'instead of imagining herself a crusader or a viking or an American spy in Cuba, she began to imagine how she would feel if she were a sweat-shop woman, making shirts for twenty-nine cents a dozen, or a working girl at two dollars a week ...' Again, the story had all the ingredients of a *Companion* piece – heroism, patriotism, pathos, instruction, and morality – and again it ran as the lead story.[40]

By the beginning of the 1910s McFarlane had seen two of his *Companion* serials reprinted in book form and published some twenty short stories in adult magazines, including *Munsey's*, *Cosmopolitan*, the *Atlantic Monthly*, *McClure's*, the *Century*, *Everybody's*, and *Harper's* (the last in August of 1910, in the same issue that launched Conrad's 'The Secret Sharer'). Also by this time, however, he had begun to move away from adventure stories towards a genre hinted at by the social conscience of 'Cissy Make-Believe.'

In August of 1909, *Saturday Night* reported that while McFarlane 'can still produce meritorious tales to order at any time, and does so occasionally, he devotes most of his energy to the manufacture of special articles. They pay better.' By this time designating the signed essay of the twentieth-century magazine rather than the anonymous special of the late-nineteenth-century paper, the 'special article' had acquired higher status and pay as a result of the muckraking boom of the century's first decade. McFarlane had in fact been writing investigative magazine articles for some time, including a series on the origins of great fortunes called 'Where the Money Came From' for the *Saturday Evening Post* of 1903, the year *McClure's* began Steffens's 'The Shame of the Cities,' after Tarbell's history of the Standard Oil Company the most famous of the muckraking exposés. According to *Saturday Night*, McFarlane had also contracted with 'a certain journal to write something about Barnum and Bailey's circus,' for which he travelled with the show for several weeks. By the time of their report, he was commanding prices for his magazine articles that would 'fairly stagger some Canadian editors.' McFarlane's real arrival as what *Saturday Night* called a 'special article' expert, however, the moment that seems to have confirmed his transition from fiction to reform-minded journalism, came two years after their report.[41]

On 25 March 1911, a fire broke out at the Triangle Shirtwaist Factory near New York's Washington Square. The fire escapes were desperately inadequate, and the fire department's hoses could reach only to the seventh of the building's ten floors. One hundred and forty-six employees died, almost all of them young women; the factory's owners were later indicted for manslaughter. That summer, McFarlane wrote the story of the fire up for *McClure's* in an impassioned polemic against inadequate building codes and fire-prevention methods for the city's new skyscrapers. McFarlane's earlier articles had shown he could assemble facts and witnesses into a readable narrative, but 'Fire and the Skyscraper' is in a different class. Some credit has to go to the magazine: it ran McFarlane's article as its lead story, embellished it with photographs and carefully chosen pull-quotes, and promised a series of subsequent articles to expose further this 'national shame.' The prose, atypically crisp for McFarlane, suggests a strong editorial hand. But the editors had something to work with: 'Fire and the Skyscraper' is an excellent piece of writing, the equal of the best magazine prose of its day. As promised, McFarlane followed it up with two more articles for *McClure's* that year on New York's fire problem, and in 1913 published a second series in *Collier's* on the complicity of North American insurance companies with professional arson. Again this series debuted as the lead story, with *Collier's* billing it on its cover as an 'Astounding Series / by Arthur E. McFarlane' beneath an illustration of a guilty-looking arsonist, gas can and torch in hand. 'Mr. McFarlane,' the editors announced, 'is the first journalist to pierce the heart of the matter ... for the past eighteen months he has been working to get the facts of the arson situation for *Collier's*.'[42] What fire had given O'Higgins in 1902, it had now given McFarlane: a genre, a culture, and a name.

Sometime early in the new century, Stringer, O'Higgins, and McFarlane left their Fifth Avenue attic. The impetus for the breakup of the 'Three Musketeers' seems to have been romantic as much as literary. Stringer married Gibson Girl model turned actress Jobyna Howland, an Indiana native he met in 1899 while she was debuting opposite Canadian lead James K. Hackett in *Rupert of Hentzau* at the New York Lyceum.[43] In 1901, O'Higgins married Anna G. Williams, daughter of a Toronto manufacturer, and three years later McFarlane married University of Toronto graduate Margaret Emma Hunter, with whom he occasionally co-wrote. The McFarlanes moved back to Toronto for a time but by 1913 returned to New York, to the Long Island neighbourhood of Forest Hills. Here, McFarlane's career as a 'special article' expert seems to have ended, with just a mystery novel and a short children's book in his known bibliography between 1914 and his death in New York's St Luke's Hospital on 11 April 1945. For the last ten years of his life, he served as literary editor of the Carnegie Endowment's Division of Economics and History, directed by James Shotwell, the young Canadian student with whom he and the other denizens of the attic had once shared milk-punch.[44]

By 1906 O'Higgins had moved to a home in the Catskills, where he wrote and that year published *Don-A-Dreams*, an autobiographical novel about three young friends who quit college in Toronto to try their luck as writers in New York.[45] Up to about 1909 he occupied himself largely with stories of New York's East Side Irish, but that year he shifted literary gears, collaborating with others on muckraking exposés of political corruption in Denver and religious corruption in Utah's Mormon community and contributing to *McClure's* popular series of 1911–12 on the cases of William J. Burns, a former Secret Service operative turned private detective. Beginning with *The Argyle Case* in 1912, he also co-wrote with American playwright Harriet Ford eleven stage plays, mostly mysteries and domestic comedies. Late in life, O'Higgins became convinced that psychoanalysis offered the most effective cure for an illness he had contracted, an interest that produced the pop psychology books *The Secret Springs* (1920) and *The American Mind in Action* (1924), as well as the fictional case studies collected in *From the Life* (1919) and *Some Distinguished Americans* (1922) and the well-reviewed psychological novels *Julie Cane* (1924) and *Clara Barron* (1926). He died at his country home in Martinsville, New Jersey, on 28 February 1929, leaving behind a reputation as the prose laureate of New York's working-class Irish and a widely shared memory of a generous man who worked tirelessly to advance and protect his fellow writers.[46]

Arthur Stringer also left New York, moving with Jobyna in 1903 to a fruit farm on the north shore of Lake Erie. He continued to write the crime stories and novels for which he had become recognized, as well as what to his biographer was his best novel, *The Wine of Life* (1921), and the trilogy for which he is best known in Canada, *The Prairie Wife* (1915), *The Prairie Mother* (1920), and *The Prairie Child* (1922). Eventually, Jobyna tired of fruit and returned to the New York stage. In 1921 Stringer sold the farm, moving permanently to Mountain Lakes in northern New Jersey with his second wife, Margaret Stringer. In 1923–4, he spent a year working as an anonymous 'movie doctor,' fixing and filling out weak scripts. Also in 1924, he published the lost-in-the-wilds romance *Empty Hands*, the first of a dozen novels set in the Canadian and later Alaskan wilderness and probably his best-selling novel in any setting. These are just highlights: from *The Silver Poppy* in 1903 to *The Devastator* in 1944 Stringer published on average just under a novel a year. According to Lauriston, some thirty of his novels and short stories were themselves made into movies, including *Empty Hands* (1924), which starred

Montreal-born Norma Shearer, and the Metro-Goldwyn production of *The Prairie Wife* (1925), starring Dorothy Devore as Chaddie, with a young Boris Karloff as Diego. He also contributed poetry to dozens of periodicals, with ten collections appearing between 1903 and 1948, wrote four works of non-fiction and at least a dozen short plays, and served as first president of the Mountain Lakes Theatre Guild. In September 1950, the last of the musketeers passed away at age seventy-six.[47]

Of the dozens of literary cultures that flourished in America of the second half of the nineteenth century, regionalism, says Richard Brodhead, was the most accessible. For both known and new writers, so-called local colour provided an open door to an established literary culture: its heavily conventionalized formulas barely changed from the 1860s to the end of the century, and the only other prerequisite was 'familiarity with some cultural backwater,' something possessed by many traditionally distanced from literary circles. As Brodhead puts it, marginality had become an 'authorial advantage.' American men and women not from Boston or New York could enter the culture, as could recent immigrants, among them the Lithuanian journalist Abraham Cahan, whose 'region' was the Jewish community of New York's Lower East Side.[48] And, of course, Canadians could enter: expatriates or not, Canadian writers grew up on the same stories that taught American regionalists the conventions of the genre, and they certainly possessed the all-important 'familiarity with some cultural backwater.' In the literary culture of regionalism, being Canadian had its advantages.

Oddly, this advantage has more often than not been seen as bad for Canadian writers and Canadian writing, a constraint rather than an opening. According to the *Literary History of Canada*'s survey of the period, for instance, 'there was no market for "Canadian" nationalism in the great publishing centres in New York or London, although there was a lively market for stories about the past or present in French Canada, maritime Nova Scotia, New Brunswick, domestic Prince Edward Island, rural Ontario, or the various localities of the great West.' In one way, the claim is self-evident: American editors certainly weren't interested in supporting Canadian nationalism for its own sake. But neither were they dogmatically averse to publishing nationalist Canadian work if it satisfied on other grounds, such as reader interest or literary quality. The *Century* reprinted Charles G.D. Roberts's poem 'Canada' in January of 1886 and that July provided the first home for his equally nationalist 'Collect for Dominion Day.' In 1896, the *Bookman* accepted D.C. Scott's pro-imperialist essay on Canadian-American relations, and eight years later *Munsey's* published Will Roberts's laudatory article on Canadian prime minister and ardent nationalist Sir Wilfrid Laurier.[49] And although American publishers did value Canadian writers' direct experience of their particular regions, nativity wasn't itself enough to guarantee publication, as Lucy Maud Montgomery discovered when American publishers repeatedly rejected what would become Canada's most famous contribution to the regionalist mode. In fact, as Montgomery discovered years later, *Anne of Green Gables* was accepted only when a Prince Edward Island woman on the staff of Boston's L.C. Page and Company overcame her boss's objections to the book. Lewis Page was generally a bastard, but forcing regionalism on Montgomery or any other Canadian writer wasn't among his sins.[50]

More fundamentally, to complain that the American market confined Canadian writers to regional at the expense of national expressions is to misunderstand how Canadian as well as American advocates of regionalism saw its function: for them, the local was the means to the national. In 1886, Canadian editor George Stewart Jr told an audience at the Canadian Club in New York that 'A mine of literary wealth is to be had in every section of the dominion, and it only awaits the hand of the craftsman. Bret Harte opened up a new phase of American character as he discovered it in wild California. Miss Murfree found the Tennessee mountains rich in incident and strong in episodes of an intensely dramatic color, and Mr. Cable developed in a brilliant and picturesque way life and movement among the Creoles of the South. Have we no Canadian authors among us, who can do as much for us?' At century's end, Ontario critic Lawrence J. Burpee reminded writers that Canada was still home to a number of 'definite types' untouched by novelists, among them the 'picturesque habitant,' the 'simple-minded Acadian,' the 'breezy and unsophisticated' North-Westerner, the 'degenerate aborigine,' and 'the Prince Edward Islander, who believes that the whole Dominion circles around his little island.' Both Stewart and Burpee were echoing arguments advanced by American writers and editors, especially Hamlin Garland, who by the mid-1880s had begun to believe that writers from the southern, eastern, and western states were unknowingly working in concert to create a national literature. As Garland explained his theory to William Dean Howells on their first meeting, 'the stories of Joel Chandler Harris, George W. Cable, Sarah Orne Jewett, and Mary E. Wilkins, like the work of Joaquin Miller and Bret Harte, are but varying phases of the same movement, a movement which is to give us at last a vital, original, and national literature.'[51] Like Garland, many Canadian writers of the period saw in regionalism not only a prime literary opportunity, but also a way to give voice to their region and thus character to their nation, which for both Canadians and Americans more often meant distinguishing their respective literatures from those of the Old World than from each other. As Stewart's examples make clear, American literature at the end of the nineteenth century wasn't an obstacle but a model for Canadian literary nationalism. Although all but one of the eighteen stories collected in Gilbert Parker's *Pierre and His People* are set in the Canadian North-West, Carman's article on the book carefully avoided characterizing it as local colour because of the genre's by then traditional associations with genteel or 'effeminate' realism. Instead, he emphasized the self-assured virility of Parker's characters and the excitement of his plots, qualities that accorded with the new romance movement he sought to champion. Carman's choice of critical emphases points to the one key respect in which the regionalist formula did change over its heyday. Still concerned to achieve realism or what Garland called Veritism, regionalists by the mid-1890s were increasingly more interested in adventure and pathos, in telling striking stories and invoking strong emotions. First-wave regionalists played a significant role in the antimodern rebellion, their rural or small-town protagonists modelling a more stable identity than the hectic urban self. But with the advent of the new romanticism that Carman heralded, regionalism acquired the additional antimodern quality of fashioning more vital modes of existence than those determined by official culture. This post-realist revision of the regionalist formula is especially evident in so-called tenement literature, a species of regionalism born in New York in the mid-1890s that tended to exploit the new romantics' fondness for pathos more than their love of adventure. Both Stringer and O'Higgins contributed to this urban answer to local colour, but its first conspicuous Canadian writer was yet another University of Toronto student in the city.

A Solomon of Little Syria

In August of 1900, the New York *Bookman* noted that although the great New York novel had yet to be written, certain districts in the city had been the subject of 'a great many very charming stories.'

> We have had picturesque and romantic tales of the old French quarter to the south of Washington Square from the pens of Mr. Janvier and Mr. Bunner and others; Mr. Cahan has written of the Ghetto, Mr. Townsend and Mr. Norr of Chinatown, and Mr. Thomas, in his recently published *The Last Lady of Mulberry*, has given us considerable insight into the curious life among the Italians down by the Bend. It would seem as if, under the circumstances, the foreign population of New York had been pretty well covered by the literary seeker for originality. However, a book is announced for the autumn which deals with a quarter which until the present time has been ignored in fiction. New Yorkers who have spent any time

roaming about the lower end of Manhattan Island cannot have failed to notice the curious little colony of Syrians in Washington Street. A collection of stories of this colony by Mr. Norman Duncan is soon to be published under the title *The Soul of the Street*.

The subject of this notice, the *Bookman* added, was 'another native of Canada engaged in literary work in this country.'[52]

Born in 1871 near Brantford, Ontario, Norman Duncan studied for several years at the University of Toronto but like Stringer and O'Higgins left without a degree in the spring of 1895. While still a student he contributed to the *Toronto Globe*, and upon moving to Auburn in upstate New York after leaving university (apparently to join his older brother Robert, a chemistry instructor at the Auburn High School), he found reporting work on the Auburn *Bulletin*. In 1897, Duncan moved to New York City, again following brother Robert, who two years before had accepted a position at a school in the city. Robert changed jobs yet again in 1898, moving to Pottstown, Pennsylvania, and by 1899 Norman had his own apartment, a small suite in the Cumberland bachelor apartments located in the triangular plot where Broadway and Fifth cross at Madison Square Park. Shortly after his arrival, the twenty-six-year-old Duncan landed a position on the New York *Evening Post*, a job that would introduce him to the 'curious little colony of Syrians' that launched his literary career.

The *Evening Post* was then a relatively small circulation but respected daily under the editorship of Edwin Lawrence Godkin, an Irish-born reformer of whom an opponent had once said that he had approved of nothing since the birth of Christ. Lincoln Steffens, who started his career on the *Post*, later recalled it as a conservative paper that generally avoided 'crime, scandal, and the sensational' and maintained a strictly enforced style of impersonal journalism.[53] Duncan began work on the *Post* as a city reporter, but when war broke out between the United States and Spain in April of 1898 the paper assigned him to Roosevelt's preparations for the invasion of Cuba, and that fall he covered the returned hero's successful campaign for governor. According to the *Bookman*, Duncan had recently declined an offer to become the *Post*'s assistant city editor, at his own suggestion sticking instead to specials. The *Bookman* explained Duncan's decision as an aversion to desk work, but another factor may have been Godkin's rigid personality and editorial policies. In any case, it's not surprising that the always subjective Duncan would turn down an editorial job for specials, in which he would have had more freedom in subject and style.

Duncan discovered Lower Manhattan's Syrian colony during his first year with the *Post*. Established in the early 1890s along Washington Street from

Rector south to the Battery, 'Little Syria' or the 'Hoochee-Koochie precinct' (the latter after a popular midway at the Chicago Fair) was by the new century home to some five thousand Christian Syrians with their own churches, schools, newspapers, publishers, restaurants, and social and political clubs. From this colony was born the 1890s' fad for all things Mideastern that made Betts's poem about a Persian brass-worker his most popular book, gave Roberts his penchant for Egyptian cigarettes, and put a 'Turkish nook' in Ernest and Grace Seton's Bryant Park apartment.[54] In the course of collecting material for a series of sketches on the colony for the *Post* and later for his stories, Duncan befriended the colony's leaders, including a newspaper editor upon whom he based one of his recurring characters. Apparently he became something of a local Solomon for the community, asked to settle disputes and give the 'principal speech of the evening' on a visit to the colony by the Turkish Minister in Washington.[55]

Duncan worked on his first story about the Syrian colony for a year before submitting it to *McClure's*; the magazine rejected it, but recommended that he try the *Atlantic Monthly*, which published the story in its February 1900 issue. In the story, an old Syrian newspaper editor, Khalil Khayat, tells a young Irish boy, Billy Halloran, a legend from his country. The legend Khayat recounts is familiar enough: a young knight saves a beautiful princess from a dragon. But the story derives its dramatic tension not from its plot, but from the reader's awareness of the pathetic contrast between the Manhattan frame and the Syrian legend. The knight is, well, a knight, a dragon-slayer. Billy is a cripple, and his mother is a drunk who beats him daily. His only escape from these beatings is in his mother's absence, when the old editor takes pity on him and tells him stories. As an adventure story, 'In the Absence of Mrs. Halloran' has little to hold the reader's attention: Khalil doesn't even bother to finish his tale, though he hardly needs to. What it does have is a concrete if sentimental evocation of the inhabitants of a New York district, which perhaps explains why *McClure's* suggested sending it to the more sober *Atlantic*. Duncan makes much out of little, for instance, by playing up the different dialects of the Syrian editor and his Washington Street auditor: 'Was y'u pinched?' asks Billy after Khalil alludes to his own adventures in his homeland; 'I escape,' answers Khalil. The story also makes effective use of pathos. When Khalil and Billy hear his mother staggering up the stairs, the impassioned editor vows to defend Billy: 'I, Khalil Khayat, say eet. My arm shall defend you. The Lord God Almighty, the poor servant of heem I am, geeve me strength an' courage to prevail against the woman!' Read next to Khalil's story, the allegory is plain: Khalil is the modern-day knight, rescuing his charge from an alcoholic dragon. But the moment he has established the allegory, Duncan undercuts it: Billy

chuckles at Khalil's speech, and asks, 'Know w'at she done t' de ol' man? ...
'E's in de 'ospital.' The story ends not in romantic triumph but in pathetic
acquiesence, with Khalil creeping back to his own flat, Mrs Halloran uncon-
scious on her mattress, and Billy left alone on the fire escape.[56]

In 1900 Duncan published two more stories of the Syrian colony in the
Atlantic and one in the now convinced *McClure's*. Late that same year, McClure,
Phillips and Company brought out in New York and London Duncan's four
published Syrian stories and two new stories under the title *The Soul of the
Street: Correlated Stories of the New York Syrian Quarter*. As the *Bookman's*
notice of the collection's release indicates, *The Soul of the Street* was invited
by a rush of previous local colour books set in various New York districts.
More specifically, both the slum setting and the pervasive note of pathos in the
collection identify it as a product of tenement literature, a recently established
urban version of regionalism.

Led and justified by Jacob Riis's quasi-sociological study of New York's
slums, *How the Other Half Lives* (1890), a number of books were by mid-
decade 'dar[ing] to overleap the "barbed-wire fence" which separates the nice
people of our literary Vanity Fair from the low life of the great Unwashed, and
to draw on the slums for their material.'[57] Riis himself wrote *Out of Mulberry
Street* (1898), also the setting for Edward W. Townsend's *A Daughter of the
Tenements* (1895); Julian Ralph wrote about a Forsythe Street tenement in
People We Pass (1896) and Stephen Crane about a Lower East Side prostitute
in *Maggie: A Girl of the Streets* (1893). James W. Sullivan gave the Irish their
day in his popular *Tenement Tales of New York* (1895), while Abraham Cahan
launched the immigrant novel in America with his *Yekl, A Tale of the New York
Ghetto* (1896). Arthur Stringer ventured into the genre with his first book, *The
Loom of Destiny*, whose bathetic New York street urchins prove if nothing else
that Stringer had neither the temperament for pathos nor the patience for
protest. Much more successfully, Harvey O'Higgins came late to the culture,
writing some dozen stories about the city's Lower East Side Irish between
1904 and 1912, collected in *Silent Sam and Other Stories of Our Day*. Although quantitatively speaking the least productive of the several literary
cultures O'Higgins mined over his career, these stories were his best remembered work and established his reputation as the prose laureate of the common
man, a title that to my knowledge first appeared in *Current Opinion* in October
of 1914. 'Harvey O'Higgins's stories,' the editors wrote, 'are the romances of
the average. He is the prose laureate of the exiles from Ireland, of the poor
servant girl, the hod carrier and the day laborer, the old washerwoman and the
night watchman, the teamster and the policeman ... [His] Irish romances ... are

the most enlightened and illuminating studies of the Irish in America that have come to print.'[58]

Duncan's *The Soul of the Street* was a product of several literary cultures: the New York colour the *Bookman* located it in, the Mideastern vogue that Betts had tapped into with *The Perfume-Holder*, and the rising tide of tenement literature. Ultimately, however, the focus of these stories is not the Syrians or the poor Irish with whom they share the street, but the confluence of these two cultures. 'In the Absence of Mrs. Halloran' pits a Syrian romance against the harsh realities of an Irish street boy's plight. In 'The Lamp of Liberty,' a Syrian publisher aspires to the power and profits of the district's Irish alderman, and to achieve his goal mimics the Tammany boss's self-serving rhetoric and corrupt politics. A love story, 'For the Hand of Haleem,' explores the courting rituals of an Irishman and a Syrian as they vie for the hand of the same girl. In 'The Spirit of Revolution,' a story that hardly needs its title or its reference to Washington to reveal its intended comparison, Syrian elders gather in a coffee-house to plan a revolution in their homeland. Against the formal Arabic of their speeches Duncan sets the street sounds of contemporary New York, of trucks on cobblestones, of the roar of the elevated trains, of Irish street kids singing 'Hello, mah baby!' The revolution is soon forgotten; the street sounds persist into the story's final paragraphs.[59] *The Soul of the Street* was billed as stories about an unwritten immigrant culture, and Duncan himself described his work on the colony as 'little windows through which you may catch a glimpse of the lives they live in this land.'[60] But although Duncan worked hard to convey the uniqueness of that culture, his collection is more a window on the modern process of acculturation and assimilation, on how the foreign slowly but inevitably becomes the familiar.

Duncan's first book was well received. The *New York Times Saturday Review* called it 'a charming book, and replete with human sympathy,' while the *Nation* thought it 'a noteworthy document upon a little-known phase of our city history.' Only Hutchins Hapgood in the *Bookman* raised a dissenting voice, complaining that Duncan was too much the soulful lyricist and too little the objective realist – the very qualities that made Duncan choose specials over an editorial job, and that identify him as one of Carman's new romantics.[61] More important for him, Duncan's entrance into regionalism via Little Syria set him on the road (or rather, the sea) to the equally lyrical stories for which he is best known. Duncan made his first visit to Newfoundland in the summer of 1900 under contract for *McClure's*: this trip and subsequent visits, most spent in the small fishing outport of Exploits, gave him the raw material for over eighty articles and stories and eleven books set in Newfoundland, notably the ten stories collected in *The Way of the Sea* (1903), the book that made his reputation.

Duncan didn't abandon the culture with which he had begun his career: he later had some of his New York Syrians emigrate rather improbably to Newfoundland, and wrote a series of impressionistic Middle East travel articles for *Harper's* that became *Going Down From Jerusalem*. By 1902, a year after quitting his job on the *Evening Post*, he had moved to Pennsylvania to teach English at Washington and Jefferson College. From 1906 to his death in 1916 he moved often, lecturing at the Lawrence campus of the University of Kansas, travelling in search of material for his writing to Newfoundland, the Middle East, Minnesota, Australia, and the Far East, and living with friends and relatives in various towns in Pennsylvania, Ontario, Ohio, and New York. An alcoholic and a chain-smoker, he died at age forty-five of a heart attack while golfing near his home in Fredonia, New York.

The Bewitchment of Charles G.D. Roberts

On the second day of February in 1897 Charles G.D. Roberts moved from New Brunswick to New York, leaving behind his wife of sixteen years and their four children to accept a position with the *Illustrated American*. He had long contemplated the move. Passionately committed to a leading role in the creation of a distinct but world-class Canadian literature, Roberts struggled throughout the 1880s and 1890s to sustain by any means possible – among others, an editing job in Toronto, a professorship in Windsor, freelance writing in Fredericton – what some part of him seems to have known from the beginning was an impossibility, a literary career in his own country.

As far back as 1879, the 'Father of Canadian Poetry' had elected to send his first important poem to an American magazine.[62] Five years later, in September of 1884, Roberts announced his intention to move to New York in the wake of his departure from the editor's desk of the Toronto *Week*. He visited New York that fall, meeting with editors and writers such as Richard Watson Gilder, Thomas Bailey Aldrich, and Edgar Fawcett, but couldn't find definite employment and returned to Canada to make equally unfruitful inquiries in Ottawa into that customary resort of the starving poet, a job in the civil service. While teaching at King's College from 1885 to 1895 Roberts made at least seven more trips to the States, giving readings, placing manuscripts, visiting Carman and other stateside friends, and looking for work. Towards the end of this period he mounted an extensive campaign for an American position, writing to Gilder at the *Century* that he was 'available, sound & trusty,' competing for an editorial job on Boston's *Youth's Companion*, and asking *Chap-Book* publisher

Herbert Stone to 'keep an eye open' for positions in Chicago. Neither these nor attempts to secure a chair at several American and Canadian universities materialized, and by November of 1895, Roberts had not unhappily resigned himself to a winter of writing in Fredericton: 'I can live there cheaply,' he explained to his former teacher, '& write without hindrance, running on to Boston & New York whenever business makes it necessary.'[63]

Measured by the page, Roberts's year and a half in Fredericton were productive, allowing him time to finish an entry for the Dominion History Competition, write his first novel, and put the finishing touches on his fourth collection of verse, as well as produce some dozen articles and stories for American magazines. But the same money problems that had prompted his resignation from King's continued to plague him. Late in 1896, pressed by creditors, he accepted the offer of a friend, Francis Bellamy from the *Youth's Companion*, to become his assistant on a New York magazine that had recently taken him on as managing editor.

Founded in 1890 by Lorillard Spencer, the *Illustrated American* was by the time of Roberts's arrival in the city a ten-cent general-interest weekly with a circulation of around forty thousand. Spencer's penchant for top-name illustrators had built his magazine a solid reputation but lost him a fortune, and in 1897 he sold the foundering weekly to A.B. de Guerville. It was probably this second owner who hired Bellamy, who in turn appointed Roberts, assigning him a range of editorial duties, including editing its book columns. In a letter written to Craven Langstroth Betts five months after joining the magazine, Roberts denied having charge of its literary department, but he may just have been diplomatically avoiding reviewing some books Betts had asked him to use the magazine to promote; certainly by November, Roberts was telling another correspondent that 'I am doing the literary page for them now.'[64] Besides his editorial work Roberts contributed at least four signed reviews, two short stories, and a dozen articles in his first year with the *Illustrated American*. He also wrote reviews for the New York *Bookman*, including reviews of Seton's friend Elliott Coues's edition of Alexander Henry's journals and Carman's *Ballads of Lost Haven*.

The offices of the *Illustrated American* were at 401 East Twenty-third Street, about two miles south of the boarding house on East Fifty-eighth where Roberts, his brother Will, and cousin Carman stayed during Roberts's first year in the city. In October, Mitchell Kennerley moved in, staying for a few crowded weeks before he and Carman found their own apartment on East Sixteenth. By at least December, another of Roberts's brothers, Theodore Goodridge, was also a resident at Miss Kelly's. (Theodore had come to New York for an editorial position on the *Independent*, but returned home in the summer of 1898 after contracting a nearly fatal fever as the weekly's war correspondent in Florida and Cuba.) As Roberts remembered this period for his biographer Elsie Pomeroy, his friends included Bellamy and another staffer at the *Illustrated American*, explorer Albert White Vorse; Carman's friends Richard and Henrietta Hovey; *Century* editor Richard Gilder and Gilder's assistant Robert Underwood Johnson; New York poet and playwright Edgar Fawcett; Edmund Clarence Stedman, with whom Roberts had been corresponding for a decade; the English poet Richard Le Gallienne; and Canadian Peter McArthur, then in the final months of his editorship of *Truth*.[65] Especially, Roberts spent what little free time he had in the company of Carman, Hovey, and Le Gallienne: this was the year that earned the four hirsute poets their reputation as 'The Angora School of Poets,' and that caused an embarrassed Roberts to cut his hair and adopt the trademark black ribbon that forever after adorned his eyeglasses.

Within just a few months of joining the *Illustrated American* Roberts found the salary unequal to the workload, writing to Stedman that he would even prefer editorial work on one of the big dailies, 'where my work would at *least* be done when it is done,' and asking for a recommendation for a rumoured opening on the *North American Review*. On 11 October, he wrote Stedman again, this time for support in his bid to replace George Washington Cable as the editor of *Current Literature* – a position, he wrote, that 'ought to be better than this thing of mine here, which is but $30.00 a week & *no prospects!*'[66] Both applications came to nothing, so Roberts stayed on with the *Illustrated American* over the fall and into winter before resigning in mid-January of 1898, again to attempt a freelance career.

Roberts's first book as a New York freelancer, the appropriately titled *New York Nocturnes and Other Poems*, appeared early that April. Published by the small Boston house of Lamson, Wolffe and Company, this fifth collection of Roberts's verse contained for the first time a substantial number of love poems (about half the volume), the urban setting of which suggests personal as well as literary reasons for his residence in New York. The book had mixed reviews, partly because, as James Doyle suggests, Roberts was by then an established enough poet not to merit 'the indulgence sometimes granted promising neophytes.'[67] Although it too met critical opposition, Roberts's first novel, *The Forge in the Forest*, had the year before become a popular success, making it on to the *Bookman*'s best-seller lists in May of 1897, where it stayed for the next three months. Perhaps because of this better reception as a novelist, that spring and summer of 1898 Roberts turned his energies away from poetry to fiction, in particular to his Acadian romances. Working in New York and for a few weeks in August in Fredericton, Roberts quickly completed a follow-up novel to *The Forge in the Forest* and several short stories with the same setting and some of the same characters.

Fiction set in the present or historical Maritimes wasn't new to Roberts: his first published prose, a series for the University of New Brunswick's *University Monthly* of 1882–3, had pretended to narrate a late-eighteenth-century excursion on the Squatook waterway. In 1884–5, he published a series of sketches of 'Old Acadia' in Chicago's *Current*, and his first short story for the *Youth's Companion* had a Maritime setting, as did many of the melodramas of tide and camp collected in *Earth's Enigmas* in 1896. His first book of fiction, the juvenile *Raid from Beauséjour*, collected 'Two Stories of Acadie.'[68] But it was Lamson, Wolffe's release of *The Forge in the Forest* in the spring of 1897 that established Roberts as one of the new romantics. The *Bookman* praised an advance copy of the novel in terms unmistakably inflected by the antimodern longings to which the school appealed: 'it is a story,' the journal said, 'to shake the torpor from the brain and to keep the soul alive. It is charged with romance, and works like wine.' A month later, the magazine's assistant editor James MacArthur reviewed *The Forge in the Forest* in phrases that could have been lifted from Carman's article, remarking that 'Nowadays, where there is so much "tooting on the sentimental flute in literature," it is inspiring to come across a book that "goes to the head of the march to sound the heady drums."' In his review MacArthur twice suggested Roberts's debt to Robert Louis Stevenson, whom Carman had cited as one of the leaders of the new romantic movement. Obviously not displeased with the comparison, Roberts later allowed Pomeroy to write in her biography that the publication of his second novel 'definitely established the Roberts tradition of prose which is, perhaps, more akin to the tradition of Robert Louis Stevenson than to that of any other school.'[69]

That second novel appeared late in 1898. In some ways a sequel to *The Forge in the Forest*, *A Sister to Evangeline* takes place a decade later, in the year of the Acadian Deportation. Like its predecessor, it is unabashedly romantic: the hero, soldier-poet Captain Paul Grande, is the best swordsman in New France; his lover Yvonne de Lamourie is the most intelligent and beautiful woman in all of Acadia; and their enemy, the evil Black Abbé, is the blackest villain in the region's history. The novel's most important literary debt is announced in its title. Like many of the countless historical romances unleashed upon North Americans in the latter half of the nineteenth century, *A Sister to Evangeline* profited from Longfellow's 1847 poem, *Evangeline: A Tale of Acadie*. Both plots turn on the separation of a pair of young Acadian lovers by the Deportation, and Roberts paints in the same pastoral strokes as his American predecessor, though his more concrete details suggest a desire to demonstrate his greater authority to write about the region (Longfellow never visited Grand Pré). Here, however, the connections end: no doubt surprisingly to the contemporary reader, neither Yvonne nor anyone else in the novel has a sister named Evangeline. In fact, the title is the only mention of Evangeline in the novel. Quite clearly, Roberts's title attempted to cash in on the success of probably the most popular of the century's historical romances: as Pomeroy admits, Roberts's first two novels benefited from the vogue for Acadian romances, 'and this success had a most salutary effect upon his finances.'[70]

Besides this ring of the familiar, Roberts's Acadian romances appealed to editors and readers because they satisfied what Richard Ohmann has described as the social voyeurism of the new professional class. American regionalism of the 1890s functioned, says Ohmann, as a kind of tour guide, 'mediating previously hidden lives to a readership of social voyeurs.'[71] As with Carman's new romantics, the particular setting of these stories didn't matter – what mattered was that they were stories of 'elsewhere,' of places outside or beyond the social or geographic confines of their audience, places like O'Higgins's Lower East Side, Duncan's Little Syria, or Roberts's Acadia.

One of Roberts's Acadian short stories, 'The Bewitchment of Lieutenant Hanworthy,' provides a typical example of how these stories worked to familiarize their regions to armchair tourists. Published in the reinvented *Saturday Evening Post* of 19 November 1898 with illustrations by New York artist Harrison Fisher, the story is the first-person account of an officer in the Boston expedition for the occupation of Port Royal who falls in love with an Acadian girl. A regionalist melodrama, it's also an exercise in acculturation by simile – in translating the Maritime setting to and for an American audience. In his first paragraph, Hanworthy describes the wind blowing through the Annapolis Valley as a bleaker version of that which he imagines to be blowing over 'my own hill pastures of Salem.' The story's occasion is a Thanksgiving dinner held for the occupying officers: the Acadians, we're told, don't observe this American feast, but they do have the raw ingredients, pumpkins, ducks, geese, and so on. All it takes is a little guidance for the Acadian cook to produce for the officers 'a pumpkin pie as might pass for the product of Duxbury or Dedham.' A chance encounter with a young Acadian woman delays Hanworthy from the dinner, and she instead serves him Bordeaux and 'some cakes of the country.' 'You shall have your Thanksgiving dinner, but translated into French!' she says. The phrase captures the story's project in small, a process of acculturation rendered concrete by the union of the future American officer and the French woman. Just as the Acadian pumpkins can be made into American pumpkin pie, so too can the exotic Acadian woman be made into an American bride. Fisher's illustrations reinforce this idea: turkeys, nowhere mentioned in the story itself, strut across the bottom of one page, literally underlining the foreign setting with the comfort of the familiar. The combination must have appealed to the *Post*'s new management, who ran Roberts's romance as their cover story during a subscription drive that by three weeks after his prose debut in the weekly had brought its circulation to 250,000, by far the highest it had ever seen, though a fraction of what it would later achieve.[72]

After completing the manuscript of *A Sister to Evangeline* in Fredericton, Roberts returned to New York in September of 1898, moving with William to a flat at 105 East Seventeenth Street, a block north of Carman and Kennerley's rooms. According to Frank Pollock, himself then staying on East Nineteenth, by that winter Maria's restaurant had become 'too self-consciously brilliant,' and Canadians and their friends in the city were instead gathering at the Roberts's top-floor residence, where, 'at all hours of the day and night, one is likely to meet poets, painters, novelists, editors and publishers, either hailing from or dealing with the great Dominion.' At work during most of this fall and winter on a third Acadian romance that appears to have been abandoned for, or perhaps transformed into, the backwoods fable *The Heart of the Ancient Wood*, Roberts continued to write short Acadian stories and sketches for the *Post* and the *Atlantic Monthly*, as well as reviews for Scribner's *Book Buyer*. The following May, the Boston house of Silver, Burdett and Company (for whom Frank Bellamy had gone to work after quitting the *Illustrated American*) sent Roberts to England on an all-expenses-paid contract to write a history of England for young American readers. Accompanied by Will and his second son Lloyd, Roberts spent his seven months in England 'chiefly dissipating' and failed to produce the contracted history, but he made some important connections, notably with the *Windsor Magazine*, a few years later to become his most loyal outlet for his animal stories, and began work on *The Heart of the Ancient Wood*.[73]

On his return to New York in early January of 1900 Roberts occupied an address on West 103rd, but that December he moved downtown again, renting a furnished top-floor flat at 22 West Ninth Street from Mark Twain's friend and later biographer Albert Bigelow Paine, then staying in the South. A two-minute walk from storied Washington Square, and next door to the Casa Napoleon, the Franco-Spanish hotel used as a setting in William Dean Howells's *The World of Chance*, Roberts's flat in the staid old brownstone was an 'airy-looking, sky-lighted, well-furnished studio apartment' littered with Paine's collections of rare prints, chinaware, and books.[74] Again, Roberts's home became a centre for New York *literati*, as well as a more permanent home for others: Carman shared the space when not summering with Mrs King in the Catskills, Will moved in after his return from England, the artist Frank Verbeck occupied the flat's other half, Lloyd joined his father in 1903, and Irish war correspondent George Lynch stayed nearly a year. Cramped but romantically located in the centre of the Bohemian district, the flat was Roberts's home for five years, after which he, Will, and Lloyd moved to a more spacious top-floor studio at 226 Fifth Avenue, a block away from the *Outing* offices where Lloyd as well as Edwyn Sandys worked.

In Roberts's first year back in New York his new publisher Silver, Burdett (Lamson, Wolffe failed the previous March) brought out a collection of his Acadian stories, *By the Marshes of Minas*, and reprinted his novel *The Heart of the Ancient Wood* from *Lippincott's Magazine*. The novel, about a young girl growing up with animals for company in the New Brunswick wilderness, was well reviewed, especially in Canada, but the historical tales had a more lukewarm reception. These reviews may have been partly responsible for Roberts's move around this time away from Acadian romances and towards the animal stories that dominated the rest of his career. According to biographer John Coldwell Adams, however, the main incentive for the switch was the phenomenal success of Seton's *Wild Animals I Have Known*. Roberts had been publishing animal stories since the early 1890s, well before Seton's book and even before Lobo's first appearance in *Scribner's* in 1894. Although the present consensus is that the earliest of these stories represent his best efforts in the genre, at the time Roberts had difficulty placing them with editors, and he gave them up for other subjects. After *Wild Animals I Have Known*, however, animal stories were suddenly in demand, and Roberts was 'quick to take advantage of the ready market.'[75]

He couldn't have known it, but by the time Roberts returned to the animal-fiction market there weren't many years left in its boom. He made the most of it, publishing some forty animal stories between 1900 and his departure from New York in 1907 in magazines like *Outing*, the *Youth's Companion*, *Frank Leslie's Popular Monthly*, *McClure's*, and the *Saturday Evening Post*. Many of these were reprinted in English magazines, especially the *Windsor Magazine*, and a few in Canadian magazines. Although he continued to publish work in other genres during this period – including his collected *Poems* in 1901, the historical novel *Barbara Ladd* in 1902, a book of new verse in 1903, and the autobiographical novel *The Heart That Knows* in 1906 – none of it attracted the praise or even the attention his animal stories were receiving. The *Nation*, for instance, called Roberts's first collection completely devoted to the genre, 1902's *The Kindred of the Wild*, 'a masterpiece of its kind,' while the *Dial* remarked of the same book that 'Mr. Roberts's animal stories are unsurpassed.' Two more collections, *The Watchers of the Trails* in 1904 and *The Haunters of the Silences* in 1907, generated equal enthusiasm. Probably his most widely reviewed book in the genre was the 1905 animal novel *Red Fox*, which the *New York Times* called 'a rare thing among animal biographies,' the *Independent* thought 'as charming in style as it is in atmosphere,' and the *Outlook* described as having 'one of the most interesting characters in all the annals of woods life.' In what must have been a difficult moment for Seton, when his own *Biography of a Silver Fox* appeared four years later, the *Times* compared it to Roberts's book, concluding that 'Mr. Roberts's chief advantage over Mr. Seton, aside from priority of publication, is that his is the better, more vivid, and more dramatic story.'[76]

Most of Roberts's animal stories during this period were literary hybrids that combined the animal story with the Maritime setting of his regionalist romances. This combination, together with Roberts's superior writing ability and his comparatively lesser pretence to documentary accuracy, explains why he weathered the nature faker storm better than Seton, and why he was able to continue selling animal stories after their fall from fashion. As a regionalist, Roberts was generally less interested than Stringer, O'Higgins, or even Duncan in bolstering his authority with local details of speech, dress, and so on, and this trait carried over into his animal stories, of which Stringer once remarked that 'we sniff no taint of the midnight oil, catch no sight of the plodding and quibbling naturalist, chained to the tyranny of facts and laws.' Like the other new romantics, Roberts was more interested in telling a dramatic story than in telling the truth, and his romanticism saved him from criticisms of his realism. Burroughs largely exempted Roberts from his 1903 attack on the new school of nature writing, remarking that unlike Seton's, Roberts's animal stories never deceived the reader into thinking that they were true. Even Theodore Roosevelt, who had particular objections to the abilities of one of Roberts's animals (an especially heroic lynx), nonetheless allowed that many of his animal stories were 'avowedly fairy tales, and no one is deceived by them.'[77] What Burroughs and Roosevelt couldn't do, however, public taste could: after Roberts's move to England, the *Windsor Magazine* became typically his first and increasingly his only outlet for the genre.

Roberts sailed for Europe in November of 1907; it would be nearly eighteen years before he returned to North America, this time to a hero's welcome in Canada, where, if still not paid, he was at least fêted, cheered, medalled, and eventually knighted. Roberts wasn't the most successful of the Canadian expatriates: he came late to both of the literary cultures that sustained him during his expatriate years, and other Canadians in New York appeared earlier and more often in the city's best new magazines. He never attained the wealth of Cox, Seton, or even his brother William; in fact, he lived one step ahead of his creditors for most of his life. But Roberts's move to New York was the most important symbolic loss for Canadian literature of his day, an importance hinted at by his reception upon his return and by the *Week*'s ardent denial of rumours of his departure back in the spring of 1895. 'Owing to the lack of a literary career in Canada,' the *Week* had said, 'it is necessary that one's literary work should be marketed in the States, but Roberts is too thorough a Canadian to leave his own country permanently. His tastes and sympathies are all Canadian, and however lofty a place he may win in the literary world Canada will be able to claim him as her son.'[78]

In 1955, Desmond Pacey quoted from this notice in his introduction to *The Selected Poems of Sir Charles G.D. Roberts*, using it as evidence of the nationalism that he argued kept Roberts for so long from heeding his reasons for leaving Canada. Those reasons, said Pacey, were Roberts's innate restlessness, his insufficient salary at King's, his estrangement from his wife, the 'insidious suggestion' that he was wasting his talents describing Maritime scenes, and the general decline of Canadian idealism in the 1890s. These are all good reasons, but as an explanation of Canada's literary exodus (which Pacey intended the last to be) they left out much more than they included. They also left out the reason Roberts himself gave for his departure, or rather they recast that reason in Pacey's terms. Expressing a viewpoint typical of his generation of Canadian critics, Pacey ultimately said Roberts abandoned Canada because he was 'bewitched by the goddess of Success.' Expressing a viewpoint typical of his generation of Canadian writers, Roberts said: 'I did my literary work in New York where my market was.'[79]

Chapter 5

Exodus Lost

Canada's literary exodus has attracted nothing like the attention paid to the most well-known expatriate literary community of modern times, the Americans in Paris of the next century. It's not that scholars don't know of it: past and present Canadian literary histories and biographies note the departure of writers in these years for other countries, and are individually if not collectively aware of most of the better-known names involved. But with the exception of James Doyle and a few others, Canadians have shown little interest in this phenomenon beyond acknowledging that it happened.

There's a perfectly valid reason for this. In 1926, Thomas Beer remarked that the literary legacy of America's magazine boom was 'an amassed competence of journalism, some wit and an enormity of tiresome fiction.'[1] For readers whose aesthetic was formed in the crucible of modernism, that remark could have titled this book. Most days, I'm one of those readers: I try to resist judging anything but modernism by modernist values, but I'm not always successful, and in any event I'm not going to try to make a case for an overlooked Gertrude Stein or even a Morley Callaghan among Canada's literary expatriates. Canadian or not, most writers of their time wrote for a larger audience and under shorter deadlines than is conducive to the creation of what we generally think of as *literature*, innovative art as against imitative craft. In the 1920s, writers went to Paris to escape the market; in the 1890s, they went to New York to find it.

But if the expatriates' skill in answering and creating the demands of a mass market prevented them from themselves attaining canonical importance, this same skill was responsible for their vital historical importance to the development of a Canadian literature. That a writer has been forgotten by posterity because she chose to write for a popular market, or chose to leave his country, doesn't automatically make that writer worthy of recovery. Marginalization doesn't confer value: it just hides it, sometimes. With a few exceptions, the bulk of the writings of Canada's expatriates of these years belongs exactly where I found it, in university libraries, on microfilm, in periodical indexes. The expatriates matter to Canadian literary history as a commercial and cultural phenomenon, not as individual artists. Before we explore that importance, however, I need to finish their story by looking at their fate in their adopted and native countries, and at some decidedly nonaesthetic reasons for their neglect in the latter.

During the peak years of the exodus Canadian writers figured prominently in the literary journalism of New York. The Canadian presence in the New York *Bookman* over the first five years of its existence, to take as representative the city's pre-eminent literary monthly, was proportionately much greater than the Canadian presence in the city itself. Between its premier issue in February of 1895 and the end of the century (as well as after), the *Bookman* regularly published and reviewed Canadian authors, took note of their movements in its Chronicle and Comment section, and listed their successes in its new best-seller lists. Most were expatriates: Roberts led the pack with no fewer than two dozen appearances (in 1897, the year of his arrival in New York, he appeared in seven of the twelve issues), Carman followed with twenty, and Seton appeared eight times in the two years after his first notice in the magazine in December of 1898. Arthur Stringer appeared eight times in 1899–1900, and Palmer Cox, Norman Duncan, William Carman Roberts, M. Bourchier Sanford, and publisher George Munro all managed at least one notice before the century's end.

Of course, not all of these notices were flattering: George Munro, for instance, earned the *Bookman*'s ire in the fall of 1898 for pirating a translation of Edmond Rostand's hit play *Cyrano de Bergerac*, and, what was apparently worse, using the pirated pamphlet to peddle Mrs Winslow's Soothing Syrup.[2] Nor was it only the New York Canadians who received the magazine's attention: Gilbert Parker, Robert Barr, Grant Allen, and Sara Jeannette Duncan in England were all featured repeatedly, the first two as often as Roberts. Other expatriate Canadians appearing at least once over these years included E.W. Thomson in Boston, Ethelwyn Wetherald in Philadelphia, Thomas O'Hagan in Chicago, and Cecilia Viets Jamison in New Orleans, as well as stay-at-homes Wilfred Campbell, Ralph Connor, Lily Dougall (who settled in England in 1900), E. Pauline Johnson, Archibald Lampman, T.G. Marquis, Jean McIlwraith (expatriated to New York in 1902), William McLennan, J. Macdonald Oxley, Duncan Campbell Scott, and Francis Sherman. In one issue, for December of 1896, the *Bookman* praised Sherman's *Matins*, reported that the eldest Roberts had completed his first novel, and puffed new books by Roberts, Thomson, Oxley, and Jamison in its Christmas survey of 'Books for Boys and Girls.' This was an unusually high Canadian content, but on average two to three Canadians appeared in each issue of the *Bookman* in this period.

Besides entries in contemporary American reference books like *Who's Who in New York City and State* and Adams's *Dictionary of American Authors*,[3] the New York expatriates also appeared more substantially in American literary chat books and memoirs of the period. Francis Whiting Halsey featured Seton in his *American Authors and Their Homes*, while Edward F. Harkins included a chapter on Roberts in his *Little Pilgrimages Among the Men Who Have Written Famous Books*, and both Roberts and Carman won chapters in Jessie B. Rittenhouse's *The Younger American Poets*. A decade later, Richard Duffy remembered Carman along with Richard Hovey and others of New York's Bohemian 1890s in the second of his 'When They Were Twenty-One' sketches for the *Bookman*. Thomas Beer recalled several Canadians in his iconoclastic history of the 1890s, *The Mauve Decade*, including the 'pink' Acton Davies, one of the 'jaunty nothings who rolled dice for drinks in the old Metrôpole, the writers of smart plays, cheap songs, forgotten reviews,' and Toronto-born actor-turned-author Clara Morris, one of the few writers and even fewer women to receive Beer's praise.[4] Two years later, New York historian and Maria's regular Henry Collins Brown included Canadians May Irwin, Clara Morris, Palmer Cox, John W. Lovell, and James Creelman in his history of the city, *In the Golden Nineties*. Hamlin Garland, as a final example, recorded his encounters with several stateside Canadians in his literary autobiographies, including his first meeting with his long-time friend Ernest Thompson Seton at the New York Player's Club in October of 1896. Garland was also a friend of Roberts and Carman, and met Basil King during the novelist's residence in New York near the end of the war, as well as Gilbert Parker, Grant Allen, and Robert Barr on trips to England.

In scholarly America, Canadian writers appeared regularly in still the single most authoritative record of magazine publishing in America, the five-volume library of American culture that is Frank Luther Mott's *History of American Magazines*, published between 1930 and 1968. In fact, the frequency of their appearances charts the history of the Canadian literary exodus: the volume covering the period from 1865 to 1885 contains eleven mentions of seven expatriate Canadian writers, while the 1885–1905 volume contains seventy-five mentions of twenty-three expatriates, and the 1905–1930 volume contains just six mentions of five expatriates. All told, twenty-four known expatriate Canadian writers, editors, and publishers appear almost a hundred times in Mott's last three volumes, with Carman appearing most often, followed by

Roberts, Stringer, and Walter Blackburn Harte. After their number and frequency, the most striking aspect of the Canadian presence in Mott's history is the number of times he lists now forgotten or nearly forgotten Canadian names alongside still well-known American names as 'notable' contributors to a particular magazine.

In 1964, four years before the posthumous publication of the final volume in Mott's *History*, a doctoral candidate at the University of Michigan completed a two-volume account of past and present Canadian authors in American libraries, university curricula, publishers' lists, anthologies, magazines, literary awards, best-seller lists, and reviews. As the first systematic study of its kind, Amos Robert Rogers's labours were presumably intended to facilitate more analytical studies of the reception of Canadian authors in the United States. Ironically, however, at the same time Rogers was busy building its foundations, barriers were being erected on both sides of the border against further study of the transnational connections his and Mott's research abundantly demonstrated.

Partly because of the settling of the American canon, but mostly because of the division of academic labour that is a necessary by-product of cultural nationalism, the 1960s marked the beginning of the disappearance of the Canadian expatriates of the 1880s and '90s from American studies of the period's literature. A few continued to appear in specialized works – Cox, for instance, maintained a reduced mention in the fourth edition of May Hill Arbuthnot's textbook *Children and Books*, and Seton and Roberts both figure prominently in independent scholar Ralph H. Lutts's history of the nature faker controversy – but in general, Canadian authors began to be left to Canadian scholars. Of the studies of American literature that have been most useful to me, no Canadians appear in Larzer Ziff's *The American 1890s*, Herbert F. Smith's *The Popular American Novel, 1865–1920*, or Richard H. Brodhead's *Cultures of Letters*. Carman appears in T.J. Jackson Lears's *No Place of Grace* as a prominent antimodernist, but the only stateside Canadians in Richard Ohmann's 1996 study of American magazines and mass culture in the 1890s are Munro (brief references) and Thomson (a short story). Similarly incidental, the only Canadians in Ronald Weber's 1997 survey of professional writers in America, *Hired Pens*, are Munro and novelist May Agnes Fleming.

Critical discussion isn't the only index of the expatriates' place in American literary history. Some have survived in the longer memory of reference works like the *Dictionary of American Biography*, which retains entries on Cox, O'Higgins, and Seton, or *The Oxford Companion to American Literature*, whose current edition includes Carman, Cox, O'Higgins, Roberts, and Seton, as well as a later Canadian arrival in New York, Constance Lindsay Skinner. For the expatriates themselves, arguably the most important legacy would be the extent to which their books are still being sold. Here, those few who have survived in print would rediscover one of their reasons for leaving Canada in the first place. At the time of writing, Carman's popular *Songs from Vagabondia* is still in print, but from a Connecticut publisher. Two of Cox's Brownie books are available from different American houses, while two more are available from European publishers. Kessinger Publishing of Montana currently lists six of Charles Brodie Patterson's New Thought books. It might be fun to ask the young Margaret Atwood why, if Ernest Thompson Seton's animal stories are so 'distinctively Canadian,' only two of his more than thirty books are in print in Canada today – and why twenty-one of those books are in print in America, from publishers spanning the gamut from mass-market children's book companies to scholarly reprint houses.[5]

The older Atwood might reasonably reply that this discrepancy is simply a consequence of the much larger American market, the same reason her own books sell more copies south than north of the border. But if the disappearance of the expatriates from Canadian publishers' lists can be justified by economics, their absence from both American and Canadian literary history is more the result of an artificial division of critical labour. Fully at home in neither country, many of the expatriates have slipped between the continental divide of North American literary history, a history that has also obscured significant transnational influences and connections. The problem, for instance, with Atwood's survivalist thesis wasn't that it presented an inaccurate claim about Canadian literature. The problem was rather that Atwood's ignorance of *American* literature beyond its canonical touchstones allowed her to conclude that the victims she found in Canadian literature were unique to Canada: that, for instance, Seton's doomed animals were a Canadian invention rather than the product of a continental literary culture with members (and models) from both sides of the border. In the United States, a greater confidence in American literature and its history has until recently meant that American critics and historians have felt even less pressure than Canadians to consider transnational influences, with similar consequences. Herbert Smith's discussion of the 'American girl abroad' motif in popular American novels, for instance, suffers from its omission of Sara Jeannette Duncan's *An American Girl in London*, surely a paradigmatic and, to judge by his descriptions, a more successful example of the genre than those Smith discusses. Ronald Weber's chapter in *Hired Pens* on American writers of the outdoors fails even to mention Seton, for a generation of Americans *the* writer of the outdoors.[6] In both cases, these omissions are the result of long-accepted disciplinary boundaries rather than of chauvinism, but however understandable the cause, the result turns literary history into something other than it really is, something neater but less true.

Apart from the stereotype of the robustly virile Canadian, which created preferential acceptance rates for Canadian contributors to some American magazines, there are no discernible trends in the American reception of the Canadian expatriates: they were received as equals, and until the lowering of the nationalist barrier in the 1960s they were published and discussed alongside American writers. From the beginning, it was a very different story in Canada.

The earliest defining note in Canadian references to their literary expatriates is assertions of their continued loyalty to Canada, assertions that seem all the more anxious for their confidence. When Henry Morgan's *Canadian Men and Women of the Time* first appeared in 1898, for instance, it appended declarations of national loyalty to its expatriate entries with a frequency and phrasing that suggests an answer to a pointed question rather than volunteered information. A sample:

Although living in the U.S., Miss B[rodlique] has a most lively faith in her own country. She is an anti-annexationist, and a believer in 'Home Rule' for Can[ada], with only more amicable commercial relations with the Republic.

Mrs. H[ensley] describes herself as 'a Can[adian] in thought, feeling, and expression.' She is also an Imp[erial] Federationist.

He [Daniel Logan] is a citizen of the republic of Hawaii, but has not waived his native allegiance.

Other examples abound. When the Toronto *Week* reviewed Arthur Wentworth Eaton's *Acadian Legends and Lyrics* in 1889, it assured readers that Eaton's 'heart [is] in the Dominion, though his bodily presence belongs to the literary circle of the American metropolis.' Writing in the *Canadian Magazine*, H.A. Bruce said of Arthur Stringer that 'His work, no matter whereof he writes or sings, is fundamentally and characteristically Canadian.' (Bruce, by this time himself an expatriate, skirted the New York setting of Stringer's recent *Loom of Destiny* by describing it only as a 'series of studies in child life.') One of the few notices of Constance Lindsay Skinner in the Canadian press, a 1913 article in the *Ottawa Evening Citizen*, argued that though all her work had been written and published in the United States, 'she is Canadian above all else, and it is our right to claim her as such.' Perhaps the most self-contradicting reclamation of a Canadian writer occurred in an 1896 *Canadian Magazine* interview with expatriate journalist Eve Brodlique, which opens with a bathetic story of the homesick writer sitting on the steps of her Chicago home, sadly setting off fire-crackers in lone celebration of the Queen's birthday. 'I am sure I now have your attention,' writes the interviewer, 'and that you are as anxious to hear anything more there is to be told of your patriotic little countrywoman as I am to tell it.' This, about a professional journalist who had told her interviewer she left Canada because of the sexism of its newspapers.[7]

Whether their subject was a writer or not, assertions of the enduring Canadianness of successful expatriates had the same two objectives: to assuage fears that migration to the United States was draining Canada of its best citizens, and to assure Canadians that there *was* something 'fundamentally and characteristically Canadian,' something that couldn't be lost by crossing a border. Many of the expatriates participated in this project, especially early in their stateside careers, when the bridges to Canada were still there to risk burning. Sophie Hensley asked Canadians several years after arriving in New York not to forget that Canadian writers who had removed to other countries 'still assert their claim to be sons and daughters of Canada.' Stringer wrote home that 'On the whole the Canadian in New York is not here for the fun of the thing. He has not left his native country for nothing, and feeling that the only compensation for the loss of old friends and old ties is that golden word "Success," he works, in his exile, like a Trojan ...' Desmond Pacey has suggested that the notice in the *Week* denying rumours of Roberts's departure for the States and proclaiming his loyalty to Canada was authorized by Roberts himself, and though there is no evidence to support this, there is no reason to doubt it either.[8]

The most elaborate public statement by one of the New York expatriates on his ties to Canada was Stringer's poem 'The Sons Beyond the Border,' published in a two-page spread in the *Canadian Magazine* for December of 1899. The poem affects to speak for Canada's stateside writers collectively, offering both an explanation for their departure and a promise of their return. Unlike in his prose, Stringer doesn't stress financial motives for the literary exodus, choosing instead to represent it as the natural departure of youth:

But of old it was writ that the Son must turn from the roof of his sires,
In quest what the Morrow demands, and not what his heart desires.
So they who are born of our Homeland, e'en they whom the North gave birth,
Must mingle with sons of the Southlands in the far-off ends of the earth ...

The poem's classical metre and echoes are common in Stringer's poetry, but here they're employed specifically to invoke the exiles of Odysseus and

Aeneas, and thus to lend the Canadian exodus a patina of tragic but noble necessity. Like Hensley, Stringer pleads for Canadians to understand that although their writers reside elsewhere, they remain 'Canadians to the heart-core, Canadian, blood and bone.' For 'all of the gold they lavish' upon them in the south, he says, the exiles need 'the more enduring praise' of their Northern kin, and they pledge to 'work for you, till the name that is ours be yours,' and until the time shall come to 'turn to our Homelands, and some day know our own!'[9]

Stringer returned to the homeland as promised, but later moved back to the States and in 1937 became an American citizen. Palmer Cox also became an American citizen (perhaps to join its militia), as did publishers John W. Lovell and George Doran. After several aborted applications, Seton became an American citizen in 1931 when his lawyer suggested the courts might favour his American wife in their impending divorce. The citizenship decision for many of the New York expatriates isn't known, but for those that are, about an equal number seem to have remained Canadian (that is, British) subjects, a group that included Charles G.D. Roberts, Norman Duncan, and Carman.

Whether they changed their citizenship or not, the facility with which the expatriates met the demands of the American literary market suggests that most would have endorsed Stringer's sense of a shared North American culture. 'We happen to speak the same language,' said Stringer in his 1927 Dominion Day address to the Canadian Club of New York, 'and have to sit through the same atrocious movies; we can claim the same currency and the same chewing gum, the same love of liberty and ice water. We have the same social problems and the same slang; the same political ideals and the same baseball and peanuts and breakfast food and comic strips.'[10] A few turned these shared realities into political convictions, such as Graeme Mercer Adam, who became an advocate for free trade while still in Canada, or Craven Langstroth Betts, who contrarily described himself for Morgan's biography as 'An Annexationist, a Free Trader, a Populist and a Unitarian.' But their political answers aside, the fact of their migration as well as the evidence of their work indicates that the expatriates' pragmatic answer to the 'Canadian Question' was overwhelmingly continentalist, a literary version of free trade that crossed the border without precluding other political options. Nationalist or commercial unionist, annexationist or imperialist, Canada's literary expatriates paid their daily allegiance to transnational literary cultures, not to any nation or any of the projected forms of political union.

The signs of citizenship in one such transnational culture are paradoxically evident in the lyrics of exile produced by virtually all of the expatriate poets. In Carman's 'The Ships of St. John,' for instance, the speaker laments having to leave home for 'far alien countries.' Stringer's 'Northern Pines' expresses the homesickness brought on by a stack of Christmas trees in a city street, while in a later poem, 'The Voyageur on Broadway,' the speaker has packed all through the Northern Barrens, but never seen anything so desolate as New York's 'Babel of Steel / With its thousand towers of stone!' Roberts's 'A Nocturne of Exile' fuses physical exile amid 'the city's endless throng' with spiritual exile, while in Pollock's 'The Lost Trail' the city's 'slimy pavement' and 'yellow gutters' awake 'the desire of a homesick heart' for the northern woods. Some of these were sent home to Canadian magazines, but interestingly, as many were printed or reprinted in American magazines.[11]

There are several possible reasons why these poems found favour with American editors. First, their evocation of home scenes easily accommodated itself to the culture of regionalism, in which the actual region was less important than the fact of region. Second, they weren't the product of imagined emotions or borrowed philosophies; they were, or seemed to be, sincere, and sincerity is an attractive quality to an editor. But third, and I suspect most salient, although invariably uttered by 'Northern' (rarely Canadian) speakers and structured around a north-south if never precisely Canadian-American division, these poems are in fact the product of what was by then a traditional *continental* discourse, namely the criticism of the City. They are nostalgic elegies for the space left behind, yes, but they are also implicitly, and often explicitly, criticisms of the space their speakers now inhabit. As such, far from being alien to New York editors and readers, they were instantly familiar. By the 1890s New York had for half a century been held up as the archetypal unfeeling, overcrowded, immoral metropolis against which poets, novelists, dramatists, and country editors championed the virtues of rural life. According to Herbert Smith, 'A sample listing of the works that satirize New York society in the last half of the nineteenth century and beginning of the twentieth would probably run nearly to book length.' To this list belong these Canadian poems, as well as Stringer's novel *The Silver Poppy*, in which New York's corrupt literary industry sends an English writer home in defeat, or O'Higgins's *Don-A-Dreams*, a romance about the trials of a young Ontario dreamer in 'cold, unfriendly' New York.[12]

That this archetypal city is the focus of the expatriates' literary distress is evident from a case in Frank Pollock's bibliography. In December of 1897, after returning to his desk job in Toronto from a four-month camping and hunting trip in northern Ontario, Pollock privately printed in Toronto a lyric called 'Where I Shall Hunt No More' expressing his regret at the end of the hunting trip and his return to 'the city's reek and fume and thunder.' In the context of its publication, the city in question is clearly Toronto. Six years later, in December of 1903 (at which time Pollock was probably living in New York), Pollock published the same poem in *Everybody's Magazine*, but with some significant changes. He changed the title from 'Where I Shall Hunt No More' to 'The Northern Trail,' sharpening the poem's emphasis from a farewell to hunting to a farewell to hunting in the North. He also replaced two lines in the second stanza,

> Now the hounds run large, but for me no more for ever,
> The fox goes safe and the ducks rise full in view.

with the lines,

> Now the trail leads long, but for me no more forever,
> Through the Northland that I knew.

Again, this change helped shift the focus from hunting to hunting specifically in 'the Northland.' All that remained was to change 'grey' to 'gray' in lines nine and seventeen, publish the revised product in a New York magazine, and a Canadian poem complaining about Toronto's 'reek and fume and thunder' had become an American poem complaining about New York's 'reek and fume and thunder.'[13]

As it turned out, it didn't matter whether the expatriates stayed Canadian at heart or not. During the exodus itself their achievements (as well as the generational bond with a million or so departed friends and relatives) made it expedient for Canadians to celebrate their expatriate writers, but soon after, they and their movement began to be erased from the historical record. In 1913, Thomas Guthrie Marquis concluded his survey of English Canadian literature for the massive *Canada and Its Provinces* series with a brief admission of the extent to which Canadian literature had suffered from expatriation, whether to the States or England. 'In either case,' wrote Marquis, 'these self-expatriated Canadians shape their style and feelings into harmony with their new conditions. They in time lose their Canadian colour and atmosphere and become a literary part of the country in which they have made their home. Parker, Carman, and [Norman] Duncan have lost to a large extent their Canadian identity.'[14] In addition to that factual but misleading neologism 'self-expatriated,' which obscured the causes of the literary exodus with just four letters and a hyphen, this short passage introduced a recurring element into Canadian references to the expatriates: before, when the leading Canadian authors were almost all living in other countries, the task had been to assert that both their identity and their work remained 'fundamentally and character-istically Canadian'; now, with a domestic literary scene finally in place, the task became to deny the Canadian identity of the expatriates, to downplay their achievements, and to celebrate instead those writers who stayed in Canada.

The crystallization of national and anti-American sentiment that followed the outbreak of war in 1914 was no doubt more broadly influential than Marquis's argument in fostering the estrangement of the expatriates, most of whom had moved to a country that dragged its feet on the way to England's aid.[15] Within the nascent field of Canadian literary history, however, Marquis's argument seems to have directly influenced his successor Archibald MacMechan, for whom the series in which Marquis's survey appeared was an 'indispensable storehouse of information' and a 'conspicuous monument of Canadian pride.'

Recalling the emigration of 'men of letters' to the United States in the final chapter of his 1924 *Head-Waters of Canadian Literature*, MacMechan noted that after those 'long lean years,' Canada experienced a period between 1900 and 1914 of prosperity for the nation and best-sellers for its authors. During this period, his book's 'fifth literary movement,' Canadian writers were 'no longer compelled to exile themselves in Boston or New York; they remained at home, and were still able to market their wares outside of Canada to great advantage.' After discussing two examples of this new home-produced success (Ralph Connor and L.M. Montgomery), MacMechan quickly listed the other Canadian novelists of his fifth movement: Basil King, Arthur Stringer, Norman Duncan, Lily Dougall, J. Storer Clouston, W. Albert Hickman, E.W. Thomson, J. Macdonald Oxley, Robert Knowles, Marshall Saunders, and Alice Jones. The problem should be obvious: the chapter argues that Canada's long-awaited literary prosperity came from writers who stayed home, but almost half of MacMechan's examples of domestic literary success were by his own argu-ment expatriates who 'treated non-Canadian themes in their books.'[16] Less obviously, MacMechan also left out of his fifth movement many well-known expatriate Canadian writers of the period, including Robert Barr, Sara Jeannette Duncan, Winnifred Eaton, Gilbert Parker, Harvey O'Higgins, Charles G.D. Roberts, and Ernest Thompson Seton. MacMechan knew of most of these authors, but ignored them or hid them in earlier 'movements.' Roberts, for instance, is part of the Ontario movement, because he once edited a Toronto magazine. Carman appears in the same chapter, presumably because he was related to someone who once edited a Toronto magazine. Like Marquis, MacMechan was concerned at every ripple in his *Head-Waters* to establish the Canadianness of Canadian literature, and such a literature could no longer admit expatriates.

In this first phase of constructing an English Canadian literary tradition the easiest means of removing the expatriates from that tradition was to assert, as Marquis had, that they were no longer real Canadians. At bottom, Marquis's and MacMechan's criterion for a Canadian author was nothing more than residency, what MacMechan dressed up by calling 'birthright.'[17] The problem with using residency as the passport to a national canon is that it's too blunt an instrument: it accepts or rejects categorically, with no allowance for writers or works the canon might like to admit for its own reasons. Especially in the early stages of canon creation, its creators need more flexible tools, criteria that will allow them to select the monuments they want and exclude those they don't. Fame works well enough in the short term: whatever their dignitaries might have said about enriching the 'traditions of our literature,' the main reason Canadians fought to have Carman's body returned home in 1929 was the popularity of his recent reading tours. But over the long haul, fame is an inadequate basis for immortality, and so Canadian canon-builders turned to the concept of *place*, to the requirement that Canadian literature should show the influence of the Canadian environment.

The important to Canadian literary history of what Leon Surette called its 'topocentric axiom' and its origins in European and American models of literary history have been well documented.[18] But perhaps because critics of this concept themselves followed too closely the lead of its European and American critics, they have overlooked some of its specifically Canadian history, namely that in Canada the first and best laboratory for topocentrism was the literary exodus. For the first fifty or so years of its existence in Canada, topocentrism was just a wish: it began life as a nationalist imperative, in for instance D'Arcy McGee's argument that to be distinct from other national literatures, Canadian literature 'must assume the gorgeous coloring and the gloomy grandeur of the forest,' or in Charles Mair's claim that an authentic national literature 'must taste of the wood.'[19] From its beginnings to the end of the nineteenth century all of this was just theory, since there wasn't yet a body of Canadian literature against which to test its validity. That literature finally arrived with Canada's literary expatriates, and after allowing themselves to bask in its glow for a time, Canadian critics used it to hone the definition of Canadian literature by setting its limits. A novel written by a Canadian resident, set in Canadian territory, and published by a Canadian publisher was evidently a Canadian novel: *too* evidently, because such criteria takes in a swath what the canon wants to pick by hand. The writings of the expatriates didn't fit some or all of these basic criteria, and yet there was something Canadian about at least some of it. Sorting through the written products of the exodus helped Canadian critics pin down what that something was, that essential quality that elevated the merely Canadian to the authentically Canadian.

This canonical process worked itself out over decades through anthologies, criticism, and literary awards, beginning with moments like MacMechan's *Head-Waters* and Carman's state funeral and culminating in the English Canadian canon that readers recognize enough to argue about today. Its largest single archive is the *Literary History of Canada*, published in 1965 and updated in 1976. By the 1960s much of the canonical spadework had already been done, so that even with the ambitious reading of general editor Carl F. Klinck and his team, many of the expatriates had long since disappeared from Canada's literary memory and didn't appear in the *History* at all (notably Palmer Cox, Sophie Hensley, and Charles Brodie Patterson), while others were remembered only for their works with Canadian settings or subjects.

In part because of Klinck's decision to delegate the work of writing Canada's literary history by genre rather than by period, the *History* also helped Canadians to forget the literary exodus as a whole: instead of discussing the expatriates as a collective phenomenon, as would presumably have resulted from a chronological approach, the *History* scatters them among its generically organized chapters, making it hard for readers to see them as a group and almost impossible to grasp their historical importance. And in those moments when history did rear its head, in the pages or paragraphs that introduce their lists, Klinck's team downplayed the exodus or found ways around it. Roy Daniells's introduction to the post-Confederation section described the period as the 'Golden Age of high colonialism' and studiously avoided any mention of migration to the United States, literary or otherwise. The chapters on the period's fiction mention several times a literary emigration to large American and English cities, but stress that not all Canadian writers left, and minimize both the problems with the Canadian literary scene and the importance of other scenes by arguing that for young Canadian writers of the period 'much the strongest influence was that of being native to a small town or rural community.'[20]

But if the exodus would seem from the *Literary History of Canada* to have been of little historical importance, its surviving products were of great help to its contributors in their efforts to separate the canonical wheat from the historical chaff. To give some shape to the long list that is 'The Kinds of Fiction, 1880–1920,' for instance, Gordon Roper and his colleagues argued from the outset that what most distinguished Canadian from American and British fiction of the period was the Canadian writers' 'experience of place.'[21] Fiction set in Canada obviously showed this experience, so that gave Roper's team their first and largest 'kind of fiction,' a list that fills seventeen of the chapter's twenty-eight pages. But when it came to sorting through the kinds of fiction *not* set in Canada, the topocentric axiom proved more difficult to deploy, and it's here that the works of the expatriates proved especially useful by helping the contributors separate books that belong to a Canadian tradition from books that belong to a generic tradition, and thus not necessarily Canadian books at all. For example, Arthur Stringer's novel about his boyhood in Ontario, *Lonely O'Malley*, is to the *History* an Ontario and so a Canadian kind of fiction, but his novel about crime in New York, *The Wire Tappers*, is a crime kind of fiction, although Stinson Jarvis's Toronto-set detective novel *Geoffrey Hampstead* is a Canadian kind of fiction. Ralph Connor's novel about religion in an Ontario lumber community (*The Man from Glengarry*) is a Canadian kind of fiction, but Norman Duncan's novel about religion in a Minnesota lumber community (*The Measure of a Man*) is a clergy kind of fiction. Sara Jeannette Duncan's novel about politics in small-town Ontario is a Canadian kind of fiction, but her novels about politics in India and England are a political kind of fiction. They weren't the only test cases, but precisely because the expatriates' books weren't self-evidently Canadian, they provided Canadian critics with something they'd been looking for since before Confederation: a literature upon which to test the topocentric axiom and prove its value.

This process didn't stop with the *Literary History of Canada*. If anything, the *History*'s entrenchment of the importance of 'experience of place' (rendered more memorably by Northrop Frye in the *History*'s conclusion as the riddle 'Where is here?') made it even more necessary to demonstrate this quality in the work of those expatriates whom the canon wished to claim for its own. Because they had each produced a body of early work that offered conspicuous answers to Frye's riddle, the canon had long been attracted to three expatriates in particular: Roberts, Carman, and Seton. Roberts had conveniently repatriated himself by returning to Canada and allowing himself to be knighted before his death, but Carman's and Seton's irritating decision to die on the American side of the border made reclaiming them more of a challenge: their long American residency meant that claiming them for Canada would require not only demonstrating their essential Canadianness, but also explaining or explaining away any dilution of that essence by their years in America.

The fight for Carman began with the rescue of his corpse from the clutches of Mary Perry King and reached its apotheosis in Muriel Miller's 1985 biography, *Bliss Carman: Quest and Revolt*. In her opening chapter, Miller tells the story of six-year-old Bliss and his cousin Charles mutilating the lawn of the Carman family home to build a miniature of the projected Inter-Colonial Railway. For Miller, the stunt and its punishment marked the beginning of the cousins' long friendship, but more important it marked them as Canadians for life. 'That Confederation summer,' she wrote, 'the Canadian dream of a country stretching from sea to sea across a continent became the reality in the minds of both of them that was to keep them Canadian all their lives and was eventually to bring them home in the 1920s from their courtesy-countries, the United States and Britain.' The notion of kindergarten nationalists suggests Miller's ambitions on its own, but what this remark obscures is more revealing: as the rest of her book shows (though never admits), the movements in Carman's life were consistently from north to south, not from 'sea to sea.' To offset her subject's frustrating habit of embarking for Boston or New York rather than Toronto or Vancouver, Miller repeatedly emphasized Canadian and, when those ran out, British influences upon Carman's life and career. Especially, she stressed the importance of his return visits to the Maritimes: Carman may have been forced to live in his 'courtesy-country,' but returning to Canada and spending time in his canoe 'was like recharging a battery.' 'Wherever his wanderings carried him,' Miller concluded, 'there had remained in Carman's work a "mystical essence," a "nascent religious flavour" of his Canadian heritage – that uniqueness which emanates from the spirit of the land itself and is no narrow provincial or racial thing.'[22] Besides its erasure of the many and arguably more profound American influences upon Carman's career, this passage highlights the ultimate goal of Miller's biography: to reclaim Carman not for 'provincial' New Brunswick, but for Canada.

Perhaps chastened by his own autobiographical excesses, Seton's biographers have generally been more objective than Carman's, but he too has excited some over-earnest Canadianization. For Fred Bodsworth in a 1959 *Maclean's* flashback, Seton was a 'restless wanderer,' but his Canadian-acquired love of the outdoors kept luring him back to the frontiers. 'Here,' said Bodsworth, 'he found his real inspiration among birds and animals. And here the fame, fortune and artistic success that had eluded him in the cultural capitals of the world eventually overtook him.' Putting aside his I trust rhetorical suggestion that Paris, New York, and London came looking for Seton in the wilderness ('Mr Seton, I presume?'), Bodsworth, like Miller, aimed to locate his subject's 'real inspiration' in the Canadian landscape and downplay the importance to his work of any international influences or rewards. He was at least willing, however, to discuss Seton's stateside years, which is more than can be said for Magdalene Redekop's *Ernest Thompson Seton*, a short biography for younger readers remarkable mainly for its determination to remove America from Seton's life. Chapters in which Seton is in Manitoba, London, or Paris, for instance, are titled as such, but chapters in which he's in America are titled by non-geographic keys, such as 'The Naturalist as a Young Man,' or 'The Story-Teller,' while his first decisive visit to New York gets a few paragraphs at the end of a chapter called 'Manitoba: The Golden Years.' Most incredibly, Redekop truncates Seton's account of hearing a Voice urging him to leave London and return to the Canadian prairies *and then to move to New York* into a Voice urging him to 'leave London and go to the plains of western Canada,' full stop.[23]

These are scattered examples, meant to suggest the means and the intensity of the desire to repatriate for Canada the right kind of literary ancestors. Not all of the expatriates were reclaimed, however, and before exploring in more detail how the rest were excluded, it's worth asking again why one expatriate author in particular failed to win a place in Canada's memory: Palmer Cox. With the possible exception of Lucy Maud Montgomery, Cox achieved more fame in his day than any other Canadian author before him, or since. And yet today, while every tree, stream, and shack remotely associated with the Anne legend is a designated heritage site, Cox's Brownie Castle is an apartment building, his body lies under a tombstone paid for by American school children, and his name is entirely absent from Canada's literary history. Why? After all, the main reason for Anne's continued popularity isn't her literary but her economic merits, and Cox's Brownies offer as many possibilities as Anne has to exploit the tourist and collector market – the Brownies once adorned everything from lunch boxes to fine china, and there's no reason why they couldn't be doing it still. Further, although Cox became an American citizen, he was born and educated in Canada, and he returned to Canada to build his home: over his life he spent as many or more years in Quebec than Montgomery did in Prince Edward Island. As Cox's American biographer puts it, 'Although Palmer Cox achieved his fame in the United States, he kept returning to Canada. Both countries shaped his career, and to both he belonged.'[24]

I bring up the example of Cox not because I'm especially enamoured of his work, but because for me the comparison to Montgomery puts to rest my own nagging doubt that the real criteria for excluding the expatriates and their work from the Canadian literary tradition was literary quality, or the lack thereof. Both Cox and Montgomery had skill: it takes a rare talent to create characters so many readers embraced. But both are also marred by such descents into cliché and formula that I can neither respond to their work aesthetically nor make an aesthetic judgment between them. Whatever it was that kept Montgomery in the canon and shut Cox out, it wasn't literary greatness.

I can think of three reasons why Canada has remembered Montgomery and forgotten Cox. First, Cox left Canada, and although Montgomery toyed with the idea of moving to the States, she never did, because, she said, of her preference for her island's rural pleasures, but also because the phenomenal success of *Anne* meant that America was uniquely willing to come to her.[25]

Second, Montgomery's Scottish-settled community stayed Scottish, but Cox's Scottish-settled community became a largely Francophone town, and although there were some local efforts in the 1970s by a non-profit group 'qui travaille depuis deux ans à la réévaluation de l'oeuvre de Cox,' I doubt his English-speaking Brownies could ever rank high on Quebec's cultural agenda.[26] Finally, although Cox twice sent his Brownies into Canada, they went as tourists. Unhappily for Cox, his work manifests experience of the wrong kind of place – places urban, modern, and American rather than places rural, quaint, and Canadian.

As Cox's fate suggests, the wrong kind of literary expatriates and the wrong works by the right expatriates were generally excluded from Canadian literature by recourse to the canonical axiom that Canadian writing is informed by the Canadian soil, and that writing severed from that soil ceases to be truly Canadian. Frequently, the corollary suggestion arose that the expatriates did their best work in Canada, and that their American experiences were either of no real importance or, more often, detrimental to their artistic development. For T.G. Marquis, the Manhattan stories in Norman Duncan's *The Soul of the Street* were 'as fine as anything done in the short story in America, and indeed compare favourably with the short-story work of the greatest of British short-story writers.' But the Newfoundland-set *Doctor Luke*, added Marquis, gave Duncan his place in modern literature, and when he turned away from that setting, he 'lost something of his power.' Fifty years later, this kind of judgment had become so internalized in Canadian criticism as to prevent the *Literary History of Canada* from even mentioning *The Soul of the Street*, and to preserve in its place Marquis's argument about the necessity of Duncan's Newfoundland experiences, experiences that according to the *History* 'provided him with feeling and material which brought out his best writing.'[27]

The expatriate this argument hit the hardest was the returned hero himself, Sir Charles G.D. Roberts. As early as the year of Roberts's return, James Cappon argued that Roberts's Canadian nature poems were his most important work, and that the move to New York 'did little for him as a poet.' In mid-century, Desmond Pacey said in his introduction to Roberts's *Selected Poems* that 'as far as his poetry is concerned, these years from 1897 to 1925 are the lost years.' Pacey was especially critical of Roberts's first stateside book of verse: 'If there is a slight decline in *The Book of the Native*, there is a positive descent in *New York Nocturnes*. The poet himself seems conscious of weariness and a lack of true inspiration now that he has left his native Maritimes and become a New York journalist: many of the poems strike the note of ennui and frustration.' Not until after his return to Canada would Roberts enjoy what

Pacey called a 'late revival' of his poetic ability. By 1982, this argument had become so accepted that W.J. Keith could count on everyone present at that year's Roberts Symposium being 'aware' that 1897 marked the end of Roberts's 'extraordinary promise in verse.'[28] It's probably true that Roberts's poetry became less interesting after his move to New York: certainly American critics weren't much kinder to *New York Nocturnes*, and also wished he had stuck to home scenes. But *post hoc* doesn't equal *propter hoc*: the underlying assumption in these judgments isn't that Roberts simply ran out of poetic steam, but that New York itself detrimentally affected his poetry.

Besides a romantic anxiety about the contamination of art by commerce, the recurring suggestion that the expatriates' American experiences blocked or weakened their artistic abilities owes much of its existence to topocentrism's more powerful and pervasive older brother, what Carl Berger called the 'myth of the north.' An especially virulent (and persistent) strain of Canadian nationalism, this myth depends on a racist ideology which argued in its strongest version that northern races were by nature robust, self-reliant, and vigorously moral, while southern races were by nature weak, effeminate, and immoral. In its softer version, the northern or southern climates developed the accompanying characteristics regardless of racial origin. Rooted in age-old racial stereotypes inherited from Europe, and bolstered late in the century by a popularized version of social Darwinism, the myth was first given full voice in Canada by an associate of the Canada First movement, Robert Grant Haliburton, and subsequently manifested itself in discussions of the Canadianness of everything from art to agriculture, history to health.

From its beginnings, the myth provided a basis for anti-Americanism. On the one hand, Canada's northern climate positively shaped the national character and discouraged immigration from weaker southern nations. On the other, America's southern climate negatively shaped its national character and encouraged massive immigration by the weaker races of southern Europe. As one of the myth's most forceful proponents noted thankfully in 1908, Italians, Greeks, Armenians, and Bulgarians were pouring into the United States, but not Canada, and the climate would weed out those few who did slip through because the 'Canadian winter exercises upon the tramp a silent but well-nigh irresistible persuasion to shift to a warmer latitude.' (These words were written by George Parkin, teacher and mentor to two Canadian 'tramps' who had earlier heeded that 'well-nigh irresistible persuasion': Roberts and Carman.)[29] Ironically, the expatriates themselves helped foster this myth. Stringer drew a clear distinction in 'The Sons Beyond the Border' between the hardy northern exiles and the rich but 'feverish' southerners among whom they worked, and although she apologized for her hero, Sara Jeannette Duncan had Lorne

Murchison describe America in his climactic speech in *The Imperialist* as the 'daughter who left the old stock to be the light woman among nations, welcoming all comers, mingling her pure blood, polluting her lofty ideals.'[30]

There is, I think, a more than coincidental similarity between the terms of this nationalist myth and those used to describe the waning of the expatriates' creative powers after their removal to the United States. Where George Parkin said that in the south 'the tendency of the climate is toward deterioration,' Desmond Pacey a half-century later found a 'positive descent' in Roberts's poetry after his move to New York. Where the Toronto *Globe* in 1869 noted the 'effeminacy' engendered by a southern climate, the *Literary History of Canada* regretted that Norman Duncan's American journalism encouraged the 'sentimental' in his work, 'especially when he dealt with "mother love."' Where the *Week* declared in 1889 that Canadians were 'broader shouldered, deeper chested, more heavily built,' than their American neighbours, Pacey in 1950 concluded that Carman's poems 'written under Hovey's influence seem to me to present us with the embarrassing spectacle of an effeminate man flexing his flabby muscles and pounding his skinny chest in public.' And where Canadian ministers decried the loose morality of southern climes, former expatriate Peter McArthur reviewed his old friend Arthur Stringer's *The Prairie Mother* in the *Globe* as 'a little too revealing about the intimacies of women.'[31] The common element in these criticisms is the 'relaxing influence' of a southern climate; repeatedly, Canadian critics represented America as the place where the existing or potential literary virtues of a northern author were corrupted by the insidious softness of southern culture. In a final ironic twist of the cultural screw, the same stereotype that had once given Canadians preferential access to New York editors and publishers had now helped condemn them to obscurity.

More recent Canadian criticism has generally been much more open than its predecessors to discussing American literary connections and influences, a development that dates from conferences on Roberts and Carman at the University of Ottawa in the 1980s, and that continues today.[32] In work specifically on late-nineteenth-century Canadian writers who moved or published south, however, the suggestion has again arisen that the American literary market was responsible for their failure to develop as writers. According to this argument, the economic rewards of publishing in genres familiar to American editors and their readers confined Canadian authors (expatriates or not) to traditional literary vehicles and discouraged them from experimenting with newer or more individual forms. As James Doyle put it in a 1990 essay on Canadian women writers of the period, 'The influence of American editors and critics was probably strong enough to make [Canadian women writers] conform to their expectations willingly, perhaps even with unquestioning acceptance of the literary assumptions involved. Still, one wonders what individual-istic tendencies were suppressed in this authoritarian cultural climate – espe-cially when the authorities were foreign.' Four years later, Carole Gerson agreed, arguing that American market forces encouraged most Canadian women writers of the 1880s and after 'to aim their sights at the popular romantic market rather than the loftier realms of high modernism.'[33] (It isn't entirely accidental that both these essays focus on women writers of the period, but their authors have elsewhere discussed the effect of these market forces on male Canadian writers. I quote from their work on women writers because it happens in both cases to be their latest articulation of the argument.)

There is some truth to this argument, but it overlooks what the preceding chapters have tried to demonstrate: that in several cases Canada's literary expatriates led rather than chased literary markets, that many more helped develop existing literary genres and cultures, and that, for all, the sheer variety of their literary and extra-literary stateside activities (as well as the range of success and failure) makes it difficult to think of them as displaying anything but 'individualistic tendencies.' According to Richard Ohmann, the mass mar-ket to which Doyle and Gerson refer was the product of mutually sustaining objectives in the fields of capital, publishing, and literary labour: Ohmann stresses that he found no evidence of direct collusion between American magazine editors and their advertisers, and little evidence that these editors commissioned or even suggested particular kinds of fiction. Book historian Clarence Karr reports from his study of Arthur Stringer's correspondence with *Saturday Evening Post* editor George Horace Lorimer that although the two frequently argued about the content and Canadian references in Stringer's submissions, Stringer 'appears to have won as often as Lorimer did,' and throughout his career 'maintained a guarded creative independence in spite of his reliance on the [magazine] industry for income.'[34] These findings don't refute the power of the market in which the expatriates worked, but they do suggest that no less than their American counterparts, the expatriates' role in that market was more collaborative than conformist.

My main concern with Doyle's and Gerson's argument, however, is that it could be misinterpreted to suggest that the Canadian literary market would have served the expatriates better – that if they had only stayed home, they would somehow have developed from Victorians into Moderns. As both critics have themselves documented, all evidence points to the contrary. Doyle tells us that aside from two short-lived little magazines in Toronto and Fredericton, *fin de siècle* Canada had no avant-garde literary scene to speak of. Gerson showed in her book on nineteenth-century English Canadian fiction that aside from a brief and qualified enjoyment of American (emphatically not French) realism in the mid-1880s, the taste of Canadian fiction publishers and their readers throughout the 1880s and 1890s ran almost exclusively to light romances. D.M.R. Bentley has recently made the same observation about the Canadian readership for poetry in these years, demonstrating its preference for 'poems of a descriptive and realistic cast whose meaning is relatively accessible and enlightening,' and suggesting that this 'conservative predilection for poetry in the high Romantic-Victorian tradition over poetry in the emerging *symboliste*-Modernist line' helps explain Lampman's relative popularity in Canada of the 1890s and Carman's relative obscurity. American market forces may have impelled Canadian writers towards popular modes, but Canadian market forces gave otherwise inclined Canadian writers little choice but to submit their work elsewhere, or move south and start their own little magazines, as Walter Blackburn Harte did. As late as 1922, expatriate Isabel Paterson complained at length in the New York *Bookman* about the dominance of Canadian fiction by 'machine-made romanticism.' New Canadian writing, warned Paterson, diverged from this formula at its peril. 'As for me,' she said in closing, 'I'm going to write about New York.'[35]

'With Confederation,' wrote Graeme Mercer Adam in 1887, 'Canadian literature burst into blossom, but the fruit, it must be said, has not quite borne out its spring-time promise. For a time literary enterprise felt the glow of national aspiration and the quickening of a new birth. But the flush on its face ere long passed off, and mental activity once more engrossed itself with material affairs.'[36] For Adam and many of his contemporaries, the exodus of Canadian writers in the 1880s and 1890s was a lamentable consequence of this unfulfilled literary promise. But what Adam did not foresee was that the fulfilment of Canada's literary promise *was* the exodus: the 'fruit' he despaired of, to borrow one of his several metaphors, was about to ripen on an American vine.

As Adam and the other expatriates knew only too well, there were few significant literary models and no professional literary community in Canada during the years they came of age. But soon after the exodus began in earnest, young Canadian writers began to come together around the personal, social, and professional addresses of prominent Canadian expatriates. Especially in New York, there were many such addresses: the Robertses' family colony at Miss Kelly's boarding house, for instance; the Art Students' League where Seton, Broughton, Hambidge, and McKellar studied; Erastus Wiman's Canadian Club; Maria's where Carman and Roberts held court; McArthur's offices at *Truth*; or the Fifth Avenue attic of Stringer, O'Higgins, and McFarlane.

Canadian writers and illustrators gathered at these and other New York settings to study, discuss each other's work, curse witless reviewers, borrow and occasionally pay back money, celebrate their successes, and drown their failures. Here, Canadians found literary models: American and English models, to be sure, but also Canadian models, especially the convivial Roberts, 'chief' of New York's Canadian artistic colony, and the aloof Seton, who kept to more elevated circles but whose photograph staring bushily from the city's magazines was by century's end a regular reminder of the success a Canadian could achieve with pen or pencil. Here too, Canadians found living literary communities, social and professional associations of writers and artists whose memberships reached back into Canada. In 1886, the Canadian Club of New York sponsored a series of readings for its more than two hundred members and their guests at the club's East Twenty-ninth Street home by visiting Canadian speakers, including Goldwin Smith, J.W. Bengough, George Stewart Jr, George Grant, and Charles G.D. Roberts. Four years later, Bliss Carman's desk at the New York *Independent* became the focal point of an epistolary exchange of poems and criticisms with Roberts in Windsor and Campbell, Lampman, and Scott in Ottawa. As the editor of the Ottawa poets' letters to Carman comments, 'Collectively, the letters point to an impressive solidarity among the Confederation poets, who truly were a "school" of poets at this time.'[37]

The most tangible evidence of these communities is how much stateside Canadians helped resident as well as expatriate Canadians into American print and American positions. For generations of Canadians, arguably the most important effort of this kind came from the otherwise unsung 'Miss Arbuckle,' the expatriate Islander who convinced her Boston employers to accept a manuscript from an unknown author about a red-haired orphan girl.[38] Bliss Carman published Roberts, Lampman, Campbell, Scott, Parker, and E. Pauline Johnson in the *Independent*, the *Chap-Book*, or both, and during the 1890s reviewed or wrote about Roberts, Lampman, Parker, Seton, Francis Sherman, and Isabella Valancy Crawford for American newspapers and magazines.[39] He pitched Lampman's second book of poems to Stone and Kimball and a collection of McArthur's short stories to Small, Maynard, and helped bring Wolfville native Minnie Prat to New York, where she and her sister established an arts and crafts influenced book binder.[40] Carman was especially active in his support of Parker, whom he met in the summer of 1890 when Parker visited the *Independent* offices during a trip to New York. Shortly afterward the *Independent* published Parker's 'The Patrol of the Cypress Hills,' and other stories followed in the weekly from the collection later issued in London as *Pierre and His People*, which Carman tried (unsuccessfully) to place with American publishers Charles Webster and Company in 1892 and (successfully) with Stone and Kimball in 1894. Sophie Hensley claimed that Parker was 'comparatively unsuccessful in London' until his meeting with Carman, who 'with his usual quiet perspicacity singled him out for special commendation in the columns of the *Independent* and predicted the success that has since so persistently followed him.'[41]

Peter McArthur aggressively published Canadian writers in *Truth* during his editorship of the New York weekly, including Carman, Lampman, Scott, the elder Roberts, and Leacock, as well as illustrators Jay Hambidge and Duncan McKellar. Edwyn Sandys probably had a hand in the many appearances in *Outing* by Canadian authors during his fifteen years on the magazine's editorial staff, especially those by his sister Grace Denison. Charles G.D. Roberts recommended a manuscript (a novel or perhaps stories) by Sophie Hensley to a Boston publisher, introduced Pauline Johnson to New York editors Richard Watson Gilder and Edmund Clarence Stedman, and found positions on New York magazines for his brothers William and Theodore and his son Lloyd.[42] In Boston, Walter Blackburn Harte published Peter McArthur, Susan Frances Harrison, Agnes Maule Machar, and Ethelwyn Wetherald during his tenure as assistant editor of the *New England Magazine* in 1891–3, introduced his sister-in-law Edith Eaton to Americans in his own *Fly Leaf* in 1896, and, after returning to New York, printed work by Carman, Roberts, Wetherald, and Eaton in the *Lotus*, a little magazine published in Kansas City but edited by Harte from New York.

Besides his own work, E.W. Thomson witnessed and undoubtedly influenced the publication of close to two hundred articles, poems, stories, and serialized novels by Canadian authors during his ten years as a revising editor for the *Youth's Companion*, including more than forty appearances by Wetherald, over thirty apiece by Roberts and Lampman, and around a half-dozen each by McArthur, Scott, Pollock, Campbell, Theodore G. Roberts, and Stinson Jarvis. Thomson's special cause was Lampman: he regularly passed Lampman's poems on to Boston reviewers and 'salt[ed] the press with Lampman paragraphs,' and when Stone and Kimball's edition of *Lyrics of Earth* fell through because Lampman couldn't find a Canadian publisher willing to share the costs, Thomson arranged for its publication with Boston's Copeland and Day. He also tried repeatedly to convince his friend to accept a position on the *Companion*, promising him that he 'could make a hit here,' but as the editor of their letters notes, Lampman's career passivity as well as his reluctance to exchange mind-numbing civil service work for mind-numbing editorial work kept him in Ottawa for the few years left in his life.[43]

For every stateside Canadian promoting or influencing another Canadian there were of course more and often more influential relations with American editors and authors. Seton's closest literary friend was Hamlin Garland, whose western regionalism inspired Seton's Woodcraft League. Roberts may have found work for his brothers and son on New York magazines, but it was Frank

Bellamy who brought Roberts himself to the city. Craven Langstroth Betts was closer to Edwin Arlington Robinson than any Canadian in the city known to me, and like Roberts found a mentor in Stedman; Bliss Carman reviewed or wrote about American authors more often than he did Canadian authors. However helped into print by Canadian friends, an extraordinary amount of early Canadian literature would never have existed without Americans such as Herbert Stone, Laurens Maynard, Richard Watson Gilder, or Mary Mapes Dodge. This list could be extended indefinitely: the point is that expatriate Canadians worked within transnational cultures of letters while in most cases maintaining and benefiting from associations with Canadian literary communities. The fact that Arthur Stringer mixed milk-punches for Bliss Carman in a Fifth Avenue flat is, I think, of genuine importance to a revised literary history of Canada, but it doesn't change the fact that Stringer wrote crime stories and Carman wrote poems about vagabonds. What those milk-punches reveal is that the common experience of exile brought together Canadian writers from villages, towns, and cities across central and eastern Canada. Ironically, it took moving to New York to produce the communities of authors necessary to fulfil the literary promise of Confederation.

Although their cause has escaped notice, the effects of Canada's expatriate literary communities are an established landmark in Canadian literary history. As early as 1899, Ontario historian Lawrence J. Burpee took the previous year to mark 'what promises to be the genuine and thorough awakening of the long dormant spirit of Canadian fiction,' an awakening that, though 'largely spontaneous,' seemed to Burpee to be due also to the interest in Canadian fiction created by five well-known writers – all of whom were expatriates.[44] In 1913, Marquis took 1890 as the boundary between the 'more or less provincial' early Canadian writers of fiction, and 'the modern school, influenced by world standards.' Again, of the twelve writers Marquis named as moderns, all of the most familiar names were or had been expatriates.[45] Gordon Roper later quoted this passage from Marquis to introduce his chapter on new fiction in the *Literary History of Canada*, adding in Marquis's support that 'After 1890 the number of Canadians who wrote fiction increased rapidly. The number of volumes of new fiction doubled in the eighties and quadrupled in the nineties.' And once again, of the twenty-seven writers chosen from this field for profiles in the following chapter, better than half, and all but three of the better-known names (Connor, Montgomery, and Leacock), were expatriates. A decade into the new century, the Canadian census confirmed the direction of these observations, reporting 434 'literary and scientific' persons, a marked gain on the 1901 low of 53 for the same category.[46]

The evidence suggests that something resembling Confederation's long-awaited literary promise finally arrived in Canada sometime in the late 1890s – and that it had to go through Customs to get there. On their own, the expatriates probably wrote something more than a third of the literary publications in this period; certainly they represented more than half of its more prolific writers. More important, the expatriates showed Canadian writers and publishers of their generation and the next that Canadians (and Americans) would buy books by Canadian authors. In his history of publishing in Canada, George L. Parker suggests that the string of best-selling books by Canadian authors brought out in the late 1890s and early 1900s by William Briggs of Toronto 'helped turn around the "stigma" of a colonial book, and probably ensured that other books, with equal artistry and smaller sales, would be published.' Six of the nine titles Parker instances as Briggs's decisive best-sellers were by expatriates.[47]

Whatever they might have achieved for themselves, the expatriates had clearly provided an audience and a model for professional authorship in Canada: as Roy Daniells remarked of one, 'The bald fact that Roberts made his living as a writer becomes a mark to shoot at.' Canadian readers didn't change their habits overnight: American authors continued to lead the country's best-seller lists, with British authors close behind.[48] But in numbers that would increase throughout the century, Canadians now appeared on these lists as well, and – harder to measure but of more lasting importance – borrowed from these successes the confidence and the readers necessary to attempt literary innovations as well as imitations.[49] Not all of the models for these changes were expatriates: Ralph Connor's meteoric success proved that Canada could produce and retain a best-selling novelist, and ten years later L.M. Montgomery provided another prominent example. But most successful Canadian authors of the 1890s and 1900s, and almost all from that first important decade, were living in other countries.

The influence of the expatriate model is also evident in the next generation of Canadian poets. But for poets, it was the cosmopolitanism of the expatriates more than their status as professional writers that provided an important if unacknowledged precedent. As has often been remarked, the first generation of modern Canadian poets defined themselves as such by rejecting any connection between themselves and earlier Canadian literature: young Canadian poets of his generation, wrote Leo Kennedy in 1928, had 'no worthwhile tradition of their own,' and were therefore 'inclined, and wisely, to look abroad for that which will influence them.'[50] The irony here, one lost on Kennedy and most of his generation, was that by 'looking abroad' the modernists were following the example if not the aesthetic of the previous generation of Canadian writers. By participating in international cultures of letters, by writing and publishing in the literary centres of their world, and by achieving the recognition of their American and English contemporaries, the expatriate poets of the 1880s and 1890s provided the early modernists with a domestic model of precisely the cosmopolitanism to which they aspired – which, as much as their no longer fashionable romanticism, perhaps explains why they and their contemporaries were rejected so strenuously. As the poet and critic A.J.M. Smith argued after the heat of the modernist revolt had abated, the achievement of Roberts, Carman, Lampman, and Scott was not that they had produced an especially Canadian poetry, but rather that they had 'showed that Canada could take her place in the main stream of American and English culture.'[51] Allowing for Smith's forgivable prejudice for poetry, this demonstration of literary maturity is the legacy not just of these four poets, but of the literary exodus in which in they all participated.

In the early 1990s, English Canadian literature took a transnational or what some see as a postnational turn, a shift visible in the settings and audiences of its writers and the methods and questions of its critics. Some observers celebrated Canadian literature's coming-of-age, its entry onto the world stage of international book clubs, prizes, and film deals. Others lamented the demise of an authentically national literature, most passionately Stephen Henighan in *When Words Deny the World*. But as Robert Lecker pointed out in a special, millennium issue of *Essays in Canadian Writing* that attempted (again) to answer Frye's where-is-here riddle, many of those declaring the arrival of a postnational Canadian literature seem unaware that it has been heralded before, that here as elsewhere literature's national-transnational pendulum has always swung with the needs of the state.[52]

What Canada's literary exodus of the 1880s and 1890s should tell us is that the shifting political imperatives of their country aside, Canadian writers have been *practising* transnationalism since before there was a Canadian literature. Literary cosmopolitanism didn't arrive in Canada with *The English Patient*, any more than globalization arrived with the internet. Globalization is not a uniquely postmodern phenomenon: it can be difficult to see in some periods in history, because it doesn't progress evenly, but waxes and wanes, accelerating in diasporic, cosmopolitan moments like the literary exodus and decelerating in periods of isolationism and nationalism. In predictably dialectical fashion, globalization caused its own temporary disappearance from the stage of Canadian literary history by creating the impetus for a fiercely defended national literature. Canadians wouldn't have wanted Carman's body back if its owner hadn't left in the first place.

The national literature of Canada has received a great deal of attention, while its transnational origins have not. I have tried to suggest the reasons for this, reasons I believe fall largely under the often-paired rubrics of Canadian nationalism and anti-Americanism. To admit that Canadian literature grew up thinking continentally would be to admit that Canada has derived an essential part of its identity from its continental heritage, and that's not an admission Canadian critics have always wanted to make.

Themselves a product of that continental heritage, the expatriates of the 1880s and 1890s provided Canada with models of literary success and in so doing enabled the development of a recognizably distinct national literature with its own canon and its own set of values, however contested. Instead of being remembered for that contribution, however, most have been consciously removed from Canadian literary history – perhaps necessarily. Gradually, Canadian literature became Canadian literature through its renunciation of its expatriate stage: the selective denials and assertions of the Canadianness of the expatriates were exercises in canon formation, in Canadian critics feeling their way towards what the Canadian identity should be, and what a Canadian literature should look like. In order for Canadian literature to reach its adulthood, it had to rewrite its adolescence.

Notes

Introduction

1 *New York World* quoted in Muriel Miller, *Bliss Carman: Quest and Revolt* (St John's, NF: Jesperson Press, 1985), 154, n.d., probably February or March 1896; *The Selected Journals of L.M. Montgomery*, ed. Mary Rubio and Elizabeth Waterston (Toronto: Oxford University Press, 1987), 2:35; Pound quoted in Humphrey Carpenter, *A Serious Character: The Life of Ezra Pound* (London: Faber & Faber, 1988), 150.
2 'Bliss Carman, Poet, Drops Dead in Home,' *New York Times*, 9 June 1929, 27.
3 Roberts to Lorne Pierce, 17 Sept. 1935, *The Collected Letters of Charles G.D. Roberts*, ed. Laurel Boone (Fredericton, NB: Goose Lane Editions, 1989), 498.
4 'To Honor Bliss Carman,' *New York Times*, 10 June 1929, 27.
5 'The Poet's Ashes,' *Hamilton (Ontario) Herald*, 14 June 1929, 4; Mary Perry King to Lorne Pierce, 21 June 1929, Lorne Pierce Papers, B003.F006.I004, Queen's University Archives, Kingston, ON.
6 Pierce to Mackenzie King, 11 Sept. 1930, William Lyon Mackenzie King Fonds, Series J1, National Archives of Canada; Roberts to Nathaniel Benson, 27 July 1929, *Letters of Charles G.D. Roberts*, 383. 'As you have doubtless seen by the papers': see, for instance, 'Bliss Carman's Ashes to Be Brought Home,' *Toronto Globe*, 23 July 1929, 24.
7 King to Pierce, 15 Aug. 1929, Pierce Papers, B003.F006.I013, Queen's University Archives; 'Bliss Carman Memorial,' *Saturday Night*, 23 Aug. 1930, 15.
8 John Richardson, *Eight Years in Canada* (1847; Toronto: Johnson Reprint Corporation, 1967), 107.
9 Canada, Dept. of Agriculture, *Census of Canada, 1880–81* (Ottawa: Maclean, Roger, 1882–5), 2:316; idem, *Census of Canada, 1890–91* (Ottawa: S.E. Dawson, 1893–7), 2:189; Canada, Census and Statistics Office, *Occupations of the People*,

Bulletin 11 of the 1901 Census (Ottawa: C.H. Parmelee, 1910), 12; idem, *Fifth Census of Canada, 1911* (Ottawa: C.H. Parmelee [vols. 1–3] and J. de L. Taché [vols. 4–6], 1912–15), 6:4–5. These figures are summarized, with minor differences, in *Fifth Census* 6:8–9.

10 Two caveats must be appended to Adams's number, the first upward and the second downward. First, like most works of its kind, his dictionary only lists authors of books; Canadian writers in the United States at this time who had only achieved periodical publication would not have been considered. Second, Adams does not distinguish between the kind or merit of a writer: to the *Dictionary*, Bliss Carman is an American author, and so is William Fletcher MacNutt, a Nova Scotia–born San Francisco physician who authored *Diseases of the Kidney and Bladder*. I suspect, though, that the forty or so Canadian-born professors, physicians, clergymen, et cetera whom Adams includes as 'authors' would be more than compensated for by those Canadian expatriates who had not yet achieved book publication or come to his attention.

11 Leon E. Truesdell, *The Canadian Born in the United States: An Analysis of the Statistics of the Canadian Element in the Population of the United States, 1850 to 1930* (New Haven: Yale University Press, 1943), 213.

12 M.F. Libby, 'Canadian Literature,' *Week* (Toronto), 3 Mar. 1893, 318; Archibald Lampman, 'At the Mermaid Inn,' *Globe* (Toronto), 4 Mar. 1893, 6; 'Don't Let the Yankees Have Our Poet,' *Toronto World*, 2 Jan. 1892, 4, reprinted in *An Annotated Edition of the Correspondence Between Archibald Lampman and Edward William Thomson (1890–1898)*, ed. Helen Lynn (Ottawa: Tecumseh Press, 1980), 220–2.

13 Sophie Almon Hensley, 'Canadian Writers in New York,' *Dominion Illustrated Monthly* (Montreal and Toronto), May 1893, 195; Frank L. Pollock, 'Canadian Writers in New York,' *Acta Victoriana* (Victoria College, University of Toronto), Apr. 1899, 434, 436; Arthur Stringer, 'Canadian Writers Who Are Winning Fame in New York,' *Montreal Herald*, 2 Mar. 1901, sec. 2, 11.

14 Thomson to Lampman, [July?] 1891 and 24 May 1892, *Correspondence Between Lampman and Thomson*, 8, 42.

15 Marshall Saunders, 'No Place Like Home,' *Halifax Herald*, 10 Aug. 1895, quoted in Gwendolyn Davies, 'The Literary "New Woman" and Social Activism in Maritime Literature, 1880–1920,' in *Separate Spheres: Women's Worlds in the 19th-Century Maritimes*, ed. Janet Guildford and Suzanne Morton (Fredericton, NB: Acadiensis, 1994), 246.

16 William S. Rossiter, 'Printing and Publishing,' in *Twelfth Census of the United States, Taken in the Year 1900*, vol. 9 (Washington, DC: U.S. Census Office, 1902), 1057, 1084.

17 G. Mercer Adam, 'An Outline History of Canadian Literature,' in *An Abridged History of Canada*, by William H. Withrow (Toronto: William Briggs, 1887), 221;

Thomas D'Arcy McGee, 'The Mental Outfit of the New Dominion,' *Montreal Gazette*, 5 Nov. 1867 (Ottawa: CIHM, 1981), microfiche, p. 6; Walter Blackburn Harte, quoted in the *Week* (Toronto), 12 Feb. 1892, 172.

18 Sara Jeannette Duncan, 'American Influence on Canadian Thought,' *Week* (Toronto), 7 July 1887, 518.

19 T.S. Eliot, 'Tradition and the Individual Talent,' in *Selected Essays, 1917–1932* (London: Faber & Faber, 1932), 15.

20 G.M. Fairchild Jr, 'The Canadian Club,' in *Canadian Leaves: History, Art, Science, Literature, Commerce: A Series of New Papers Read Before the Canadian Club of New York*, ed. Fairchild (New York: N. Thompson, 1887), 288.

21 Mitchell Kennerley, 'Kennerley on Carman,' ed. H. Pearson Gundy, *Canadian Poetry: Studies, Documents, Reviews* 14 (1984): 72; Roberts quoted in Pollock, 'Canadian Writers,' 435.

22 Pollock, 'Canadian Writers,' 434.

23 Lawrence J. Burpee, 'Recent Canadian Fiction,' *Forum* (New York), Aug. 1899, 754; CIHM Progress Report, *Facsimile* 13 (May 1995): 16. The Institute's 1900 to 1920 collection only includes Canadian imprints, but its pre-1900 collection includes titles published in Canada and titles written by Canadians but published elsewhere, the latter a large number because of the same impediments to domestic publication that caused the exodus. The percentage of language and literature titles among its pre-1900 collection of 'Canadiana' is therefore artificially high, and the increase of these titles even greater than its figures indicate.

24 Thomas Guthrie Marquis, 'Crude Criticism,' *Week* (Toronto), 6 Mar. 1896, 350–1; idem, 'English-Canadian Literature,' in *Canada and Its Provinces*, ed. Adam Shortt and Arthur G. Doughty, vol. 12 (Toronto: Glasgow, Brook, 1914), 588–9.

Chapter 1: Lamentations

1 S. Morley Wickett, 'Canadians in the United States,' *Political Science Quarterly* 21, no. 2 (1906): 202; Herbert N. Casson, 'The Canadians in the United States,' *Munsey's Magazine*, July 1906, 486.

2 G.E. Jackson, 'Emigration of Canadians to the United States,' *Annals of the American Academy of Political and Social Science* 107 (1923): 28; Marcus Lee Hansen, *The Mingling of the Canadian and American Peoples*, Volume 1, *Historical* (New Haven: Yale University Press, 1940), 183. See also Randy William Widdis, *With Scarcely a Ripple: Anglo-Canadian Migration into the United States and Western Canada, 1880–1920* (Montreal and Kingston: McGill-Queen's University Press, 1998), esp. 64–5.

3 Goldwin Smith, *Canada and the Canadian Question* (Toronto: Hunter, Rose, 1891), 233.

4 John A. Macdonald, House of Commons, *Debates,* 7 Mar. 1878, 854.

5 June Callwood, *The Naughty Nineties, 1890–1900,* Canada's Illustrated Heritage Series (Toronto: Natural Science of Canada, 1977), 37.

6 J.H.S., 'Emigration of the Young Men of Canada to the United States,' *Week* (Toronto), 8 May 1884, 361. J.H.S. may be James Henry Stevenson (1860–1919), an Ontario-born clergyman who himself emigrated in 1893 to become professor of Hebrew at Vanderbilt University in Nashville, Tennessee.

7 *Week,* 15 Nov. 1889, 787; K.L. Jones, 'Causes of the Canadian Exodus,' *Week,* 11 Apr. 1890, 293; Redfern [pseud.], letter, *Week,* 1 Aug. 1890, 554.

8 Samuel E. Moffett, *The Americanization of Canada* (1907; Toronto: University of Toronto Press, 1972), 13.

9 Fairchild, *Canadian Leaves,* 284; Truesdell, *Canadian Born in the United States,* 35.

10 Truesdell, *Canadian Born in the United States,* 44. French-Canadian emigration to the United States peaked earlier than English-Canadian emigration (probably by 1880, and certainly by 1890), and by the 1910s had begun to reverse itself, with more French Canadians returning from than emigrating to the States. For a bibliography of 'la diaspora,' see Pierre Anctil, *A Franco-American Bibliography: New England* (Bedford, NH: National Materials Development Center, 1979).

11 Moffett, *Americanization of Canada,* 14.

12 Notes and Announcements, *Publishers' Circular* (London), 16 Feb. 1895, 181–2.

13 For the printing industry figures in this paragraph, see Canada, *Fourth Census of Canada, 1901* (Ottawa: S.E. Dawson, 1902–6), 3:290–1, and *Fifth Census,* 6:6–7.

14 George L. Parker, *The Beginnings of the Book Trade in Canada* (Toronto: University of Toronto Press, 1985), 166–7.

15 Ibid., 195.

16 Lampman to E.W. Thomson, 31 Mar. 1896, *Correspondence Between Lampman and Thomson,* 172; Duncan to John Willison, 18 Sept. 1902, *The Imperialist,* ed. Thomas E. Tausky, Canadian Critical Editions (1904; Ottawa: Tecumseh Press, 1996), 306.

17 Harte quoted in the *Week,* 12 Feb. 1892, 172; Harvey O'Higgins, *Don-A-Dreams: A Story of Love and Youth* (New York: Century, 1906), 158.

18 James Doyle, *The Fin de Siècle Spirit: Walter Blackburn Harte and the American/ Canadian Literary Milieu of the 1890s* (Toronto: ECW Press, 1995), 86.

19 Casson, 'Canadians in the United States,' 478.

20 George Stewart Jr, 'Views of Canadian Literature,' letter, *Week,* 30 Mar. 1894, 415.

21 Listed in R.G. Moyles, 'Young Canada: An Index to Canadian Materials in Major British and American Juvenile Periodicals, 1870–1950,' *CCL* 78 (1995): 7–63.

22 Carl F. Klinck, *Wilfred Campbell: A Study in Late Provincial Victorianism*

(Toronto: Ryerson, 1942), 84; Carole Gerson, 'Canadian Women Writers and American Markets, 1880–1940,' in *Context North America: Canadian/U.S. Literary Relations*, ed. Camille R. La Bossière (Ottawa: University of Ottawa Press, 1994), 112.

23 Sara Jeannette Duncan, Saunterings, *Week*, 30 Sept. 1886, 707; Harte quoted in the *Week*, 12 Feb. 1892, 172; Robert Barr, 'Literature in Canada,' *Canadian Magazine*, Nov. 1899, 4.

24 Canada, *Census of Canada, 1890–91*, 2:viii–x; U.S., Census Office, *Twelfth Census of the United States, Taken in the Year 1900* (Washington, DC, 1901–3), 2:xcviii. Both censuses define as literate those individuals ten years of age or over who can read and write in the language they ordinarily speak.

25 Parker, *Beginnings of the Book Trade*, 131, 145; John A. Wiseman, 'Silent Companions: The Dissemination of Books and Periodicals in Nineteenth-Century Ontario,' *Publishing History* 12 (1982): 26, 31.

26 Heather Murray, *Come, Bright Improvement! The Literary Societies of Nineteenth-Century Ontario* (Toronto: University of Toronto Press, 2002), 78.

27 See Carl Spadoni, 'The Dutch Piracy of *Gone With the Wind*,' *Papers of the Bibliographical Society of America* 84, no. 2 (1990): 131–50. Thanks to Eli MacLaren for alerting me to this article.

28 Parker, *Beginnings of the Book Trade*, 211.

29 'No Interference: Sir Charles H. Tupper on the Copyright Question,' *Toronto Globe*, 10 Sept. 1895.

30 Hensley, 'Canadian Writers,' 197.

31 'Canadian Literature,' *Week*, 4 July 1890, 486.

32 Stringer, 'Canadian Writers'; Marshall Saunders, Address to the Women Teachers Association of Toronto, 26 Nov. 1921, corrected TS, Vaughan Memorial Library, Acadia University, Wolfville, NS; Constance Lindsay Skinner to Snowdon Dunn Scott, 8 Jan. 1920, quoted in Jean Barman, *Constance Lindsay Skinner: Writing on the Frontier* (Toronto: University of Toronto Press, 2002), 225; Thomas O'Hagan, 'The Future of Canadian Poetry,' letter, *Week*, 24 July 1896, 834–5.

33 Ernest Thompson Seton, *Trail of an Artist-Naturalist: The Autobiography of Ernest Thompson Seton* (New York: Charles Scribner's Sons, 1940), 63; Marian Fowler, *Redney: A Life of Sara Jeannette Duncan* (Toronto: Anansi, 1983), 26; Barman, *Constance Lindsay Skinner*, 24.

34 McGee, 'Mental Outfit of the New Dominion,' 2; Duncan, 'American Influence,' 518.

35 'Canadian Publications and Native Intelligence,' *Canada Bookseller* (Toronto), Apr. 1871, 22.

36 *Ottawa Free Press*, 20 Sept. 1905, quoted in Moffett, *Americanization of Canada*, 96.

37 *The Canadian Centennial Guide to New York and Philadelphia by Thirty Different Routes ... from Every Large Town in Canada* (Brockville, ON: Leavitt and Southworth, Printers, 1876).
38 James W. Bell, 'The Future of Canada,' *Week*, 26 July 1889, 537.
39 Sara Jeannette Duncan, *Cousin Cinderella*, Early Canadian Women Writers Series (1908; Ottawa: Tecumseh Press, 1994), 51, 213.
40 'An Appeal for Justice,' *Toronto Evening Telegram*, 23 Jan. 1889.
41 Duncan Campbell Scott, 'Canadian Feeling Toward the United States,' *Bookman* (New York), June 1896, 335; Scott to Edgar, 23 Feb. 1905, *More Letters of Duncan Campbell Scott*, ed. Arthur S. Bourinot (Ottawa: A.S. Bourinot, 1960), 27.
42 Moffett, *Americanization of Canada*, 102–3.
43 Quoted in H.F. Angus, ed., *Canada and Her Great Neighbour: Sociological Surveys of Opinions and Attitudes in Canada Concerning the United States*, (Toronto: Ryerson; New Haven: Yale University Press, 1938), 29.
44 Scott, 'Canadian Feeling Toward the United States,' 334; Moffett, *Americanization of Canada*, 114.
45 *Toronto Globe*, 15 Aug. 1905, quoted in Moffett, *Americanization of Canada*, 93.
46 For the development in nineteenth-century Canada of continental frames of reference in the natural sciences as well as in agriculture, forestry, journalism, literature, history, and social reform see Allan Smith, 'The Continental Dimension in the Evolution of the English-Canadian Mind,' in *Canada: An American Nation?* (Montreal and Kingston: McGill-Queen's University Press, 1994).
47 Thomas O'Hagan, 'Canadian Students at Cornell,' *Week*, 15 Dec. 1893, 62–3; *Canadian Club of Harvard University* (Cambridge, MA, 1890).
48 Casson, 'Canadians in the United States,' 477; Truesdell, *Canadian Born in the United States*, 213.
49 News Notes, *Bookman* (New York), Oct. 1895, 93–4.
50 U.S., Census Office, *Twelfth Census*, 7:13; Wickett, 'Canadians in the United States,' 199.
51 Rossiter, 'Printing and Publishing,' 1043.
52 An Outsider, 'A Comparison: An Epistle to the Canadian People by a New York Journalist,' *Week*, 6 Dec. 1895, 31.
53 Hansen, *Mingling of the Canadian and American Peoples*, 261; Sophie Almon Hensley, 'Canadian Nurses in New York,' *Dominion Illustrated Monthly*, Apr. 1892, 161–70.
54 Pollock, 'Canadian Writers,' 434.
55 Duncan quoted in Marjory Lang, *Women Who Made the News: Female Journalists in Canada, 1880–1945* (Montreal and Kingston: McGill-Queen's University Press, 1999), 38–9; Brodlique quoted in Mary Temple Bayard, 'Eve Brodlique,' *Canadian Magazine*, Oct. 1896, 516–17.

56 Statistics from U.S., Census Office, *Twelfth Census*, 2:cxliv (journalists and authors) and 7:13 (printers) and Canada, *Fifth Census*, 6:6–9, and *Occupations of the People*, 12 (authors only).

57 Truesdell, *Canadian Born in the United States*, 207, 209, 213. Truesdell's figures are from the first American enumeration of foreign-born white workers by occupation, recorded as part of the 1910 census but not published.

58 *Canadian American* quoted in Hansen, *Mingling of the Canadian and American Peoples*, 206; U.S., Census Office, *Twelfth Census*, 1:796; Rossiter, 'Printing and Publishing,' 1051, 1084.

59 Our New York Letter, *Prince Edward Island Magazine*, Apr. 1899, 82; Gary Burrill, *Away: Maritimers in Massachusetts, Ontario, and Alberta: An Oral History of Leaving Home* (Montreal and Kingston: McGill-Queen's University Press, 1992), 4–5; Truesdell, *Canadian Born in the United States*, 35.

60 Rossiter, 'Printing and Publishing,' 1057, 1070–1.

61 The best overall history of American magazines remains Frank Luther Mott's five-volume *History of American Magazines* (Cambridge: Harvard University Press, Belknap Press, 1930–68): see, for this period, vol. 4, esp. chaps. 1 and 2. For a more recent analysis along Marxist lines, see Richard Ohmann, *Selling Culture: Magazines, Markets, and Class at the Turn of the Century* (London: Verso, 1996).

62 Duncan, 'American Influence on Canadian Thought,' 518; Pollock, 'Canadian Writers,' 438–9; Stringer, 'Canadian Writers.'

Chapter 2: Agents of Modernism

1 Mott, *History of American Magazines*, 4:2; Ohmann, *Selling Culture*; T.J. Jackson Lears, *No Place of Grace: Antimodernism and the Transformation of American Culture, 1880–1920* (1981; Chicago: University of Chicago Press, 1994), 4, 20.

2 'Inside a New York Newspaper Office,' *Week* (Toronto), 21 Feb. 1884, 183; 'Reporting in New York,' *Week*, 13 Mar. 1884, 233–4. John Coldwell Adams attributes the second of these sketches, like the first credited only to 'R.,' to Charles G.D. Roberts ('A Preliminary Bibliography,' *The Sir Charles G.D. Roberts Symposium*, ed. Glenn Clever [Ottawa: University of Ottawa Press, 1984], 239), but this seems unlikely: their styles are very different, and 'R.' knows his subject much more intimately than Roberts could have.

3 Lincoln Steffens, *The Autobiography of Lincoln Steffens* (New York: Harcourt, Brace, 1931), 314.

4 Hensley, 'Canadian Writers,' 204. Herbert Sinclair may be the J.H. Sinclair who contributed 'Canadians in New York' to the Toronto *Week* of 19 August 1886, an article partly about the founding of the city's Canadian Club. J.H. Sinclair is listed as a resident member of the club for 1887 (Canadian Club, *Constitution and By-*

Laws of the Canadian Club, With a List of Its Officers and Members [New York, 1887]).

5 'Acton Davies Dead,' *New York Times*, 13 June 1916, 11. See also Literary and Personal Gossip, *Week* (Toronto), 16 Oct. 1891, 740; Richard Harding Davis, 'Our War Correspondents in Cuba and Puerto Rico,' *Harper's Magazine*, May 1899, 940; 'Actress's Husband and Critic Engage in Fight,' *New York Times*, 20 Jan. 1904, 1; and 'Death of Acton Davies,' *New York Dramatic Mirror*, 17 June 1916, 8.

6 Sydney Reid, 'New York's Early History,' letter, *New York Times*, 13 Nov. 1914, 10. See also Henry James Morgan, ed., *The Canadian Men and Women of the Time: A Hand-Book of Canadian Biography*, 2nd ed. (Toronto: William Briggs, 1912); *Who's Who in New York City and State* (New York: L.R. Hammersly, 1904); and Raymond A. Schroth, *The 'Eagle' and Brooklyn: A Community Newspaper, 1841–1955*, Contributions in American Studies, no. 13 (Westport, CT: Greenwood Press, 1974).

7 Sydney Reid, 'A Profitable Journey,' letter, *New York Times* 12 July 1933, 16; 'Sydney Reid Dies; Journalist Was 78,' *New York Times*, 22 July 1936, 19.

8 Herbert N. Casson, *The Story of My Life* (London: Efficiency Magazine, 1931), 60–1.

9 Mott, *History of American Magazines*, 4:38–41, 120; Arthur Stringer, 'Wild Poets I've Known: Bliss Carman,' *Saturday Night*, 1 Mar. 1941, 29.

10 G. Mercer Adam, 'Trade Relations with the United States,' letter, *Week*, 28 Dec. 1888, 58; idem, review of *Tangled Ends*, by Alice Maud Ardagh, *Week*, 4 Jan. 1889, 74; idem, 'Literature, Nationality, and the Tariff,' *Week*, 27 Dec. 1889, 59–60.

11 Henry James Morgan, ed., *The Canadian Men and Women of the Time: A Hand-Book of Canadian Biography* (Toronto: William Briggs, 1898).

12 Madeleine B. Stern, ed., *Publishers for Mass Entertainment in Nineteenth-Century America* (Boston: G.K. Hall, 1980), 309.

13 Hensley, 'Canadian Writers,' 198; John Tebbel, *The Expansion of an Industry, 1865–1919*, vol. 2 of *A History of Book Publishing in the United States*, 4 vols. (New York: R.R. Bowker, 1972–81), 350–2.

14 See Mott, *History of American Magazines*, 4:54–5, and the entry under *Modern Culture* in the *Union List of Serials*.

15 Morgan, *Canadian Men and Women of the Time*, 2nd ed.

16 G. Mercer Adam, 'An Interregnum in Literature,' *Week*, 12 June 1884, 439.

17 E.M. Pomeroy, *Sir Charles G.D. Roberts: A Biography* (Toronto: Ryerson Press, 1943), 150; John Coldwell Adams, *Sir Charles God Damn: The Life of Sir Charles G.D. Roberts* (Toronto: University of Toronto Press, 1986), 77.

18 *Literary Digest*, 2 Jan. 1904; Mott, *History of American Magazines*, 4:569–79.

19 Pollock, 'Canadian Writers,' 436; Roberts to Hamilton Wright Mabie, 24 Jan.
    1906, to Charles Bruce, 25 Jan. 1928, and to Harrison Smith Morris, 4 Nov. 1932,
    Letters of Charles G.D. Roberts, 278, 364, 430; 'W.C. Roberts Dies; Ex-Magazine
    Aide,' *New York Times*, 23 Nov. 1941, 51.
20 Roberts to Carman, 1 Mar. 1890, *Letters of Charles G.D. Roberts*, 115. The poem
    was 'Sicilian Octave,' so far as I know unpublished.
21 'Mrs. W.C. Roberts, Writer, Editor, 85,' obituary, *New York Times*, 15 Oct. 1956,
    25.
22 'Syndicate Buys Garden,' *New York Times*, 3 Jan. 1917, 4; 'W.C. Roberts Dies.'
23 Mary Roberts to Charles G.D. Roberts, 4 October 1941, quoted in Adams, *Sir
    Charles God Damn*, 201–2; 'Mrs. W.C. Roberts.'
24 Van. [pseud.], 'Jokes and How They Make Them,' *Saturday Night*, 20 Dec. 1890,
    7; Modris Eksteins, *Rites of Spring: The Great War and the Birth of the Modern
    Age* (Toronto: Lester & Orpen Dennys, 1989).
25 Morgan, *Canadian Men and Women of the Time*.
26 Eastern Letter, *Bookman* (New York), July 1897, 441.
27 Sanford to Rev. W.A. Laughlin, 5 Apr. 1909, M. Bourchier Sanford fonds, F 1104,
    Archives of Ontario, Toronto, Ont. See also Sanford to Laughlin, 20 Jan. 1909,
    ibid. (Thanks to Carole Gerson for alerting me to these letters and for sharing her
    notes on Sanford from her database on Canada's Early Women Writers.) Sanford
    eventually recovered her strength and with it her literary ambitions, writing at least
    five more novels between 1913 and 1930, all published in London, England.
28 Hensley, 'Canadian Writers,' 204; *Life* editor quoted by Daniel McArthur in Alec
    Lucas, *Peter McArthur* (Boston: Twayne, 1975), 105.
29 William Arthur Deacon, *Peter McArthur* (Toronto: Ryerson Press, 1923), 10.
30 Hensley, 'Canadian Writers,' 204; Van., 'Jokes and How They Make Them.' The
    timing of this and other articles by 'Van' in *Saturday Night* invite identification
    with Duncan McKellar, by then the weekly's assistant editor.
31 Lucas, *Peter McArthur*, 105.
32 'McArthur-Waters,' *New York Times*, 12 Sept. 1895, 2. Ill health later forced
    Duncan McKellar to leave New York and return to his home in Penetanguishene
    on Georgian Bay, where he died of consumption in 1899.
33 *Truth*, 31 Aug. 1895, 2. For histories of *Truth* see Mott, *History of American
    Magazines*, 4:83–4, and Richard Samuel West's essay at http://www.oldmagazines
    .com/private/history6.htm.
34 Stringer, 'Canadian Writers.'
35 Jay Hambidge, *The Elements of Dynamic Symmetry* (New York: Brentano's,
    1926).
36 Gerald Wade, 'When Bliss Carman Wrote "Advertising,"' *Western Home Monthly*
    (Winnipeg), Apr. 1930, 30.

37 Christian Gauss, 'The Summer's Vintage of Verse,' *New York Times Saturday Review of Books*, 10 Aug. 1907, 492; William Morton Payne, 'Recent Verse,' *Dial*, 16 Aug. 1907, 93.

38 Peter McArthur, 'To My Fashionable Fiancée,' in *The Prodigal and Other Poems* (New York: Mitchell Kennerley, 1907), 55.

39 I date Cox's departure from Canada by his final entry in *Squibs of California*, a date he calls 'the anniversary of my departure from my native fields' (486). For details of Cox's life not otherwise cited see Roger W. Cummins's *Humorous but Wholesome: A History of Palmer Cox and the Brownies* (Watkins Glen, NY: Century House, 1973).

40 Joyce Kilmer, 'Palmer Cox of Brownie Castle Comes to Town,' *New York Times*, 16 Jan. 1916, sec. 4, p. 19.

41 A.W. Munkittrick, letter, *New York Times*, 10 Aug. 1924, sec. 7, p. 8.

42 Kilmer, 'Palmer Cox of Brownie Castle,' 19–20. The poem was 'The Wasp and the Bee,' published in *St. Nicholas* in March of 1879.

43 Stanley J. Kunitz and Howard Haycraft, eds., *The Junior Book of Authors* (New York: Wilson, 1934), 97.

44 'Palmer Cox,' *New York Times*, 25 July 1924, 12.

45 Kunitz and Haycraft, *Junior Book of Authors*, 97.

46 Palmer Cox, *The Brownies Around the World* (New York: Century, 1894), 20.

47 Wayne Morgan, 'Now, Brownies Seldom Idle Stand: Palmer Cox, the Brownies and Curiosity,' in *The Brownie World of Palmer Cox: An Exhibition* (Montreal: McGill University Libraries, 1997), 7.

48 Cox, 'The Brownies in the Academy,' *St. Nicholas*, Apr. 1888, 465–7.

49 Cox quoted in Kilmer, 'Palmer Cox of Brownie Castle,' 19–20.

50 Review of *The Brownies: Their Book*, by Palmer Cox, *New York Times*, 24 Oct. 1887, 2.

51 'The Brownies,' *Week* (Toronto), 6 Mar. 1896, 359.

52 For more on Brownie products and advertisements by their leading authority, see Wayne Morgan, '"If Your Grocer Does Not Keep the Ivory Soap": Palmer Cox, the Brownies, and Nineteenth-Century Marketing,' in *The Romance of Marketing History: Proceedings of the Eleventh Conference on Historical Analysis and Research in Marketing*, ed. Eric H. Shaw (Boca Raton, FL: Association for Historical Research in Marketing, 2003), 22–7; and idem, 'Cox on the Box: Palmer Cox and the Brownies; the First Licensed Characters, the First Licensed Games,' *Game Researchers' Notes* 23 (June 1996).

53 Wayne Morgan, 'Palmer Cox, the Brownies Craze and the Brownie Camera' (paper presented at *The Brownie at 100*, Rochester, New York, 12 Oct. 2000); Brownie camera sales from Douglas Collins, *The Story of Kodak* (New York: Harry N. Abrams, 1990), 97.

54 'The Brownie Man at Home,' *Saturday Night*, 13 May 1922, 3; Cox quoted in Kilmer, 'Palmer Cox of Brownie Castle,' 20.

55 'Palmer Cox Dead, "Brownies" Author,' *New York Times*, 25 July 1924, 13; *Le Brownie* (Granby, QC) 1, no. 1 (June 1979): n.p.; 'The Father of the Brownies,' *Nation* (New York), 6 Aug. 1924, 137.

56 Palmer Cox, *Squibs of California*, 486.

57 An unsigned review of the first Brownie book in Toronto's *Pleasant Hours* begins, 'One of the most popular features of *St. Nicholas Magazine* during the past few years has been the Brownie poems and pictures by Palmer Cox ... We can bear personal testimony to the delight with which one boy, at least, followed the Brownies' career from month to month in *St. Nicholas*' (10 Dec. 1887, 197).

Chapter 3: Living the Significant Life

1 Tebbel, *Expansion of an Industry*, 350.

2 Henry Collins Brown, *In the Golden Nineties* (Hastings-on-Hudson, NY: Valentine's Manual, 1928), 384–5, 391; Pollock, 'Canadian Writers,' 435; Richard Duffy, 'A New York Group of Literary Bohemians,' *Bookman* (New York), Jan. 1914, 521–2.

3 Richard Le Gallienne, *The Romantic '90s* (New York: Doubleday, Page, 1925), 271.

4 Frank Lillie Pollock, 'The Lost Trail,' *Atlantic Monthly*, May 1901, 722.

5 Bliss Carman to Maude Mosher, 9 Apr. 1890, *Letters of Bliss Carman*, ed. H. Pearson Gundy (Kingston and Montreal: McGill-Queen's University Press, 1981), 37; Carman to Gertrude Burton, [Aug. 1894], ibid., 76; Bliss Carman, 'Mr. Charles G.D. Roberts,' *Chap-Book*, 1 Jan. 1895, 169; Carman to Charles G.D. Roberts, n.d., quoted in Miller, *Bliss Carman*, 28; Carman to Muriel Carman, 17 Apr. 1887, *Letters of Bliss Carman*, 15. The panned poem was 'Corydon,' published in the London *Universal Review* in November 1889.

6 Literary and Personal Gossip, *Week*, 7 Mar. 1890, 221.

7 Stringer, 'Wild Poets I've Known: Bliss Carman.' Edwin Tappan Adney had been studying art in New York for several years before looking Carman up at the *Independent*. He later became *Collier's* Alaskan correspondent: see his 'The Klondike Gold Fields' in *Collier's* of 30 Dec. 1899 and subsequent reports in 1900–1.

8 Just how troublesome has only recently been discovered: for Collins's anonymous role in the 'War among the Poets,' in which Wilfred Campbell accused Carman and Roberts especially of plagiarism and boosterism, see D.M.R. Bentley, *The Confederation Group of Canadian Poets, 1880–1897* (Toronto: University of Toronto Press, 2004), 289–90.

9   Carman to Annie Prat, 26 July 1892, *Letters of Bliss Carman*, 47; Carman to
    Richard Hovey, [August or July 1892], quoted in Miller, *Bliss Carman*, 87.
10 Miller, *Bliss Carman*, 87; Bliss Carman, 'The Vagabonds,' *Independent*, 8 Dec.
    1892, 1. Miller actually says, erroneously, that the poem was 'The Vagabond
    Song,' an altogether different poem published three years later in the November
    1895 *Bookman*.
11 Charles G.D. Roberts, 'More Reminiscences of Bliss Carman,' *Dalhousie Review*
    10 (1930–1): 3.
12 Bliss Carman and Richard Hovey, *Songs from Vagabondia* (Boston: Copeland &
    Day, 1894). The poems in *Songs from Vagabondia* are all unsigned, suggesting
    joint authorship: in fact, Hovey contributed twenty poems, and Carman the
    remaining thirteen plus the end-paper verses.
13 Carman to Gertrude Burton, [Aug. 1894], *Letters of Bliss Carman*, 74; Carman to
    George Parkin, 2 Oct. 1894, ibid., 77; Library Table, *Week*, 16 Nov. 1894, 1218;
    Thomas Wentworth Higginson, 'Recent American Poetry,' *Nation*, 20 Dec. 1894,
    468.
14 Lears, *No Place of Grace*, 119; Henrietta Hovey to Harriet Spofford Hovey, date
    unknown, quoted by Miller and misdated July 1894, two months before *Songs
    from Vagabondia* was published (*Bliss Carman*, 127).
15 Carman to Susan Ward, 1 Mar. 1894, *Letters of Bliss Carman*, 64.
16 For the *World* article see note 1 to chap. 1 above; Carman to Richard Hovey, 7 Jan.
    1895, *Letters of Bliss Carman*, 83.
17 Bliss Carman, 'A Spring Feeling,' *Saturday Night*, 4 Apr. 1896, 14.
18 Charles G.D. Roberts, 'Some Reminiscences of Bliss Carman in New York (1896–
    1906),' *Canadian Poetry Magazine* 5, no. 2 (1940): 8–9; Stringer, 'Wild Poets I've
    Known: Bliss Carman'; idem, 'Wild Poets I've Known: Richard Le Gallienne,'
    Saturday Night, 25 Oct. 1941, 33.
19 Canadian papers lapped up these reports: *Saturday Night* quoted extensively from
    the *New York Sun* article in its issue of 2 Mar. 1901 (p. 7), and 'Kilmeny' copied
    the report on the Hubbard dinner into her column for the *Ottawa Evening Sun* of
    6 Apr. 1901 (p. 8).
20 Miller, *Bliss Carman*, 185; *Halifax Chronicle* quoted in ibid., 204–5, but misdated
    1907 (see Carman to Muriel Carman Ganong, 28 Feb. 1906, *Letters of Bliss
    Carman*, 153, and Gundy's note to same).
21 Hamlin Garland, *My Friendly Contemporaries: A Literary Log* (New York:
    Macmillan, 1932), 97–8.
22 Robinson to Edith Brower, 5 Aug. 1900, *Edwin Arlington Robinson's Letters to
    Edith Brower*, ed. Richard Cary (Cambridge: Harvard University Press, Belknap
    Press, 1968), 122–4; W.G. MacFarlane, *New Brunswick Bibliography: The Books
    and Writers of the Province* (St John, NB: Sun Printing, 1895), 10.

23 Hensley, 'Canadian Writers,' 203; Roberts to Craven Langstroth Betts, 18 Nov. 1888, *Letters of Charles G.D. Roberts*, 94. This, the earliest letter to Betts in Roberts's known correspondence, is clearly the response of a friend: perhaps the two met in 1876 or 1877 in Fredericton, where they were both then students at different institutions.

24 *The National Cyclopædia of American Biography* (New York: J.T. White, 1891–1984), 38:228; Morgan, *Canadian Men and Women of the Time*; Canadian Club, *Constitution and By-Laws of the Canadian Club*.

25 Craven Langstroth Betts, *The Perfume-Holder: A Persian Love Poem* (New York: Saalfield & Fitch, 1891), 6–7; Hensley, 'Canadian Writers,' 203. Ernest and Grace Thompson Seton had a 'Turkish nook' in their Bryant Park apartment as late as 1900 (John J. a'Becket, 'Mr. and Mrs. Seton-Thompson at Home,' *Harper's Bazar*, 3 Feb. 1900, 89.)

26 *The Perfume-Holder* saw five printings; Betts and Eaton's *Tales of a Garrison Town* was never reprinted, though it did show up in the *Literary History of Canada*, 2nd ed., vol. 1 (Toronto: University of Toronto Press, 1976), 304, 318.

27 Edith Brower, 'Memories of Edwin Arlington Robinson,' in ibid., 211. For Roberts's friendship with Coan see his note of 5 Feb. 1901 inviting Albert Bigelow Paine to join himself, Coan, and others at a Broadway restaurant, and his later letter to Betts expressing regret at 'dear old Coan's death' (*Letters of Charles G.D. Roberts*, 262, 358).

28 Emery Neff, *Edwin Arlington Robinson* (New York: Russell, 1948), 91; Brower, 'Memories of Edwin Arlington Robinson,' 212.

29 Robinson to Brower, 10 Nov. 1900, *Edwin Arlington Robinson's Letters to Edith Brower*, 131; Robinson to Brower, 14 Oct. 1901, ibid., 145.

30 Robinson to Betts, 3 Jan. 1934, *Selected Letters of Edwin Arlington Robinson*, ed. Ridgely Torrence (New York: Macmillan, 1940), 174; Craven Langstroth Betts, *A Garland of Sonnets: In Praise of the Poets* (New York: M.F. Mansfield & A. Wessels, 1899), n.p.

31 Jarvis's claim repeated in Morgan, *Canadian Men and Women of the Time*; review of *Geoffrey Hampstead*, by Thomas Stinson Jarvis, *Nation* (New York), 25 Dec. 1890, 507; ibid., *New Haven Morning News*, 23 Aug. 1890, 7; E.W. Thomson, letter, *Toronto Globe*, 23 Sept. 1890, 7; Editor's Table, *Dominion Illustrated*, 11 Oct. 1890, 247.

32 Stinson Jarvis, 'For Explanation and Record,' TS, quoted in Jeffrey Wollock, 'Anatomy of a Grudge Novel,' *Journal of Canadian Fiction* 20 (1977): 96.

33 See Wollock, 'Anatomy of a Grudge Novel,' 88–9.

34 [Benjamin Orange Flower], 'Prospectus of the *Arena* for 1894,' *Arena*, Dec. 1893 supplement, xliv; Stinson Jarvis, 'The Ascent of Life; or, Psychic Laws and Forces in Nature,' *Arena*, Dec. 1893, 7; idem, 'The Truly Artistic Woman,' *Arena*, Dec.

1897, 814. See also Jarvis's anti-decadent essay 'The Priesthood of Art,' *Arena*, Apr. 1897, 735–41.

35 Stinson Jarvis, *She Lived in New York: A Novel* (New York: Judge Publishing Co., 1894), 300–1, preface n.p.; Jeffrey Wollock, 'Stinson Jarvis: A Bio-Bibliography,' *Papers of the Bibliographic Society of Canada* 8 (1969): 40; review of *The Ascent of Life*, Library Table, *Week*, 7 Dec. 1894, 40.

36 Wollock, 'Anatomy of a Grudge Novel,' 103.

37 Klinck, *Literary History of Canada*, 335; Stinson Jarvis to Henry James Morgan, 10 Mar 1895, in Wollock, 'Stinson Jarvis,' 50.

38 [Flower], 'Prospectus of the *Arena* for 1894,' xlvii; Horatio W. Dresser, *A History of the New Thought Movement* (New York: T.Y. Crowell), 1919, 2, 9.

39 P[aul] T[yner], 'Metaphysical Organization,' *Arena*, Mar. 1899, 398.

40 D.M.R. Bentley, 'Carman and Mind Cure: Theory and Technique,' in *Bliss Carman: A Reappraisal*, ed. Gerald Lynch (Ottawa: University of Ottawa Press, 1990), 85; Carman to H.D.C. Lee, 27 Apr. 1910, *Letters of Bliss Carman*, 176; Bliss Carman, *The Making of Personality* (Boston: L.C. Page, 1908), 28.

41 Miller, *Bliss Carman*, 210; reviews of *The Making of Personality*, Dial, 16 May 1908, 313–14; *New York Times Saturday Review of Books*, 20 June 1908, 356; *Literary Digest*, 24 Oct. 1908, 599; and the *Independent*, 3 Dec. 1908, 1311. Of the known reviews, only *Putnam's* offered a dissenting voice, complaining that 'Mr. Carman's prose – if it be understood as his – is as clumsy and cacophonous as his verse is nimble and sweet' (Oct. 1908, p. 108).

42 Carman to James Carleton Young, 26 Oct. 1909, *Letters of Bliss Carman*, 172. Carman adds, 'I talk as if it were all mine, but I want you to know that most of the inwards of it, the pith and philosophy, come from a better brain than mine – the friend whose name you will read in the preface.'

43 Morgan, *Canadian Men and Women of the Time*.

44 Advertisement for the *Metaphysical Magazine*, *Arena*, June 1898 advertising section.

45 *Who's Who in New York* (McLean); Morgan, *Canadian Men and Women of the Time* (Norraikow); 'A "Nobleman" in Poor Business,' *New York Times*, 30 July 1890, 8.

46 'Count Adolphus Norraikow,' *New York Times*, 7 Mar. 1892, 8; 'Count Norraikow Dead,' *New York Times*, 14 Oct. 1892, 3; Countess Norraikow, 'Nihilism and the Famine,' *Lippincott's* 49 (1892): 471.

47 *Who's Who in New York*.

48 Advertisement for the Alliance Company, *Arena*, Oct. 1899 advertising section.

49 Advertisement for *Mind*, *Arena*, May 1899 advertising section.

50 Special Notice, *Arena*, June 1899 advertising section; Announcement, *Arena*, Oct. 1899, n.p.

51 Mott, *History of American Magazines*, 4:414; advertisement for the Alliance School, *Arena*, Dec. 1899, n. p.; Charles Brodie Patterson, 'One from the Beginning: A Psychological Story,' *Arena*, Dec. 1903, 627. By 1902 the Alliance School had relocated to the Schuyler building at 59 West Forty-fifth Street, also the home of John and Ella McLean. It continued offering classes, with Patterson as principal, until at least the 1902–3 school year.

52 Charles A. Montgomery, Publisher's Notes, *Arena*, Nov. 1903, 559; B.O. Flower, Notes and Comments, *Arena*, Apr. 1904, 444.

53 Morgan, *Canadian Men and Women of the Time*, 2nd ed. (McLean, Mrs).

54 'Dr. Patterson Dies; "New Thought" Leader,' *New York Times*, 23 June 1917, 9; Dresser, *History of the New Thought Movement*, 153–4, 157; Charles Brodie Patterson, 'What the New Thought Stands For,' *Arena*, Jan. 1901, 9.

55 Houdini's copy of *New Thought Essays* has been microfilmed by the Canadian Institute for Historical Microreproductions.

56 Almon Hensley, 'The Society for the Study of Life: I. Its Organization and Aims,' *Arena*, Nov. 1899, 614–20.

57 Pomeroy, *Sir Charles G.D. Roberts*, 83. Hensley's first appearance in the *Dominion Illustrated*, for instance, came at the behest of Roberts, who sent editor Jean Talon Lesperance a copy of her poem 'Tout pour l'amour' (Red and Blue Pencils, *Dominion Illustrated*, 10 Nov. 1888, 295).

58 *Portland Transcript* notice reprinted in Literary Notes, *Dominion Illustrated*, 27 July 1889, 51; review of *Poems*, by Sophie M. Almon, Our Library Table, *Week*, 23 Aug. 1889, 604.

59 For Hensley's letter to Lighthall see Gwendolyn Davies, 'Sophie Almon Hensley,' in *Dictionary of Literary Biography*, ed. W.H. New, vol. 99 (Detroit: Gale, 1990), 163.

60 Review of *A Woman's Love Letters*, by Sophie M. Almon-Hensley, *Week*, 17 Apr. 1896, 502; Thomas O'Hagan, 'Some Canadian Women Writers,' *Catholic World*, Sept. 1896, reprinted in the *Week*, 25 Sept. 1896, 1053. It's possible, even likely, that the stories and novel or novels that O'Hagan credits to Hensley were published under a pseudonym – as her first known fiction, the novella *Love and Company*, was the next year.

61 Charles G.D. Roberts to Archibald MacMechan, 19 Dec. 1892, *Letters of Charles G.D. Roberts*, 162.

62 Sophie M. Almon Hensley, New York Letter, *Week*, 8 Apr. 1892, 296; ibid., *Week*, 5 June 1896, 668.

63 See Hensley's detailed knowledge of the Guild's aims in her New York Letter to the *Week*, 5 June 1896, 668.

64 Sophie M. Almon-Hensley, *A Woman's Love Letters* (New York: J. Selwin Tait, 1895), 21.

65 Hensley, 'Society for the Study of Life,' 614–15.
66 Hensley, New York Letter, 8 Apr. 1892 p. 296, and 5 June 1896 p. 668. Walter
    Blackburn Harte and Bliss Carman were both associated with the *Philistine* around
    the time of Hensley's notice, Harte as contributor and short-lived partner and
    Carman as an editorial assistant whom Hubbard soon fired with the explanation
    that 'Ignorance (which is Bliss) was so bright that he would not get up mornings
    until noon, as he said he wished to give the Dawn a chance' (quoted in Mott,
    History of American Magazines, 4:645).
67 Hensley, 'Canadian Writers,' 204; Sophia M. Hensley, 'Repatriated,' *Dalhousie
    Review* 13 (1934): 434.

Chapter 4: The New Romantics

 1 Bliss Carman, 'Mr. Gilbert Parker,' *Chap-Book*, 1 Nov. 1894, reprinted in the
    Week, 16 Nov. 1894, 1214–15; Chronicle and Comment, *Bookman*, Dec. 1898,
    305. The *Bookman*'s remark alludes to a trend-setting novel by another Canadian
    expatriate, Grant Allen's *The Woman Who Did* (1895).
 2 Seton, *Trail of an Artist-Naturalist*, 145–8. Like many stories in Seton's autobi-
    ography, this account is contradicted by other sources. *Who's Who in New York*
    (which claims to have compiled its entries at first hand) doesn't mention an
    illness, saying instead that Seton abandoned his scholarship at the Academy
    because he was 'dissatisfied with the methods of instruction.' Seton's most recent
    biographer says he wanted to leave England anyway and was provided with an
    excuse when a doctor suggested he be sent home (Betty Keller, *Black Wolf: The
    Life of Ernest Thompson Seton* [Vancouver: Douglas & McIntyre, 1984], 90).
 3 Seton, *Trail of an Artist-Naturalist*, 249.
 4 Ibid., 280.
 5 Seton made several conflicting claims for his first animal story and the first of the
    genre: see, for starters, *Trail of an Artist-Naturalist*, 353; and William Wallace
    Whitelock, 'Ernest Seton-Thompson,' *Critic*, Oct. 1901, 324–5.
 6 Klinck, *Literary History of Canada*, 399; John Burroughs, 'Real and Sham Natural
    History,' *Atlantic Monthly*, Mar. 1903, 300.
 7 John Henry Wadland, *Ernest Thompson Seton: Man in Nature and the Progressive
    Era, 1880–1915* (New York: Arno Press, 1978), 452.
 8 For Mavor's role see Chronicle and Comment, *Bookman*, Apr. 1899, 101.
 9 Seton, *Trail of an Artist-Naturalist*, 351–2. The problem with Seton's account is
    that most of the eight stories were not, as he claimed, previously published in
    magazines, but new: although he tries hard in *Trail of an Artist-Naturalist* to
    establish 'precursors' for the stories in *Wild Animals I Have Known* from
    among his earlier sketches to fortify his claim as originator of the genre, only two

had actually seen print before, 'Lobo' in 1894 and 'Silverspot' in February 1898.

10 James MacArthur, 'Wolf Thompson and His Wild Animals,' *Bookman*, Mar. 1899, 72; review of *Wild Animals I Have Known*, *Nation*, 15 Dec. 1898, 454–5; other reviews quoted in Critical Notices, *Wild Animals I Have Known* (Toronto: Morang, 1900), n.p., and later Scribner's editions.

11 *Wild Animals* sales reported in *Literary Digest*, 20 Feb. 1904, 251; Seton, *Trail of an Artist-Naturalist*, 352; Ernest Seton Thompson, Note to the Reader, *Wild Animals I Have Known* (New York: Scribner's, 1898), 9.

12 *Zoölogist* quoted in Critical Notices, *Wild Animals I Have Known* (Toronto: Morang, 1900), n.p.; D.J.'s letter quoted in review of *Some Children's Letters Concerning Ernest Seton-Thompson's 'Wild Animals I Have Known*,' compiled by D.P. Elder and Morgan Shepard, *New York Times Saturday Review*, 6 Jan. 1900, 7; Carman, 'Mr. Gilbert Parker,' 1215; Wadland, *Ernest Thompson Seton*, 453.

13 A'Beckett, 'Mr. and Mrs. Seton-Thompson at Home,' 89; Myra Emmons, 'With Ernest Seton-Thompson in the Woods,' *Ladies' Home Journal*, Sept. 1901, 3–4; Hutchins Hapgood, 'Ernest Thomson Seton at Home,' *Everybody's*, Jan. 1901, 90–5; Whitelock, 'Ernest Seton-Thompson,' 324; 'Ernest Seton-Thompson in Bryant Park, N.Y.,' *American Authors and Their Homes: Personal Descriptions and Interviews*, ed. Francis Whiting Halsey (New York: Pott, 1901), 284; Charles G.D. Roberts, 'The Home of a Naturalist,' *Country Life*, Dec. 1903, 152–6; Stringer, 'Canadian Writers.'

'I do prefer the old way': born Ernest Evan Thompson, Seton legally added Seton (purportedly the family's ancestral surname) to his name in 1883 but promised his mother he would only use it as part of the *nom de plume* 'Seton-Thompson.' After her death in 1897, he legally changed his name in October of 1901 to Ernest Thompson Seton.

14 Chronicle and Comment,' *Bookman*, Sept. 1899, 8; 'Ernest Seton-Thompson's Story of a Bear,' *New York Times Saturday Review*, 23 June 1900, 429.

15 Sydney Reid, 'Trouble in the Jungle,' *Independent*, 20 Feb. 1902, 452, 456; Burroughs, 'Real and Sham Natural History,' 298–309.

16 Seton, *Trail of an Artist-Naturalist*, chap. 39. For a less partisan discussion of the controversy, see Ralph H. Lutts, *The Nature Fakers: Wildlife, Science, Sentiment* (1990; Charlottesville: University of Virginia Press, 2001).

17 Seton, *Trail of an Artist-Naturalist*, 349. Keller identifies these 'divergent interests' as Grace's increasingly public feminism, which conflicted with Seton's biological theory of sexual identity (*Black Wolf*, 188–9).

18 Julia M. Seton, foreword, *The Gospel of the Redman* (1936; London: Psychic Press, 1970), v–vi; 'Happy Hunting Ground,' obituary, *Time*, 4 Nov. 1946, 30.

19 Ed. W. Sandys, 'A Day on Alberta Plains,' *Dominion Illustrated Monthly*, Aug. 1892, 409.

20 Advertisement for the *Canadian Sportsman*, in *Fishing Resorts Along the Canadian Pacific Railway ... From Special Explorations by Commissioners of 'The Canadian Sportsman'* (Montreal: Canadian Pacific Railway, 1887), 32; Hensley, 'Canadian Writers,' 200; Ed. W. Sandys, *Fishing and Shooting on the Canadian Pacific Railway*, 3rd ed. (Montreal: Canadian Pacific Railway, 1891).

21 Hensley, 'Canadian Writers,' 200.

22 Ed. W. Sandys, 'Woodcock Shooting in Canada,' *Outing*, Oct. 1890, 56.

23 Sandys, 'A Day on Alberta Plains,' 411; Edwin Sandys, 'Robert White Jr.,' *Canadian Magazine*, Nov. 1903, 24.

24 Edwyn Sandys, 'In the Marsh with "Reedies" and Rails,' *Collier's*, 27 Sept. 1902, 10.

25 Periodicals, *Week*, 3 Nov. 1893, 1170. Pollock's 'In Luzon' appeared in *Outing*'s June 1906 issue, followed two months later by Carman's 'Pan in the Catskills.'

26 Review of *The American Sportsman's Library*, ed. Caspar Whitney, *Dial* (Chicago), 16 Oct. 1902, 241. The contributor who condemned the game butcher in the series' first volume was Theodore Roosevelt, who, as the *Dial* reviewer noted, nonetheless 'defends vigorously' big-game hunting as 'an antidote to that softening of fibre incident to the highly complex industrialism of our life.'

27 'Edwin Sandys,' obituary, *New York Times*, 27 Oct. 1906, 9; Edwyn Sandys, 'White Woodlands,' *Outing*, Mar. 1907, 775.

28 Arthur Stringer, 'Wild Poets I've Known: Charles G.D. Roberts,' *Saturday Night*, 11 Apr. 1942, 25.

29 See Stringer's fictionalization of his time at the American Press Association in *The Silver Poppy*, in which John Hartley writes under a dozen different names for a 'Boiler-Plate Factory' called the United News Bureau (43, 94–5).

30 Review of *Don-A-Dreams*, by Harvey O'Higgins, *Saturday Night*, 6 Oct. 1906, 11; 'A "Special Article" Expert,' *Saturday Night*, 21 Aug. 1909, 10. For Small, Maynard's notice of *The Loom of Destiny* see Chronicle and Comment, *Bookman*, Aug. 1899, 492.

31 Victor Lauriston, 'Three Musketeers of the Pen in New York of the Nineties,' *Saturday Night*, 12 Jan. 1946, 32–3; Stringer, 'Wild Poets I've Known: Bliss Carman.'

32 Novel Notes, *Bookman* (New York), Dec. 1899, 382–3; other reviews of *The Loom of Destiny* quoted in H[enry] A[ddington] Bruce, 'Canadian Celebrities No. XIV: Arthur J. Stringer,' *Canadian Magazine*, June 1900, 145.

33 See 'Tale of Literary Theft,' *New York Times Saturday Review*, 29 Aug. 1903, 595; F.T. Cooper, 'The Single Idea and Some Recent Books,' *Bookman*, Oct. 1903, 164. Both these reviews allude to rumours of the woman author supposed to be Stringer's model, but neither identifies her.

34 Victor Lauriston, *Arthur Stringer: Son of the North; Biography and Anthology*

(Toronto: Ryerson Press, 1941), 142, 145; Arthur Stringer, *The Wire Tappers* (Boston: Little, Brown, 1906), 66; Arthur E. McFarlane, 'The Work of Arthur Stringer,' *Toronto Globe Saturday Magazine Section*, 30 July 1910, 4.

35 Reviews of *The Wire Tappers*, by Arthur Stringer, in the *Dial*, 16 July 1906, 38; *Critic*, Sept. 1906, 288; *New York Times Saturday Review*, 12 May 1906, 308; *Arena*, Aug. 1906, 217; *Literary Digest*, 30 June 1906, 983; *Bookman*, Aug. 1906, 642.

36 Stringer, 'Canadian Writers'; Carl Hovey quoted in *Autobiography of Lincoln Steffens*, 316; Editorial Bulletin, *Collier's Weekly*, 16 Nov. 1907. O'Higgins won the *Collier's* prize in the third quarter of 1907 for his 'The Old Woman's Story,' beating out entries from Frank L. Packard, Margaret Deland, and Rudyard Kipling, among others.

37 Harvey O'Higgins, *The Smoke-Eaters: The Story of a Fire Crew* (New York: Century, 1905), 96; Heywood Broun, 'Harvey O'Higgins,' *Bookman* (New York), Oct. 1921, 156.

38 *Book Review Digest* (Minneapolis: Wilson, 1905); *National Cyclopædia of American Biography*, 25:296; O'Higgins, *Smoke-Eaters*, 72.

39 Reviews of *The Smoke-Eaters*, by Harvey J. O'Higgins, in *New York Times Saturday Review*, 25 Mar. 1905, 178; *Critic*, May 1905, 478; *Dial*, 1 June 1905, 293; *Literary Digest*, 12 Aug. 1905, 224.

40 Arthur E. McFarlane, 'Cissy Make-Believe,' *Youth's Companion*, 8 May 1902, 233–4.

41 '"Special Article" Expert.' The 'certain journal' may be *Collier's*, to which McFarlane contributed two articles on circus animals in January of 1909.

42 Arthur E. McFarlane, 'Fire and the Skyscraper: The Problem of Protecting the Workers in New York's Tower Factories,' *McClure's*, Sept. 1911, 466–82; idem, 'The Business of Arson,' *Collier's*, 8 Feb. 1913, 8.

43 See 'Jobyna Howland, Actress, Found Dead,' *New York Times*, 9 June 1936, 29. Arthur and Jobyna married around the time of her appearance with Marie Dressler's company in George Hobart's musical *Miss Prinnt*, which opened on Christmas day of 1900 at New York's Victoria Theatre. Coincidentally, both Dressler and Hobart were Canadian expatriates: Dressler (born Leila Koerber) was a native of Cobourg, Ontario, who became a New York actress and later film star, and George Vere Hobart Philpott was a Cape Bretoner who made his name as a humour columnist in Baltimore in the late 1890s and was then on his second career as an author of Broadway musicals and revues.

44 'Arthur E. M'Farlane,' obituary, *New York Times*, 12 Apr. 1945, 23.

45 'Mr. O'Higgins in the Limelight,' Points about People, *Saturday Night*, 11 Sept. 1909, 10.

46 'Harvey O'Higgins, Author, Is Dead,' *New York Times*, 1 Mar. 1929: 25; *Dictio-*

184 Notes to pages 121–8

nary of American Biography (New York: Scribner's, 1934), 14:5. See also *New Yorker* art critic Murdock Pemberton's eulogistic letter to the *Times*, 8 Mar. 1929, 24.

47 'Doctoring of Weak Pictures Is Confessed by an Author,' *New York Times*, 17 Feb. 1924, sec. 7, p. 4; 'Arthur Stringer, Poet, Novelist, 76,' obituary, *New York Times*, 15 Sept. 1950, 25.

48 Richard H. Brodhead, *Cultures of Letters: Scenes of Reading and Writing in Nineteenth-Century America* (Chicago: University of Chicago Press, 1993), 116–18.

49 Klinck, *Literary History of Canada*, 287; Charles G.D. Roberts, 'Canada,' *Century*, Jan. 1886, 401; idem, 'Collect for Dominion Day,' *Century*, July 1886, 349; Scott, 'Canadian Feeling Toward the United States'; William Carman Roberts, 'The Strong Man of Canada,' *Munsey's*, Dec. 1904, 683–6.

50 *Selected Journals of L.M. Montgomery*, 1:331, 2:187. For Page, see Dennis Duffy, 'The Robber Baron of Canadian Literature,' *Literary Review of Canada*, Apr. 2004, 20–2.

51 George Stewart Jr, 'Literature in Canada,' in Fairchild, *Canadian Leaves*, 132; Burpee, 'Recent Canadian Fiction,' 752–3; Hamlin Garland, *Roadside Meetings* (New York: Macmillan, 1930), 59.

52 Chronicle and Comment, *Bookman*, Aug. 1900, 502.

53 Frank Luther Mott, *American Journalism: A History, 1690–1960*, 3rd ed. (New York: Macmillan, 1962), 427; *Autobiography of Lincoln Steffens*, 179.

54 Brown, *In the Golden Nineties*, 370–1; Norman Duncan, 'A People from the East,' *Harper's*, Mar. 1903, 556–8. For Roberts's taste in cigarettes, see Stringer, 'Canadian Writers'; for the Setons' Turkish Corner, see A'Beckett, 'Mr. and Mrs. Seton-Thompson at Home,' 89.

55 Chronicle and Comment, *Bookman*, Aug. 1900, 502.

56 Norman Duncan, 'In the Absence of Mrs. Halloran,' *Atlantic Monthly*, Feb. 1900, 255–61.

57 J[ames] M[acArthur], 'Slum Stories,' *Bookman* (New York), Mar. 1895, 110.

58 'The Man Who Writes Irish Stories,' *Current Opinion*, Oct. 1914, 269.

59 Norman Duncan, 'In the Absence of Mrs. Halloran'; idem, 'The Lamp of Liberty,' *Atlantic Monthly*, May 1900, 649–56; idem, 'For the Hand of Haleem,' *Atlantic Monthly*, Sept. 1900, 347–55; idem, 'The Spirit of Revolution: How the Party of Liberty Revolted Against Abdul Hamid,' *McClure's*, Sept. 1900, 466–73.

60 Duncan, 'People from the East,' 562.

61 'The Orient in New York,' *New York Times Saturday Review*, 22 Dec. 1900, 938; 'More Fiction,' *Nation*, 4 Apr. 1901, 280; Hutchins Hapgood, 'Norman Duncan's "The Soul of the Street,"' *Bookman*, Feb. 1901, 583–4.

62 Pomeroy, *Sir Charles G.D. Roberts*, 28. The poem was 'Memnon,' published in *Scribner's Monthly*, June 1879, 218–20.

63 Roberts to Charles Leonard Moore, 20 Sept. 1884, *Letters of Charles G.D. Roberts*, 42; to Richard Watson Gilder, 17 Mar. 1894, ibid., 180; to Herbert Stuart Stone, 20 Mar. 1895, ibid., 196; and to George Parkin, 6 June 1895, ibid., 204.

64 Roberts to Craven Langstroth Betts, 17 June 1897, *Letters of Charles G.D. Roberts*, 234; Roberts to Edmund Clarence Stedman, 16 Nov. 1897, ibid., 236.

65 Pomeroy, *Sir Charles G.D. Roberts*, 147–8.

66 Roberts to Edmund Clarence Stedman, 30 May and 11 Oct. 1897, *Letters of Charles G.D. Roberts*, 233, 235.

67 James Doyle, 'The American Critical Reaction to Roberts,' in *The Proceedings of the Sir Charles G.D. Roberts Symposium*, ed. Carrie MacMillan (Mount Allison University, Sackville, NB; Halifax, NS: Nimbus, 1984), 105.

68 Charles G.D. Roberts, 'Ye Truie and Faithfulle Hystorie of Ye Squattyckke Trippe,' *University Monthly* (New Brunswick), Apr. 1882–Mar. 1883; idem, 'Echoes from Old Acadia,' *Current* (Chicago), 20 Dec. 1884–14 Feb. 1885; idem, 'Indian Devils,' *Youth's Companion*, 30 June 1887, 286–7.

69 Chronicle and Comment, *Bookman*, Mar. 1897, 11; James MacArthur, 'A Gentleman of New France,' *Bookman*, Apr. 1897, 162; Pomeroy, *Sir Charles G.D. Roberts*, 152.

70 Pomeroy, *Sir Charles G.D. Roberts*, 153.

71 Ohmann, *Selling Culture*, 322.

72 Charles G.D. Roberts, 'The Bewitchment of Lieutenant Hanworthy,' *Saturday Evening Post*, 19 Nov. 1898, 321–3.

73 Pollock, 'Canadian Writers,' 435; Roberts to Bliss Carman, 13 Aug. 1899, *Letters of Charles G.D. Roberts*, 255.

74 Arthur Stringer, 'Eminent Canadians in New York: The Father of Canadian Poetry,' *National Monthly of Canada* (Toronto), Feb. 1904, 61.

75 Adams, *Sir Charles God Damn*, 82–3.

76 Reviews of *The Kindred of the Wild*, by Charles G.D. Roberts, in *Nation*, 3 July 1902, 16, and *Dial*, 16 Oct. 1902, 240; reviews of *Red Fox* in *New York Times*, 21 Oct. 1905, 710, *Independent*, 14 Dec. 1905: 1390, and *Outlook*, 25 Nov. 1905, 718; review of *Biography of a Silver Fox*, by Ernest Thompson Seton, *New York Times Saturday Review*, 10 Apr. 1909, 209.

77 Stringer, 'Eminent Canadians in New York,' 63; Burroughs, 'Real and Sham Natural History,' 299; Edward B. Clark, 'Roosevelt on the Nature Fakirs,' *Everybody's Magazine*, June 1907, 773.

78 Personal, *Week*, 17 May 1895, 595.

79 Desmond Pacey, introduction to *The Selected Poems of Sir Charles G.D. Roberts* (Toronto and Montreal: McGraw-Hill Ryerson, 1955), xiv–xviii; Charles G.D. Roberts, 'Some Reminiscences of Bliss Carman,' 6.

Chapter 5: Exodus Lost

1 Thomas Beer, *The Mauve Decade: American Life at the End of the 19th Century* (1926; New York: Vintage Books, 1961), 160–1.

2 Chronicle and Comment, *Bookman*, Nov. 1898, 198.

3 The first edition of *Who's Who in New York City and State* (1904) contained entries on Craven Langstroth Betts, Palmer Cox, Arthur Wentworth Eaton, Herbert F. Gunnison, Sophie Almon Hensley, George Vere Hobart, John Emery McLean, Charles Brodie Patterson, Sydney Reid, Charles G.D. Roberts, and Ernest Thompson Seton. Some eighty Canadian-born authors appeared that same year in Adams's *Dictionary of American Authors*, including New York expatriates Betts, Carman, Cox, Creelman, Duncan, Hensley, Jarvis, Patterson, Reid, Roberts, Seton, and Stringer.

4 Beer, *Mauve Decade*, 87, 172. In 1890s' parlance, 'pink' meant a swell, one of the smart set.

5 Margaret Atwood, *Survival: A Thematic Guide to Canadian Literature* (Toronto: Anansi, 1972), 73. Publication information from *Bowker's Global Books in Print*, February 2004, www.globalbooksinprint.com.

6 Herbert F. Smith, *The Popular American Novel, 1865–1920* (Boston: Twayne, 1980), 75–6; Ronald Weber, *Hired Pens: Professional Writers in America's Golden Age of Print* (Athens: Ohio University Press, 1997), chap. 7.

7 Alchemist [William Douw Lighthall], review of *Acadian Legends and Lyrics*, by Arthur Wentworth Eaton, *Week*, 28 June 1889, 470; Bruce, 'Arthur J. Stringer,' 143, 145; 'How a Talented B.C. Girl Became a Figure in American Literature: Miss Constance Skinner, Playwright and Novelist,' *Ottawa Evening Journal*, 3 May 1913; Bayard, 'Eve Brodlique,' 515–16.

8 Hensley, 'Canadian Writers,' 195; Stringer, 'Canadian Writers'; Pacey, introduction, xvii.

9 Arthur J. Stringer, 'The Sons Beyond the Border,' *Canadian Magazine*, Dec. 1899, 128–9.

10 'Canadians Here Celebrate,' *New York Times*, 2 July 1927, 22.

11 Carman's 'The Ships of St. John' first appeared in the *Canadian Magazine* in December 1893 and was reprinted on 13 November 1897 in Boston's *Living Age*. I could only find Stringer's 'Northern Pines' in Wilfred Campbell's 1913 *Oxford Book of Canadian Verse*, but presumably this is a reprint from an earlier source. Stringer's 'The Voyageur on Broadway' appeared in the *Canadian Poetry Magazine* in June 1937, the same year its author became an American citizen. Roberts's 'A Nocturne of Exile' first appeared in the New York *Bookman* of February 1898, and Pollock's 'The Lost Trail' was published in the *Atlantic Monthly* of May 1901.

12 Smith, *Popular American Novel*, 71; O'Higgins, *Don-A-Dreams*, 360.

13 Francis L. Pollock, 'Where I Shall Hunt No More,' *A Four-Fold Greeting in Numbers for the Festival of Christe His Masse* ... (Toronto: N.p., 1897); idem, 'The Northern Trail,' *Everybody's Magazine*, Dec. 1903, 732.

14 Marquis, 'English-Canadian Literature,' 588–9.

15 Several stateside expatriates actually helped the war effort: Carman joined the Vigilantes, a group of New York writers and artists advocating American entry into the War; John Emery McLean worked for the Allies' Hospital Relief Commission in New York; and Harvey O'Higgins served as associate chair of the counter-propaganda U.S. Committee of Public Information.

16 Archibald MacMechan, *Head-Waters of Canadian Literature* (Toronto: McClelland & Stewart, 1924), 195–6, 189–90, 213–14.

17 Ibid., 17.

18 See, for instance, Leon Surette, 'Here Is Us: The Topocentrism of Canadian Literary Criticism,' *Canadian Poetry: Studies, Documents, Reviews* 10 (1982): 44–57; Robert Lecker, 'The Canonization of Canadian Literature: An Inquiry into Value,' *Critical Inquiry* 16, no. 3 (1990): 656–71; and Jonathan Kertzer, *Worrying the Nation: Imagining a National Literature in English Canada* (Toronto: University of Toronto Press, 1998), chaps. 1–2.

19 Thomas D'Arcy McGee, 'Protection for Canadian Literature,' *The New Era*, 24 Apr. 1858; Charles Mair, 'The New Canada,' *Canadian Monthly*, Aug. 1878. Both articles are reprinted in Carl Ballstadt, ed., *The Search for English-Canadian Literature: An Anthology of Critical Articles from the Nineteenth and Early Twentieth Centuries* (Toronto: University of Toronto Press, 1975).

20 Klinck, *Literary History of Canada*, 213, 277. All references to the *Literary History of Canada* are to the more accessible second edition.

21 Ibid., 299.

22 Miller, *Bliss Carman*, 6, 75, 275–6.

23 Fred Bodsworth, 'The Backwoods Genius with the Magic Pen,' *Maclean's*, 6 June 1959, 22; Magdalene Redekop, *Ernest Thompson Seton* (Don Mills, ON: Fitzhenry & Whiteside, 1979), 21.

24 Cummins, *Humorous but Wholesome*, 15.

25 *Selected Journals of L.M. Montgomery*, 2:34. By 1910 Montgomery's importance to her publisher Lewis Page was such that Page had concluded his invitation to visit Boston with an offer to come to see her in Prince Edward Island should she be unable to make the trip – surely not an offer extended to many in Page's stable (ibid., 2:19).

26 *Le Brownie: Le trimestriel des amis de Palmer Cox Inc.* (Granby, QC) 1, no.1 (June 1979). In a letter to myself of 11 Aug. 2004, Wayne Morgan speculates that Cox's disappearance may also be due to his lack of heirs who might have protected and promoted his reputation.

27 Marquis, 'English-Canadian Literature,' 556–7; Klinck, *Literary History of Canada*, 342.
28 James Cappon, *Charles G.D. Roberts* (Toronto: Ryerson Press, [1925]), 120; Pacey, introduction, xviii, xxii, xxiii; W.J. Keith, 'Charles G.D. Roberts and the Poetic Tradition,' in *The Proceedings of the Sir Charles G.D. Roberts Symposium*, ed. Carrie MacMillan (Mount Allison University, Sackville, NB; Halifax, NS: Nimbus, 1984), 61–2. Despite Pacey's low opinion of *New York Nocturnes*, he included five poems from it in the *Selected Poems*, only one fewer than from the book that marked Roberts's 'late revival,' *The Vagrant of Time*. *The Book of the Rose*, also from Roberts' 'lost years,' is represented by seven poems.
29 Parkin quoted in Carl Berger, 'The True North Strong and Free,' in *Nationalism in Canada*, ed. Peter Russell (Toronto: McGraw-Hill, 1966), 15.
30 Sara Jeanette Duncan, *The Imperialist*, ed. Thomas E. Tausky (1904; Ottawa: Tecumseh Press, 1996), 229. See Darlene Kelly, 'Rewriting *The Imperialist*,' *Canadian Literature* 121 (1989): 33.
31 Parkin and *Globe* quoted in Berger, 'True North,' 5; Pacey, introduction, xxii; Klinck, *Literary History of Canada*, 342; J.H. Bowes, 'Canadians and Americans,' *Week*, 1 Mar. 1889, 198; Desmond Pacey, 'Bliss Carman: A Reappraisal,' *Northern Review* 3, no. 3 (1950): 3; McArthur quoted in Lucas, *Peter McArthur*, 78.
32 For transnational discussion of Canadian writers of this period see for instance the essays by John Coldwell Adams and Terry Whalen in Glenn Clever, ed., *The Sir Charles G.D. Roberts Symposium*, Reappraisals: Canadian Writers, no. 10 (Ottawa: University of Ottawa Press, 1984); by James Doyle, Whalen, and D.M.R. Bentley in Gerald Lynch, ed., *Bliss Carman: A Reappraisal*, Reappraisals: Canadian Writers, no. 16 (Ottawa: University of Ottawa Press, 1990); by Doyle, Carole Gerson, and Michael A. Peterman in Camille R. La Bossière, ed., *Context North America: Canadian/U.S. Literary Relations*, Reappraisals: Canadian Writers, no. 18 (Ottawa: University of Ottawa Press, 1994); and Bentley, *Confederation Group of Canadian Poets*, chaps. 4–5.
33 James Doyle, 'Canadian Women Writers and the American Literary Milieu of the 1890s,' in *Rediscovering Our Foremothers: Nineteenth-Century Canadian Women Writers*, ed. Lorraine McMullen (Ottawa: University of Ottawa Press, 1990), 33; Gerson, 'Canadian Women Writers,' 111.
34 Ohmann, *Selling Culture*, 293; Clarence Karr, *Authors and Audiences: Popular Canadian Fiction in the Early Twentieth Century* (Montreal and Kingston: McGill-Queen's University Press, 2000), 62–3.
35 James Doyle, 'Canadian Writers and American Little Magazines in the 1890s,' *Canadian Literature* 110 (1986): 178; Bentley, *Confederation Group of Canadian Poets*, 173; Isabel Paterson, 'The Absentee Novelists of Canada,' *Bookman*, Apr. 1922, 133–8.
36 Adam, 'Outline History of Canadian Literature,' 221.

37 Tracy Ware, ed., 'Letters to Carman, 1890–92, from Campbell, Lampman, and Scott,' *Canadian Poetry: Studies, Documents, Reviews* 27 (1990): 46.
38 *Selected Journals of L.M. Montgomery*, 2:187.
39 Bliss Carman, 'Mr. Gilbert Parker'; idem, 'Mr. Charles G.D. Roberts'; idem, review of *Matins*, by Francis Sherman, *Bookman*, Mar. 1897, 75–6; Chronicle and Comment, *Bookman*, Sept. 1899, 8–9 (Carman quoted praising Seton's 'The Trail of the Sandhill Stag'). For the remainder see Terry Whalen, 'Carman as Critic,' in Lynch, *Bliss Carman*, 79n3.
40 Lampman to E.W. Thomson, 5 Mar. 1894, *Correspondence Between Lampman and Thomson*, 108; Carman to Herbert Small, 7 July 1899, *Letters of Bliss Carman*, 126; Gwendolyn Davies, 'The Elephant and the Primrose: The Prat Sisters in New York,' *Journal of Pre-Raphaelite Studies* 6–7 (1997–8): 129.
41 Carman to Arthur Stedman, 8 Apr. 1892, *Letters of Bliss Carman*, 44; Carman to Herbert Stone, 28 Feb. 1894, ibid., 63; Hensley, 'Canadian Writers,' 201.
42 Roberts to Small, Maynard & Co., 19 Oct. 1898, *Letters of Charles G.D. Roberts*, 244; Roberts to Gilder, 12 Oct. 1895, ibid., 209–10; Roberts to Stedman, 8 Nov. 1895, ibid., 213–14. Hensley's manuscript was 'a certain romance called 'Souls,'' so far as I know unpublished, though it may have appeared under a pseudonym.
43 Thomson to Lampman, 17 Oct. 1892, *Correspondence Between Lampman and Thomson*, 51. See also Helen Lynn's introduction, ibid., esp. pp. xlvii–lii.
44 Burpee, 'Recent Canadian Fiction,' 754. The five writers were Gilbert Parker, Sara Jeannette Duncan, Robert Barr, Grant Allen, and E.W. Thomson – for whatever reason, the New York expatriates got short shrift in Burpee's survey, with only Charles G.D. Roberts receiving a mention.
45 Marquis, 'English-Canadian Literature,' 548–9. The seven expatriates in Marquis' 'modern school' were Parker, Sara Jeannette Duncan, Lily Dougall, Charles G.D. Roberts, Norman Duncan, Thomson, and Marshall Saunders.
46 Klinck, *Literary History of Canada*, 274; Canada, *Fifth Census* 6:8–9. The Census and Statistics Office had been lumping 'scientific' persons in with authors since the 1890s, so although the totals are off the figures are comparable. To the census, 'scientific' meant people working in pure rather than applied science: chemists and physicians, for instance, are listed elsewhere, as are professors.
47 Parker, *Beginnings of the Book Trade*, 237. The Briggs titles were Thomson's *Old Man Savarin* (1895), *Walter Gibbs* (1896), and *Between Earth and Sky* (1897); Roberts's *The Forge in the Forest* (1897); W.A. Fraser's *The Eye of a God* (1899); Seton's *Two Little Savages* (1903); Stringer's *The Silver Poppy* (1903); Nellie McClung's *Sowing Seeds in Danny* (1908); and H.A. Cody's *The Frontiersman* (1910). All were first or simultaneously issued in the United States.
48 Klinck, *Literary History of Canada*, 421; Mary Vipond, 'Best Sellers in English Canada, 1899–1918: An Overview,' *Journal of Canadian Fiction* 24 (1979): 108.
49 See, for instance, Colin Hill, 'As For Me and My Blueprint: Sinclair Ross's Debt

to Arthur Stringer,' in *The Canadian Modernists Meet: Essays on Modernism, Antimodernism, and Modernity,* ed. Dean Irvine (Ottawa: University of Ottawa Press, 2005).

50 Leo Kennedy, 'The Future of Canadian Literature,' *Canadian Mercury,* Dec. 1928, reprinted in Louis Dudek and Michael Gnarowski, *The Making of Modern Poetry in Canada: Essential Articles on Contemporary Canadian Poetry in English* (Toronto: Ryerson Press), 36.

51 A.J.M. Smith, 'Nationalism and Canadian Poetry,' *Northern Review* 1, no.1 (1945–6): 41.

52 Stephen Henighan, *When Words Deny the World: The Reshaping of Canadian Writing* (Erin, ON: Porcupine's Quill, 2002); Robert Lecker, 'Where Is Here Now?' *Essays on Canadian Writing* 71 (2000): 7–8.

Selected Bibliography

This bibliography lists the main works of the Canadian expatriates' Stateside careers, together with frequently consulted past and present secondary works. For a more complete list of sources, see the Notes. Works appear in the order of their publication.

Adam, G. Mercer. 'An Outline History of Canadian Literature.' In *An Abridged History of Canada*, by William H. Withrow, 179–232. Toronto: William Briggs, 1887.

– Introduction to *Classical (Imaginary) Conversations: Greek, Roman, Modern*, by Walter Savage Landor. New York: M.W. Dunne, 1901.

– *The Life of General Robert E. Lee*. Burt's Library of the World's Best Books. New York: A.L. Burt, 1905.

– ed. *A History of Our Own Times from the Accession of Queen Victoria to the General Election of 1880; by Justin McCarthy ... with an Introduction and Supplementary Chapters ... a New Index, and Additions to the Survey of the Literature of the Reign*, by G. Mercer Adam. 2 vols. New York: International Book, 1894.

– ed. *Sandow on Physical Training: A Study in the Perfect Type of the Human Form*. New York: J. Selwin Tait; London: Gale & Polden, 1894.

– ed. *The People's Standard History of the United States from the Landing of the Norsemen to the Present Time; by E.S. Ellis ... Assisted by, with Introduction, Annotation, Lists of Authorities, etc., G.M. Adam*. London: Ward, Lock, & Bowden, 1896.

– ed. *The Confessions of a Clarionet Player: A Novel; Translated from the French of M.M. Erckmann-Chatrian and Edited with Introduction by G. Mercer Adam*. New York: A.L. Burt, 1903.

– ed. *Spain and Portugal: Edited from Standard Authorities by G. Mercer Adam, with Introduction by Wilfred H. Munro*. History of Nations Series, vol. 8, ed. H.C. Lodge. Philadelphia: J.D. Morris, 1906.

Adams, John Coldwell. 'Roberts, Lampman, and Edmund Collins.' In *The Sir Charles G.D. Roberts Symposium*, ed. Glenn Clever, 5–13. Reappraisals: Canadian Writers, no. 10. Ottawa: University of Ottawa Press, 1984.

– *Sir Charles God Damn: The Life of Sir Charles G.D. Roberts.* Toronto: University of Toronto Press, 1986.

Adams, Oscar Fay. *A Dictionary of American Authors.* 5th ed. Boston: Houghton, Mifflin, 1904.

Angus, H.F., ed. *Canada and Her Great Neighbour: Sociological Surveys of Opinions and Attitudes in Canada Concerning the United States.* The Relations of Canada and the United States Series. Toronto: Ryerson; New Haven: Yale University Press, 1938.

Arbuthnot, May, and Zena Sutherland. *Children and Books.* 4th ed. Glenview, IL: Scott, Foresman, 1972.

Atwood, Margaret. *Survival: A Thematic Guide to Canadian Literature.* Toronto: Anansi, 1972.

Barman, Jean. *Constance Lindsay Skinner: Writing on the Frontier.* Toronto: University of Toronto Press, 2002.

Bayard, Mary Temple. 'Eve Brodlique.' *Canadian Magazine*, Oct. 1896, 515–18.

Beer, Thomas. *The Mauve Decade: American Life at the End of the 19th Century.* 1926. New York: Vintage Books, 1961.

Bentley, D.M.R. 'Carman and Mind Cure: Theory and Technique.' In *Bliss Carman: A Reappraisal*, ed. Gerald Lynch, 85–110. Reappraisals: Canadian Writers, no. 16. Ottawa: University of Ottawa Press, 1990.

– *The Confederation Group of Canadian Poets, 1880–1897.* Toronto: University of Toronto Press, 2004.

Berger, Carl. 'The True North Strong and Free.' In *Nationalism in Canada*, ed. Peter Russell, 3–26. Toronto: McGraw-Hill, 1966.

Betts, Craven Langstroth. *Songs from Béranger: Translated in the Original Metres by Craven Langstroth Betts.* New York: Frederick A. Stokes, 1888.

– *The Perfume-Holder: A Persian Love Poem.* New York: Saalfield & Fitch, 1891.

– *A Garland of Sonnets: In Praise of the Poets.* New York: M.F. Mansfield & A. Wessels, 1899.

– *The Promise, a Greek Idyl.* [New York]: Monarch Press, 1911.

– *Selected Poems of Craven Langstroth Betts.* New York: Associated Authors and Compilers, 1916.

Betts, Craven Langstroth, and Arthur Wentworth Eaton. *Tales of a Garrison Town.* New York and St Paul: D.D. Merrill, 1892.

Brodhead, Richard H. *Cultures of Letters: Scenes of Reading and Writing in Nineteenth-Century America.* Chicago: University of Chicago Press, 1993.

Brower, Edith. 'Memories of Edwin Arlington Robinson.' In *Edwin Arlington*

Robinson's Letters to Edith Brower, ed. Richard Cary, 203–15. Cambridge: Harvard University Press, Belknap Press, 1968.

Brown, Henry Collins. *In the Golden Nineties*. Hastings-on-Hudson, NY: Valentine's Manual, 1928.

Burpee, Lawrence J. 'Recent Canadian Fiction.' *Forum* (New York), Aug. 1899, 752–60.

Canada. Census and Statistics Office. *Occupations of the People*, Bulletin XI of the 1901 Census. Ottawa: C.H. Parmelee, 1910.

– *Fifth Census of Canada, 1911*. 6 vols. Ottawa: C.H. Parmelee (vols. 1–3) and J. de L. Taché (vols. 4–6), 1912–15.

Canada. Census Office. *Fourth Census of Canada, 1901*. 4 vols. Ottawa: S.E. Dawson, 1902–6.

Canada. Dept. of Agriculture. *Census of Canada, 1880–81*. 4 vols. Ottawa: Maclean, Roger, 1882–5.

– *Census of Canada, 1890–91*. 4 vols. Ottawa: S.E. Dawson, 1893–7.

Canadian Club. *Constitution and By-Laws of the Canadian Club, With a List of Its Officers and Members*. New York, 1887.

Carman, Bliss. *Low Tide on Grand Pré: A Book of Lyrics*. New York: Charles L. Webster, 1893.

– 'Mr. Gilbert Parker,' *Week* (Toronto), 16 Nov. 1894, 1214–15. First published in the *Chap-Book*, 1 Nov. 1894.

– 'Mr. Charles G.D. Roberts.' *Chap-Book*, 1 Jan. 1895, 163–71.

– *Behind the Arras: A Book of the Unseen*. Boston and New York: Lamson, Wolffe, 1895.

– *The Making of Personality*. Boston: L.C. Page, 1908.

– *Letters of Bliss Carman*. Ed. H. Pearson Gundy. Montreal and Kingston: McGill-Queen's University Press, 1981.

Carman, Bliss, and Richard Hovey. *Songs from Vagabondia*. Boston: Copeland & Day; London: Elkin Mathews & John Lane, 1894.

– *More Songs from Vagabondia*. Boston: Copeland & Day; London: Elkin Mathews, 1896.

– *Last Songs from Vagabondia*. Boston: Small, Maynard, 1900.

Casson, Herbert N. *The Red Light*. Lynn, MA: Lynn Labor Church Press, 1898.

– 'The Canadians in the United States.' *Munsey's Magazine*, July 1906, 473–87.

– *The Romance of Steel: The Story of a Thousand Millionaires*. New York: A.S. Barnes, 1907.

– *The Story of My Life*. London: Efficiency Magazine, 1931.

Clever, Glenn, ed. *The Sir Charles G.D. Roberts Symposium*. Reappraisals: Canadian Writers, no. 10. Ottawa: University of Ottawa Press, 1984.

Cox, Palmer. *Squibs of California; or, Every-Day Life Illustrated*. Hartford, CT: Mutual Publishing; San Francisco: A. Roman, 1874.

– *The Brownies: Their Book.* New York: Century, 1887.
– *Another Brownie Book.* New York: Century, 1890.
– *The Brownies at Home.* New York: Century, 1893.
– *The Brownies in Fairyland: A Cantata in Two Acts.* New York: T.B. Harms, 1894.
– *The Brownies Around the World.* New York: Century, 1894.
– *The Brownies Through the Union.* New York: Century, 1895.
– *The Brownies Abroad.* New York: Century, 1899.
– *The Brownies in the Philippines.* New York: Century, 1904.
– *Brownie Clown of Brownie Town.* New York: Century, 1908.
– *The Brownies' Latest Adventures.* New York: Century, 1910.
– *The Brownies Many More Nights.* New York: Century, 1913.
– *The Brownies and Prince Florimel; or, Brownieland, Fairyland, and Demonland.* New York: Century, 1918.
Creelman, James. *On the Great Highway: The Wanderings and Adventures of a Special Correspondent.* Boston: Lothrop, 1901.
Cummins, Roger W. *Humorous but Wholesome: A History of Palmer Cox and the Brownies.* Watkins Glen, NY: Century House, 1973.
Davies, Acton. *Maude Adams.* New York: Frederick A. Stokes, 1901.
– *Romance: A Novel, by Acton Davies, from the Drama by Edward Sheldon; with Pictures from the Play.* New York: Macaulay, 1913.
Davies, Acton, and Charles Nirdlinger. *The First Lady in the Land; or, When Dolly Todd Took Boarders.* New York: H.K. Fly, 1912.
Davies, Gwendolyn. 'The Literary "New Woman" and Social Activism in Maritime Literature, 1880–1920.' In *Separate Spheres: Women's Worlds in the 19th-Century Maritimes,* ed. Janet Guildford and Suzanne Morton, 233–50. Fredericton, NB: Acadiensis, 1994.
Deacon, William Arthur. *Peter McArthur.* Makers of Canadian Literature, vol. 8. Toronto: Ryerson Press, 1923.
Dickerson, Richard E. *A Brownie Bibliography: The Books of Palmer Cox, 1840–1924.* 2nd ed. Pasadena, CA: Golden Pippin Press, 1995.
Douglas, Ann. *The Feminization of American Culture.* New York: Knopf, 1977.
Doyle, James. 'Canadian Writers and American Little Magazines in the 1890s.' *Canadian Literature* 110 (1986): 177–83.
– 'Canadian Women Writers and the American Literary Milieu of the 1890s.' In *Rediscovering Our Foremothers: Nineteenth-Century Canadian Women Writers,* ed. Lorraine McMullen, 30–6. Reappraisals: Canadian Writers, no. 15. Ottawa: University of Ottawa Press, 1990.
– *The Fin de Siècle Spirit: Walter Blackburn Harte and the American/Canadian Literary Milieu of the 1890s.* Toronto: ECW Press, 1995.

Dresser, Horatio W. *A History of the New Thought Movement*. New York: T.Y. Crowell, 1919.

Duffy, Richard. 'When They Were Twenty-One: II – A New York Group of Literary Bohemians.' *Bookman* (New York), Jan. 1914, 521–31.

Duncan, Norman. *The Soul of the Street: Correlated Stories of the New York Syrian Quarter*. New York: McClure, Phillips & Company, 1900.

– 'A People from the East.' *Harper's*, Mar. 1903, 553–62.

– *Every Man for Himself*. New York and London: Harper, 1908.

– *Going Down From Jerusalem: The Narrative of A Sentimental Traveller*. New York and London: Harper, 1909. First published in *Harper's*, July 1908–Apr. 1909.

Duncan, Sara Jeannette. 'American Influence on Canadian Thought.' *Week* (Toronto), 7 July 1887, 518.

Fairchild, G.M., Jr, ed. *Canadian Leaves: History, Art, Science, Literature, Commerce: A Series of New Papers Read Before the Canadian Club of New York*. New York: N. Thompson, 1887.

Garland, Hamlin. *Roadside Meetings*. New York: Macmillan, 1930.

– *My Friendly Contemporaries: A Literary Log*. New York: Macmillan, 1932.

Gerson, Carole. *A Purer Taste: The Writing and Reading of Fiction in English in Nineteenth-Century Canada*. Toronto: University of Toronto Press, 1989.

– 'Canadian Women Writers and American Markets, 1880–1940.' In *Context North America: Canadian/U.S. Literary Relations*, ed. Camille R. La Bossière, 107–18. Reappraisals: Canadian Writers, no. 18. Ottawa: University of Ottawa Press, 1994.

Halsey, Francis Whiting. *American Authors and Their Homes: Personal Descriptions and Interviews*. New York: J. Pott, 1901.

Hansen, Marcus Lee. *The Mingling of the Canadian and American Peoples*. Volume 1. *Historical*. The Relations of Canada and the United States Series. New Haven: Yale University Press, 1940.

Harkins, E.F. *Little Pilgrimages Among the Men Who Have Written Famous Books*. Boston: L.C. Page, 1902.

Hensley, Sophie Almon. *Poems*. Windsor, NS: Printed by J.J. Anslow, 1889.

– 'Canadian Nurses in New York.' *Dominion Illustrated Monthly* (Montreal and Toronto), Apr. 1892, 161–70.

– 'Canadian Writers in New York.' *Dominion Illustrated Monthly*, May 1893, 195–204.

– *A Woman's Love Letters*. The Fleur-de-Lis Poets. New York: J. Selwin Tait, 1895.

– 'The Society for the Study of Life: I. Its Organization and Aims.' *Arena*, Nov. 1899, 614–20.

– *The Heart of a Woman*. New York and London: G.P. Putnam's, 1906.

– [Gordon Hart, pseud.]. *Woman and the Race*. Westwood, MA: Ariel Press, 1907.

Jackson, G.E. 'Emigration of Canadians to the United States.' *Annals of the American Academy of Political and Social Science* 107 (1923): 25–34.

Jarvis, Stinson. *Letters from East Longitudes; Sketches of Travel in Egypt, the Holy Land, Greece, and Cities of the Levant; by Thomas Stinson Jarvis, Student at Law.* Toronto: James Campbell & Son, 1875.

– *Geoffrey Hampstead: A Novel.* Appleton's Town and Country Library, no. 57. New York: D. Appleton, 1890.

– *Dr. Perdue: A Novel.* Laird & Lee's Prize Novels, no. 2. Chicago: Laird & Lee, 1892.

– *The Ascent of Life; or, The Psychic Laws and Forces in Nature.* Boston: Arena Publishing Co., 1894. First published in the *Arena,* Dec. 1893–May 1894.

– *She Lived in New York: A Novel.* New York: Judge Publishing Co., 1894.

Karr, Clarence. *Authors and Audiences: Popular Canadian Fiction in the Early Twentieth Century.* Montreal and Kingston: McGill-Queen's University Press, 2000.

Keller, Betty. *Black Wolf: The Life of Ernest Thompson Seton.* Vancouver: Douglas & McIntyre, 1984.

Kennerley, Mitchell. 'Kennerley on Carman.' Ed. H. Pearson Gundy. *Canadian Poetry: Studies, Documents, Reviews* 14 (1984): 69–74.

Klinck, Carl F., ed. *Literary History of Canada: Canadian Literature in English.* 2nd ed. Vol. 1. Toronto: University of Toronto Press, 1976.

La Bossière, Camille R., ed. *Context North America: Canadian/U.S. Literary Relations.* Reappraisals: Canadian Writers, no. 18. Ottawa: University of Ottawa Press, 1994.

Lampman, Archibald. *An Annotated Edition of the Correspondence Between Archibald Lampman and Edward William Thomson (1890–1898).* Ed. Helen Lynn. Ottawa: Tecumseh Press, 1980.

Lang, Marjory. *Women Who Made the News: Female Journalists in Canada, 1880–1945.* Montreal and Kingston: McGill-Queen's University Press, 1999.

Lauriston, Victor. *Arthur Stringer: Son of the North; Biography and Anthology.* Makers of Canadian Literature Series. Toronto: Ryerson Press, 1941.

– 'Three Musketeers of the Pen in New York of the Nineties.' *Saturday Night,* 12 Jan. 1946, 32–3.

Lears, T.J. Jackson. *No Place of Grace: Antimodernism and the Transformation of American Culture, 1880–1920.* 1981. Chicago: University of Chicago Press, 1994.

Lucas, Alec. *Peter McArthur.* Twayne's World Authors Series, no. 363. Boston: Twayne, 1975.

Lutts, Ralph H. *The Nature Fakers: Wildlife, Science and Sentiment.* 1990. Under the Sign of Nature: Explorations in Ecocriticism Series. Charlottesville and London: University Press of Virginia, 2001.

Lynch, Gerald, ed. *Bliss Carman: A Reappraisal*. Reappraisals: Canadian Writers,
    no. 16. Ottawa: University of Ottawa Press, 1990.
MacFarlane, W.G. *New Brunswick Bibliography: The Books and Writers of the
    Province*. St John, NB: Press of the Sun Printing Co., 1895.
MacMechan, Archibald. *Head-Waters of Canadian Literature*. Toronto: McClelland
    & Stewart, 1924.
MacMillan, Carrie, Lorraine McMullen, and Elizabeth Waterston. *Silenced Sextet: Six
    Nineteenth-Century Canadian Women Novelists*. Montreal and Kingston: McGill-
    Queen's University Press, 1992.
Marquis, Thomas Guthrie. 'English-Canadian Literature.' In *Canada and Its Prov-
    inces*, ed. Adam Shortt and Arthur G. Doughty. Vol. 12, 493–589. Toronto:
    Glasgow, Brook, 1914.
McArthur, Peter. 'Dominion Day in New York.' *Massey's*, July 1896, 24–7.
– *The Prodigal and Other Poems*. New York: Mitchell Kennerley, 1907.
McFarlane, Arthur E. 'Tales of a Deep-Sea Diver.' *Youth's Companion*, 30 Jan.,
    13 Feb., 13 Mar., and 20 Mar. 1902.
– 'Fire and the Skyscraper: The Problem of Protecting the Workers in New York's
    Tower Factories,' *McClure's*, Sept. 1911, 466–82.
– 'The Inflammable Tenement: How New York Has Placed Two and a Half Million
    People in the Worst Fire-Trap Dwellings in the World.' *McClure's*, Oct. 1911,
    690–701.
– 'The Conflagration Hazard in New York.' *McClure's*, Dec. 1911, 153–75.
– 'The Business of Arson.' *Collier's*, 8 Feb.-26 Apr. 1913.
McGee, Thomas D'Arcy. 'The Mental Outfit of the New Dominion.' Ottawa: CIHM
    microfiche, 1981. First published in the *Montreal Gazette*, 5 Nov. 1867.
McLean, Ella N. (Countess Norraikow). 'Woman's Share in Russian Nihilism.'
    Cosmopolitan, Sept. 1891, 619–27.
– 'The Russian Famine.' *Harper's Weekly*, 23 Jan. 1892, 86–7.
– 'Nihilism and the Famine.' *Lippincott's* 49 (1892): 463–71.
McLean, John Emery. *Spiritual Economics: A Plea for Christianity in Action*. Pitts-
    burgh, PA: Henry George Foundation of America, 1926.
McOuat, Mary Elizabeth [Mary Dudderidge, pseud.]. 'Embattled Housewives.'
    Independent, 28 Nov. 1912, 1230–4.
– 'New Light Upon Our Eyes: An Investigation Which May Result in Normal Vision
    for All, Without Glasses.' *Scientific American*, 12 Jan. 1918, 53, 61.
– *Normal Vision by Normal Methods*. New York: Friebele Press, 1927.
Miller, Elizabeth Russell. *The Frayed Edge: Norman Duncan's Newfoundland*.
    St John's, NF: Harry Cuff, 1992.
Miller, Muriel. *Bliss Carman: Quest and Revolt*. St John's, NF: Jesperson Press,
    1985.

198 Selected Bibliography

Moffett, Samuel E. *The Americanization of Canada*. 1907. Toronto: University of Toronto Press, 1972.

Montgomery, L.M. *The Selected Journals of L.M. Montgomery*. Ed. Mary Rubio and Elizabeth Waterston. 4 vols. Toronto: Oxford University Press, 1985–98.

Morgan, Henry James, ed. *The Canadian Men and Women of the Time: A Hand-Book of Canadian Biography*. Toronto: William Briggs, 1898.

– *The Canadian Men and Women of the Time: A Hand-Book of Canadian Biography of Living Characters*. 2nd ed. Toronto: William Briggs, 1912.

Morgan, Wayne. 'Now, Brownies Seldom Idle Stand: Palmer Cox, the Brownies and Curiosity.' In *The Brownie World of Palmer Cox: An Exhibition*. Montreal: McGill University Libraries, 1997. First published in *The Ephemera Journal* 7 (1994): 25–37.

– '"If Your Grocer Does Not Keep the Ivory Soap": Palmer Cox, the Brownies, and Nineteenth-Century Marketing.' In *The Romance of Marketing History: Proceedings of the Eleventh Conference on Historical Analysis and Research in Marketing*, ed. Eric H. Shaw, 22–7. Boca Raton, FL: Association for Historical Research in Marketing, 2003.

Mott, Frank Luther. *A History of American Magazines*. 5 vols. Cambridge: Harvard University Press, Belknap Press, 1930–68.

– *American Journalism: A History, 1690–1960*. 3rd ed. New York: Macmillan, 1962.

Moyles, R.G. 'Young Canada: An Index to Canadian Materials in Major British and American Juvenile Periodicals, 1870–1950.' *CCL* 78 (1995): 7–63.

Murray, Heather. *Come, Bright Improvement! The Literary Societies of Nineteenth-Century Ontario*. Toronto: University of Toronto Press, 2002.

New, W.H., ed. *Canadian Writers, 1890–1920*. Vol. 92 of *Dictionary of Literary Biography*. Detroit: Gale, 1990.

O'Higgins, Harvey. *The Smoke-Eaters: The Story of a Fire Crew*. New York: Century, 1905.

– *Don-A-Dreams: A Story of Love and Youth*. New York: Century, 1906.

– *Old Clinkers: A Story of the New York Fire Department*. Boston: Small, Maynard, 1909.

– *Silent Sam and Other Stories of Our Day*. New York: Century, 1914.

Ohmann, Richard. *Selling Culture: Magazines, Markets, and Class at the Turn of the Century*. London: Verso, 1996.

Pacey, Desmond. Introduction to *The Selected Poems of Sir Charles G.D. Roberts*. Toronto and Montreal: McGraw-Hill Ryerson, 1955.

Parker, George L. *The Beginnings of the Book Trade in Canada*. Toronto: University of Toronto Press, 1985.

Patterson, Charles Brodie. *Seeking the Kingdom: Sunday Evening Talks on Spiritual Science, Given at Our Home*. Hartford, CT: The Author, 1888.

- *New Thought Essays*. New York: Alliance, 1898.
- 'Mental Healing.' *Arena*, June 1899, 772–6.
- 'What the New Thought Stands For.' *Arena*, Jan. 1901, 9–16.
- *The Will to Be Well*. New York: Alliance, 1901.
- *The Measure of a Man*. New York and London: Funk & Wagnalls, 1904.
- *The Rhythm of Life*. New York: T.Y. Crowell, 1915.

Pollock, Frank L. 'Canadian Writers in New York.' *Acta Victoriana* (Victoria College, University of Toronto), Apr. 1899, 434–9.

Pomeroy, E.M. *Sir Charles G.D. Roberts: A Biography*. Toronto: Ryerson Press, 1943.

Reid, Sydney. 'Dog-Hunting in New York.' *Harper's Weekly*, 25 June 1892, 605–6.
- 'Jim Bowers's Hoss.' *Lippincott's* 58 (1896): 511–18.
- *Josey and the Chipmunk: A Tale*. New York: Century, 1900. First published in *St. Nicholas*, Jan.-May 1900.
- 'The Newest Historical Novel.' *Independent*, 5 Sept. 1901, 2092–5.
- 'New York Public Library.' *Independent*, 21 Nov. 1901, 2752–7.
- 'Trouble in the Jungle.' *Independent*, 20 Feb. 1902, 452–7.
- 'The Yacht Race.' *Independent*, 3 Sept. 1903, 2106–11.
- 'Vacation in the Leather-Stocking Country.' *Independent*, 22 Aug. 1907, 437–42.
- 'The New Grand Central Terminal.' *Independent*, 14 Mar. 1912, 550–5.
- 'The "Titanic" Disaster.' *Independent*, 2 May 1912, 936–40.

Rittenhouse, Jessie B. *The Younger American Poets*. Boston: Little, Brown, 1904.

Roberts, Charles G.D. *The Forge in the Forest: Being the Narrative of the Acadian Ranger, Jean de Mer, Seigneur de Briart; and How He Crossed the Black Abbé; and of His Adventures in a Strange Fellowship*. Boston: Lamson, Wolffe, 1896 [1897].
- *New York Nocturnes and Other Poems*. Boston: Lamson, Wolffe, 1898.
- *A Sister To Evangeline: Being the Story of Yvonne de Lamourie, and How She Went into Exile with the Villagers of Grand Pré*. Boston: Lamson, Wolffe, 1898.
- *By the Marshes of Minas*. Boston: Silver, Burdett, 1900.
- *The Heart of the Ancient Wood*. New York: Silver, Burdett, 1900. First published in *Lippincott's*, Apr. 1900.
- *The Kindred of the Wild: A Book of Animal Life*. Boston: Page, 1902.
- *The Watchers of the Trails: A Book of Animal Life*. Boston: Page, 1904.
- *Red Fox: The Story of His Adventurous Career in the Rinkwaak Wilds and of His Final Triumph Over the Enemies of His Kind*. Boston: Page, 1905. First published in *Outing*, June-Sept. 1905.
- *The Heart That Knows*. Boston: Page, 1906.
- *The Haunters of the Silences: A Book of Animal Life*. Boston: Page, 1907.
- 'More Reminiscences of Bliss Carman.' *Dalhousie Review* 10 (1930–1): 1–9.
- 'Some Reminiscences of Bliss Carman in New York (1896–1906).' *Canadian Poetry Magazine* 5, no. 2 (1940): 5–10.

– *The Collected Letters of Charles G.D. Roberts*. Ed. Laurel Boone. Fredericton, NB: Goose Lane Editions, 1989.

Roberts, William Carman. 'Smoke-Wreaths.' *Chap-Book*, 1 June 1896, 78–9.

– 'At Twilight.' *Century*, July 1897, 330.

– 'To Lilith.' *Chap-Book*, 15 Sept. 1897, 322.

– 'Nachstück.' *Bookman* (New York), July 1899, 448.

– 'Guardians of the Northwest.' *Munsey's*, Sept. 1903, 933–6.

– 'The Strong Man of Canada.' *Munsey's*, Dec. 1904, 683–6.

Roberts, William Carman, Theodore Roberts, and Elizabeth Roberts Macdonald. *Northland Lyrics*. Selected and arranged by Charles G.D. Roberts. Boston: Small Maynard, 1899.

Robinson, Edwin Arlington. *Edwin Arlington Robinson's Letters to Edith Brower*. Ed. Richard Cary. Cambridge: Harvard University Press, Belknap Press, 1968.

Rogers, Amos Robert. *American Recognition of Canadian Authors Writing in English, 1890–1960*. PhD diss., University of Michigan, 1964. 2 vols. Ann Arbor: UMI Research, 1971.

Rossiter, William S. 'Printing and Publishing.' In *Twelfth Census of the United States, Taken in the Year 1900*. Vol. 9, 1037–1119. Washington, DC: U.S. Census Office, 1902.

Sandys, Edwyn. *Trapper 'Jim'*. New York: Macmillan; London: Macmillan, 1903.

– 'Robert White Jr.' *Canadian Magazine*, Nov. 1903, 23–9.

– *Sportsman 'Joe'*. New York: Macmillan; London: Macmillan, 1904.

– *Sporting Sketches*. New York: Macmillan, 1905.

Sandys, Edwyn, and T.S. Van Dyke. *Upland Game Birds*. The American Sportsman's Library. New York: Macmillan; London: Macmillan, 1902.

Sanford, M. Bourchier. 'In Favor of the Jew.' *North American Review*, Jan. 1891, 126–8.

– 'Rescue Work Among Fallen Women.' *North American Review*, Jan. 1892, 119–22.

– *The Romance of a Jesuit Mission: A Historical Novel*. New York: Baker & Taylor, 1897.

– *The Wandering Twins: A Story of Labrador*. Chicago: A.C. McClurg, 1904.

Seton, Ernest Thompson. *Studies in the Art Anatomy of Animals: Being a Brief Analysis of the Visible Forms of the More Familiar Mammals and Birds; Designed for the Use of Sculptors, Painters, Illustrators, Naturalists, and Taxidermists*. London and New York: Macmillan, 1896.

– *Wild Animals I Have Known: Being the Personal Histories of Lobo, Silverspot, Raggylug, Bingo, the Springfield Fox, the Pacing Mustang, Wully, and Redruff*. New York: Scribner's, 1898.

– *The Trail of the Sandhill Stag*. New York: Scribner's, 1899. First published in *Scribner's Magazine*, Aug. 1899.

– *The Biography of a Grizzly*. New York: Century, 1900. First published in *Century Magazine*, Nov. 1899–Jan. 1900.

– *Lives of the Hunted: A True Account of the Doings of Five Quadrupeds and Three Birds, and in Elucidation of the Same, Over Three Hundred Drawings.* New York: Scribner's, 1901.
– *Two Little Savages: Being the Adventures of Two Little Boys Who Lived as Indians and What They Learned.* London and New York: Doubleday, Page, 1903. First published in *Ladies' Home Journal*, Jan.-Aug. 1903.
– *Life-Histories of Northern Animals: An Account of the Mammals of Manitoba.* 2 vols. New York: Scribner's, 1909.
– *Trail of an Artist-Naturalist: The Autobiography of Ernest Thompson Seton.* New York: Charles Scribner's Sons, 1940.
– comp. *The Gospel of the Redman: An Indian Bible.* Garden City, NY: Doubleday, Doran, 1936.
Smith, Allan. 'The Continental Dimension in the Evolution of the English-Canadian Mind.' In *Canada: An American Nation?* 40–64. Montreal and Kingston: McGill-Queen's University Press, 1994.
Smith, Goldwin. *Canada and the Canadian Question.* Toronto: Hunter, Rose, 1891.
Smith, Herbert F. *The Popular American Novel, 1865–1920.* Boston: Twayne, 1980.
Steffens, Lincoln. *The Autobiography of Lincoln Steffens.* New York: Harcourt, Brace, 1931.
Stern, Madeleine B., ed. *Publishers for Mass Entertainment in Nineteenth-Century America.* Boston: G.K. Hall, 1980.
Stringer, Arthur. *The Loom of Destiny.* Boston: Small, Maynard, 1899.
– 'The Sons Beyond the Border.' *Canadian Magazine*, Dec. 1899, 128–9.
– 'Canadian Writers Who Are Winning Fame in New York.' *Montreal Herald*, 2 Mar. 1901, sec. 2, p. 11.
– *The Silver Poppy.* New York: D. Appleton, 1903.
– *Lonely O'Malley: A Story of Boy Life.* Boston and New York: Houghton, Mifflin, 1905.
– *The Wire Tappers.* Boston: Little, Brown, 1906.
– *Phantom Wires: A Novel.* Boston: Little, Brown, 1907.
– 'Wild Poets I've Known: Bliss Carman.' *Saturday Night*, 1 Mar. 1941.
Tebbel, John. *The Expansion of an Industry, 1865–1919.* Vol. 2 of *A History of Book Publishing in the United States.* 4 vols. New York: R.R. Bowker, 1972–81.
Thomson, E.W. *An Annotated Edition of the Correspondence Between Archibald Lampman and Edward William Thomson (1890–1898).* Ed. Helen Lynn. Ottawa: Tecumseh Press, 1980.
Truesdell, Leon E. *The Canadian Born in the United States: An Analysis of the Statistics of the Canadian Element in the Population of the United States, 1850 to 1930.* The Relations of Canada and the United States Series. New Haven: Yale University Press; Toronto: Ryerson Press, 1943.

United States. Census Office. *Twelfth Census of the United States, Taken in the Year 1900*. 10 vols. and supplements. Washington, DC, 1901–3.

Wadland, John Henry. *Ernest Thompson Seton: Man in Nature and the Progressive Era, 1880–1915*. Biologists and Their World. New York: Arno Press, 1978.

Weber, Ronald. *Hired Pens: Professional Writers in America's Golden Age of Print*. Athens: Ohio University Press, 1997.

Who's Who in New York City and State. 1st ed. New York: L.R. Hammersly, 1904.

Wickett, S. Morley. 'Canadians in the United States.' *Political Science Quarterly* 21, no. 2 (1906): 190–205.

Wiseman, John A. 'Silent Companions: The Dissemination of Books and Periodicals in Nineteenth-Century Ontario.' *Publishing History* 12 (1982): 17–50.

Wollock, Jeffrey. 'Stinson Jarvis: A Bio-Bibliography.' *Papers of the Bibliographic Society of Canada* 8 (1969): 23–60.

- 'Further Bibliography of Stinson Jarvis (1854–1926). *Papers of the Bibliographic Society of Canada* 14 (1975): 79–89.

- 'Anatomy of a Grudge Novel.' *Journal of Canadian Fiction* 20 (1977): 83–116.

Ziff, Larzer. *The American 1890s: Life and Times of a Lost Generation*. New York: Viking Press, 1966.

Acknowledgments

I am indebted to Andrew Wainwright, Bruce Greenfield, and Karen Smith of Dalhousie University; to Gwendolyn Davies, now of the University of New Brunswick; to James Doyle of Wilfrid Laurier University; to Thomas Beer, a model of wit, style, and my opening sentence; and especially, to Frank Luther Mott, author of the *History of American Magazines*, over thirty years in the making and worth every one of them. My thanks also to teachers, colleagues, students, and friends old and new, some of whom know they contributed to this book and some of whom don't, but did all the same: Joan Weir, Nelson Smith, Misao Dean, Samuel L. Macey, Kevin Flynn, David McGimpsey, Carole Gerson, David Bentley, Jeffrey Wollock, Brian Corman, Jared Bland, and Siobhan McMenemy.

I acknowledge with gratitude the financial support of the Social Sciences and Humanities Research Council of Canada, the Killam Trusts, and the Connaught Fund at the University of Toronto, behind which stands the citizen who pays for us all. I hope it was worth it.

N.M.

Illustration Credits

Frontispiece map, detail reprinted from *Rand, McNally & Co.'s Indexed Atlas of the World*. Volume I, *United States* (Chicago and New York: Rand McNally, 1902), 58–9. Courtesy Data, Map, and Government Informatiom Services, Robarts Library, University of Toronto. Caption from Sara Jeannette Duncan, 'American Influence on Canadian Thought,' *Week* (Toronto), 7 July 1887, 518.

'The Brownies in the Studio' reprinted from *St. Nicholas*, Jan. 1890, 271.

Engraving of Richard Hovey and Bliss Carman reprinted from the *Bookman* (New York), Jan. 1897, 406. Caption from Henrietta Hovey to Harriet Spofford Hovey, quoted in Muriel Miller, *Bliss Carman: Quest and Revolt* (St John's: Jesperson Press, 1985), 127.

Stinson Jarvis photo reprinted from the *Arena*, Dec. 1893, opp. p. 1.

Ernest Thompson Seton photo by 'Watson,' reprinted from William Wallace Whitelock, 'Ernest Seton-Thomson,' *Critic* (New York), Oct. 1901, 323. Caption from Arthur Stringer, 'Canadian Writers Who Are Winning Fame in New York,' *Montreal Herald*, 2 Mar. 1901, sec. 2, p. 11.

Edwyn Sandys photo and caption from Sophie Hensley, 'Canadian Writers in New York,' *Dominion Illustrated Monthly*, May 1893, 200.

Arthur Stringer photo and caption from the *Bookman* (New York), Dec. 1899, 294.

Harvey O'Higgins photo reprinted from the *Bookman* (New York), Aug. 1908, 546.

Charles G.D. Roberts photo reprinted from Jessie B. Rittenhouse, *The Younger American Poets* (Boston: Little, Brown, 1904, © 1904 by Little, Brown, and Company), 135. Caption from Frank L. Pollock, 'Canadian Writers in New York,' *Acta Victoriana*, Apr. 1899, 434, 436.

Index

STUDIES IN BOOK AND PRINT CULTURE

General editor: Leslie Howsam

Hazel Bell, Introduction by A.S. Byatt, *Indexes and Indexing in Fact and Fiction*

Heather Murray, *Come, Bright Improvement! The Literary Societies of Nineteenth-Century Ontario*

Joseph A. Dane, *The Myth of Print Culture: Essays on Evidence, Textuality, and Bibliographical Method*

Eva Hemmungs Wirtén, *No Trespassing: Authorship, Intellectual Property Rights, and the Boundaries of Globalization*

Christopher Knight, *Uncommon Readers: Denis Donoghue, Frank Kermode, George Steiner, and the Tradition of the Common Reader*

William A. Johnson, *Bookrolls and Scribes in Oxyrhynchus*

Siân Echard and Stephen Partridge, eds., *The Book Unbound: Editing and Reading Medieval Manuscripts and Texts*

Peter Stoicheff and Andrew Taylor, eds., *The Future of the Page*

Bronwen Wilson, *The World in Venice: Print, the City, and Early Modern Identity*

Elizabeth Sauer, *'Paper-contestations' and Textual Communities in England, 1640–1675*

Nick Mount, *When Canadian Literature Moved to New York*